3,000 YEARS OF WAR

...AE QUINTUS FABIUS MAXIMUS VERRUCOSUS FABIAN STRATEGY ROMAN LEGI...
...A GAIUS JULIUS CAESAR THE BATTLE OF ACTIUM BATTLE OF TEUTOBURG FOR...
...LFRED THE GREAT VIKING LONGBOAT THE BATTLE OF HASTINGS WILLIAM I, T...
...TRAI BATTLE OF BANNOCKBURN BATTLE OF CRÉCY BOW THE BATTLE OF AGI...
...F PANIPAT ZAHIR UD-DIN MUHAMMAD BABUR SULEIMAN I TREBUCHET THE...
...LE OF OKEHAZAMA THE BATTLE OF LEPANTO GUNPOWDER THE SPANISH ARM...
...DEMOLITIONS SÉBASTIEN LE PRESTRE DE VAUBAN HERMAN MAURICE, COMTE...
...BATTLE OF QUEBEC INVASION OF CANADA THE BATTLE OF TRENTON GEORGE...
...ATTLE OF ABOUKIR BAY NAPOLEON I THE BATTLE OF AUSTERLITZ THE BATTL...
...TTLE OF LEIPZIG THE BATTLE OF WATERLOO CARL PHILIPP GOTTLIEB VON CLA...
...BATTLE OF CARABOBO SIMÓN BOLÍVAR BATTLE OF MAIPÚ JOSÉ DE SAN MART...
...FORT SUMTER THE FIRST BATTLE OF MANASSAS (BULL RUN) THOMAS JONATH...
...ATHAN BEDFORD FORREST THE BATTLE OF SHILOH THE BATTLE OF ANTIETAM...
...LE OF CHANCELLORSVILLE THE SIEGE OF VICKSBURG BENJAMIN HENRY GRIE...
...TO THE SEA WILLIAM TECUMSEH SHERMAN THE FIRST BATTLE OF SEDAN ENG...
...RAZY HORSE RORKE'S DRIFT THE SIEGE OF KHARTOUM WOUNDED KNEE TSU...
...OWIG HANS VON BENECKENDORFF UND VON HINDENBURG ERICH FRIEDRICH...
...ON STRATEGY THE BATTLE OF JUTLAND ALFRED THAYER MAHAN THE BATTLE...
...HE BATTLE OF CAMBRAI SECOND BATTLE OF THE MARNE JOHN JOSEPH PERSH...
...KHALKIN GOL POLISH CAMPAIGN TANKS HEINZ WILHELM GUDERIAN INDIRE...
...V GEORGI ZHUKOV THE BATTLE OF MOSCOW PEARL HARBOR ISOROKU YAMAI...
...IC AIR CAMPAIGN OVER GERMANY AIRPLANE THE BATTLE OF SINGAPORE THE...
...RD AMES SPRUANCE THE SECOND BATTLE OF EL ALAMEIN MINES BERNARD L...
...E BATTLE OF STALINGRAD TOTAL WARFARE STRATEGY THE BATTLE OF KASSERI...
...ON AVALANCHE THE BATTLES FOR MONTE CASSINO THE BATTLE OF ANZIO OP...
...ARLEY "HAP" ARNOLD THE BATTLE OF LEYTE GULF DOUGLAS MACARTHUR T...
...BOMB INCHON THE SIEGE OF DIEN BIEN PHU SUEZ CRISIS MOSHE DAYAN TH...
...DS WAR MISSILE OPERATION EAGER ANVIL NIGHT VISION DEVICE (NVD) GU...

3,000 YEARS OF WAR

Dwight Jon Zimmerman

Tess Press

To my friend, John D. Gresham
— D. J. Z.

Special thanks to Stratford/Tex Tech Publishing Services and Charles Merullo,
Jennifer Jeffrey, and Franziska Payer at Endeavour.

3,000 Years of War was created by Black Dog and Leventhal in conjunction with Endeavour London Limited.
Originally published as *The Book of War.*

PHOTO CREDITS

CNG: 37; **Library of Congress:** 160, 164, 168, 172, 174, 180, 194, 200, 216, 220, 222, 224, 227, 232, 238, 240, 247, 252, 254, 257,
258, 263, 266, 270, 276, 282, 289, 290, 293, 297, 298, 300, 308, 312, 316, 328, 331, 334, 336, 392, 410, 432, 434;
National Archives: 229, 342, 352, 356, 358, 362, 368, 382, 388, 405, 412, 416, 426, 428, 438, 442, 446, 447, 448, 452, 456, 460;
464, 468, 469; **NASA:** 491; **Naval Historical Center:** 386; **Shutterstock:** 18, 28, 80, 90, 102, 106, 118, 134, 142, 182, 186, 212, 406, 414;
The Granger Collection, New York: 233; **United States Department of Defense:** 203, 272, 315, 318, 323, 324, 332, 349, 395, 401, 409,
435, 437, 479, 483, 487, 493; **United States Military Academy:** 306

All other images courtesy of **Getty Images** including the following which have additional attributions —

Agence France Presse: 11 (3L), 231, 393, 455, 459, 463, 465, 481, 488, 489; **Bridgeman Art Library:** cover (2L) and 1(L)/Musée Nat.
du Chateau de Malmaison, Rueil-Malmaison; 5 (3L)/Louvre; 5 (R), 6 (3L), 7(L)/Service Historique de l'Armée de Terre, France; 7(3L)/
Louvre, Paris; 9 (L)/Private Collection; 29/Louvre, Paris; 43, 51, 55/Musée de la Revolution Française, Vizille; 69/Private Collection;
73/Musée de la Tapisserie, Bayeaux; 79, 83/Bibliotheque Nationale, Paris; 89/Courtesy of the Wardens & Scholars of New College, Oxford;
91/Private Collection; 93/Musée Dobrée, Nantes; 99, 101 Collegio del Cambio, Perugia; 105, 121/Victoria & Albert Museum, London;
141/Service Historique de l'Armée de Terre, France; 153, 175/Louvre, Paris; 191/Private Collection; 237/Private Collection; 281/Private
Collection; **De Agostini Picture Library:** 6 (2R), 107; **Fine Art Photographic:** 317; **Imagno:** 115, 129, 139, 179, 187, 189, 193, 215;
National Geographic: cover (L), 3; **Roger Viollet:** 49, 65, 103, 145, 347; **Stock Montage:** 97, 225, 255, 267, 485; **Time & Life Pictures:**
cover (2R), 1(R), 5 (L & 2L), 6 (L & R), 10 (R), 11 (L & 2L), 15, 21, 25, 33, 35, 39, 41, 53, 63, 75, 109, 111, 117, 119, 131, 133, 135,
137, 147, 149, 167, 171, 195, 209, 211, 245, 262, 265, 285, 286, 287, 305, 309, 319, 339, 343, 365, 367, 375, 383, 385, 387, 391, 399,
403, 411, 421, 423, 425, 429, 439, 441, 443, 449, 453

CONTENTS

Introduction	12	Pyrrhus of Epirus	32
Battle of Kadesh	14	Battle of Cannae	34
Chariot	16	Quintus Fabius Maximus Verrucosus	36
Siege of Troy	18	Fabian	38
Battle of Marathon	20	Roman Legion	40
Hoplite	22	Sword	42
Battle of Salamis	24	Battle of Zama	44
Sun Tzu	26	Hannibal Barca	46
Battle of Gaugamela	28	Siege of Carthage	48
Alexander III, The Great	30	Battle of Alesia	50

1274 B.C.
Battle of Kadesh

480 B.C.
Battle of Salamis

331 B.C.
Battle of Gaugamela

331 B.C.
Alexander III,
The Great

52 B.C.
Battle of Alesia

Gaius Julius Caesar	52		Battle of Bannockburn	90
Battle of Actium	54		Battle of Crécy	92
Battle of Teutoburg Forest	56		Gunpowder	94
Siege of Masada	58		Bow	96
Battle of Chalons	60		Battle of Agincourt	98
Sack of Rome	62		Halberd	100
Battle of Badr	64		Siege of Orleans	102
Battle of Tours	66		Joan of Arc	104
Alfred The Great	68		Fall of Tenochtitlan	106
Viking Longboat	70		Hernando Cortés	108
Battle of Hastings	72		Battle of Panipat	110
William I, The Conqueror	74		Zahir ud-Din Muhammad Babur	112
Siege of Antioch	76		Siege of Vienna	114
Trebuchet	78		Suleiman I	116
Siege of Jerusalem	80		Battle of Cajamarca	118
Battle of Hattin	82		Stirrup	120
Saladin	84		Francisco Pizarro	122
Genghis Khan	86		Siege of Kazan	124
Battle of Courtrai	88		Battle of Okehazama	126

44 B.C.
Gaius Julius Caesar

1000

Viking Longboat

1429

Joan of Arc

1521

Fall of Tenochtitlan

1575

Battle of Nagashino

Battle of Lepanto	128	George Washington	166
Battle of Nagashino	130	Battle of Saratoga	168
Arquebus	132	Benedict Arnold	170
Spanish Armada	134	Siege of Yorktown	172
Battle of Sekigahara	136	Battle of Valmy	174
Gustavus Adolphus	138	Battle of Aboukir Bay	176
Battle of Rocroi	140	Napoleon I	178
Battle of Blenheim	142	Battle of Austerlitz	180
Fortifications	144	Battle of Trafalgar	182
Sébastien Le Prestre de Vauban	146	Horatio Nelson	184
Hermann Maurice	148	Battle of Friedland	186
Battle of Leuthen	150	Battle of Talavera	188
Frederick II, The Great	152	Battle of Borodino	190
Battle of Plassey	154	Battle of Leipzig	192
Robert Clive	156	Battle of Waterloo	194
Brown Bess Musket	158	Carl von Clausewitz	196
Battle of Quebec	160	Baron Antoine-Henri Jomini	198
Invasion of Canada	162	Battle of New Orleans	200
Battle of Trenton	164	Rifle	202

1643

Battle of Rocroi

1776

George Washington

1792

Battle of Valmy

1805

Battle of Austerlitz

1815

Battle of New Orleans

Battle of Gqokli Hill	204	Robert E. Lee	242
Shaka	206	Telegraph	244
Battle of Maipú	208	Battle of Hampton Roads	246
José de San Martín	210	Ironclad Warship	248
Battle of Carabobo	212	Containment	250
Simón Bolívar	214	Battle of Chancellorsville	252
The Alamo	216	Siege of Vicksburg	254
Battle of San Jacinto	218	Benjamin Henry Grierson	256
Battle of Chapultepec	220	Battle of Gettysburg	258
Siege of Fort Sumter	222	James Ewell Brown ("Jeb") Stuart	260
First Battle of Manassas	224	Battle of Mobile Bay	262
Thomas "Stonewall" Jackson	226	David Glasgow Farragut	264
John Singleton Mosby	228	Sherman's March to the Sea	266
Guerilla	230	William Tecumseh Sherman	268
Battle of Fort Donelson	232	First Battle of Sedan	270
Ulysses S. Grant	234	Engines	272
Nathan Bedford Forrest	236	Count Helmuth von Moltke	274
Battle of Shiloh	238	Battle of the Little Bighorn	276
Battle of Antietam	240	Sitting Bull (Tatanka Yotanka)	278

1818
Battle of Gqokli Hill

1836

The Alamo

1862

Battle of Hampton Roads

1863

James Ewell "Jeb" Stuart

1870

First Battle of Sedan

Crazy Horse (Tashunca Uitco)	280	Battle of Passchendaele	318
Battle of Rorke's Drift	282	Poison Gas	320
Giuseppe Garibaldi	284	Machine Gun	322
Siege of Khartoum	286	Battle of Beersheba	324
Wounded Knee	288	Edmund Henry Hynman Allenby	326
Battle of Tsushima	290	Battle of Cambrai	328
Heihachiro Togo	292	Second Battle of the Marne	330
Dreadnought	294	John Joseph Pershing	332
Alfred Thayer Mahan	296	Battle of Megiddo	334
First Battle of the Marne	298	Battle of Khalkin Gol	336
Battle of Tannenberg	300	Sir Basil Henry Liddell Hart	338
Paul von Hindenburg	302	John Frederick Charles Fuller	340
Erich Wilhelm Ludendorff	304	Polish Campaign	342
Battle of Gallipoli	306	Tank	344
Battle of the Somme	308	Heinz Wilhelm Guderian	346
Barbed Wire	310	Indirect	348
Battle of Verdun	312	George Catlett Marshall	350
Attrition	314	Fall of France	352
Battle of Jutland	316	Battle of Britain	354

1876

Crazy Horse

1906

Dreadnought

1917

Battle of Beersheba

1918

John Joseph Pershing

1940
Fall of France

Operation Barbarossa	356	Mines	394
Georgi Zhukov	358	Bernard Law Montgomery	396
Battle of Moscow	360	Operation Torch	398
Pearl Harbor	362	Dwight David Eisenhower	400
Isoroku Yamamoto	364	George S. Patton, Jr.	402
Chester William Nimitz	366	Guadalcanal	404
Battle of the Atlantic	368	Battle of Stalingrad	406
Submarine	370	Total Warfare	408
Torpedo	372	Battle of Kasserine Pass	410
Radar/Sonar	374	Battle of Tarawa	412
Air Campaign Over Germany	376	Battle of Kursk	414
Airplane	378	Operation Husky	416
Battle of Singapore	380	Sutjeska Offensive	418
Doolittle Raid	382	Tito (Josef Broz)	420
William Frederick Halsey, Jr.	384	Operation Avalanche	422
Battle of Coral Sea	386	Battles for Monte Cassino	424
Battle of Midway	388	Battle of Anzio	426
Raymond Ames Spruance	390	Operation Overlord	428
Second Battle of El Alamein	392	Omar Nelson Bradley	430

1941
Operation Barbarossa

1941
Pearl Harbor

1941
Radar/Sonar

1943
Battle of Tarawa

1944
Operation Overlord

Operation Cobra	432
Air Campaign Over Japan	434
Henry Harley "Hap" Arnold	436
Battle of Leyte Gulf	438
Douglas MacArthur	440
Battle of the Bulge	442
Battle for Berlin	444
Battle of Iwo Jima	446
Hiroshima and Nagasaki	448
Atomic Bomb	450
Battle of Inchon	452
Siege of Dien Bien Phu	454
Suez Crisis	456
Moshe Dayan	458
Tonkin Gulf Incident	460
Six-Day War	462
Tet Offensive	464
Yom Kippur War	466
Operation Eagle Claw	468

Falklands War	470
Missiles and Rockets	472
Operation Eager Anvil	474
Night Vision Device	476
Global Positioning System	478
Battle of 73 Easting	480
H. Norman Schwarzkopf, Jr.	482
Armor	484
Plastic Explosives	486
First Battle of Mogadishu	488
Satellite	490
Map	492
Operation Enduring Freedom	494
Operation Anaconda	496
Radio	498
Battle of Debecka Pass	500
Index	502

1944

Douglas MacArthur

1950

Battle of Inchon

1991

Battle of 73 Easting

2001

Operation Enduring Freedom

2003

Battle of Debecka Pass

INTRODUCTION

Union General William Tecumseh Sherman minced no words when he said, "War is hell." Yet war is central to the growth of civilization. Each stage in a civilization's cycle—birth, growth, decline, and replacement by another society—includes war. Some of the greatest works of literature include war as their theme..

The eternal fascination with war is due to its wealth of extremes: Brutality, cynicism, tragedy, and absurdity go hand-in-hand with courage, comradeship, self-sacrifice, and noble purpose. Men can begin as heroes and then turn into villains, like Benedict Arnold, whose name became a synonym for treason. Or ordinary men, such as Ulysses Grant, with a humble past and a failed civilian career, find themselves redeemed by war and achieve unimaginable greatness.

With so many changes happening on the battlefields of the twenty-first century, tough editorial decisions had to be made when putting this book together. This caused eminently worthy generals or battles of previous eras to be bypassed in favor of more recent generals and battles, and we also placed an emphasis on those inventions that are still in use today. That said, *3,000 Years of War* presents some of the most important and influential battles, people, inventions, and strategies that affected the course of civilization. Its scope is vast—from ancient times to the twenty-first century—and spans the globe.

This book's framework is chronological, based on the dates of battles. The placement of the biographies is intuitive: An individual's respective role in military history influenced the placement of his or her biography; generals' biographies appear after their most famous battles. Otherwise, their stories are grouped in their milieu, as are the theorists. Inventions, for the most part, are located in the time period in which they were introduced. Exceptions were made for those inventions that endured for centuries or millennia. The universal nature of strategies allowed them to be located near conflicts or periods that highlight their principles.

Sir Walter Raleigh said, "The ordinary theme and argument of all history is war." *3,000 Years of War*, with it selection of landmark individuals, conflicts, and achievements, proves it by providing a remarkable look at the history of mankind.

Street fighting during the Battle of Berlin

Battle of Kadesh

First battle in history to be recorded in detail

The last of the great pharaohs, Ramesses II, mounted the throne at a time when Egypt, having suffered years of decline, was reasserting itself. Upon becoming pharaoh, Ramesses sent an expedition to Nubia to seize the gold mines there. He used the assets to replenish Egypt's treasury and fund a re-conquest of rebellious provinces. Ramesses II began with campaigns in Canaan and Syria and, in the fourth year of his reign (1275 B.C.), captured the Hittite vassal state of Amurru. This set the stage for battle with Muwatallis II, king of Egypt's major rival, the growing Hittite Empire.

In the spring of 1274 B.C., Muwatallis led an army that contained 2,500–3,500 chariots (accounts vary) and 37,000 infantry and marched south to retake Amurru. Ramesses, meanwhile, had formed an army of at least 2,000 chariots and 20,000 infantry and marched north. They met at roughly the border of their two empires, on the Orontes River, near the town of Kadesh.

Misled by faulty intelligence from spies, Ramesses believed that Muwatallis's forces were at the city of Aleppo, some distance away, and divided his command into four divisions. By the time he discovered that Muwatallis and his army were just on the other side of the city, his command had already separated. Before Ramesses could recall his divisions, Muwatallis's chariots attacked and routed two divisions, almost killing Ramesses himself.

Ramesses regrouped the shattered two divisions that had retreated across the Orontes River and, with reinforcements, counterattacked with his chariots and some infantry. Muwatallis responded by sending more chariots into battle. The fighting continued into the next morning before concluding.

Extensive written accounts survive telling two different outcomes. In Egypt, Ramesses scored a great victory. The Hittite record claims triumph for Muwatallis. Though the battle actually ended inconclusively, or, according to some interpretations, as a Pyrrhic victory for Ramesses, its importance in history is twofold: It's the oldest battle in the ancient world whose extensive records have survived and it's the largest chariot battle in history.

Ramesses II on a two-man war chariot

CHARIOT

Horse-drawn vehicle pivotal in the Battle of Kadesh

The word "chariot" comes from the Latin *carrus,* for car. The basic chariot was a three-sided platform on two wheels pulled by two horses. Archeological sites have revealed evidence of chariot use in almost all the major ancient civilizations in Asia, Europe, and Africa. The earliest known chariots date back to 3000 B.C. and their usage in war reached the high point about seven hundred years later at the Battle of Kadesh, the largest chariot battle ever fought.

Chariot use in war arose out of a need to be able to strike an enemy quickly and with great force. Since horses during this period were too small to carry men on their backs, horse-drawn carts were modified for use in battle. An important innovation in chariot design was the light spoked wheel. Previously wheels were solid and heavy. War chariots usually carried two people—a driver and the warrior.

Chariot tactics were designed to exploit the advantages of speed and maneuverability. Charioteers would rush forward until they were within effective bow-and-arrow or javelin range and launch their weapons. They would then rush to a new position and repeat the process before an enemy could effectively respond. Heavy chariots, carrying three people, were designed to smash into an opponent's line of infantry and disrupt it.

The most proficient charioteers of the ancient world were the Hittites. They became masters of the art of chariot warfare and introduced a number of innovations, including the three-person chariot.

The successful breeding of larger and more robust horses that could be used as mounted cavalry led to the decline of war chariots by 1200 B.C. By the fourth century B.C., the chariot's transition from use in combat was complete. Civilian use continued, and chariot races remained popular in the Mediterranean world into the sixth century A.D.

1274

B.C.

Chariot-riding warriors from the Sumerian Royal Graves of Ur

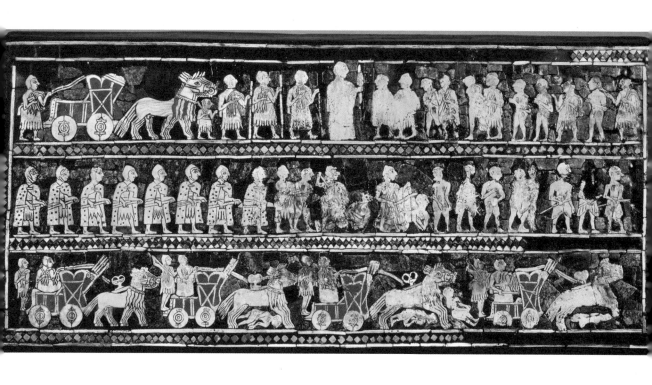

SIEGE OF TROY

Legendary siege that lasted from 1194 to 1184 B.C.

Bas-relief of Greek
chariot riders

The only written account of this epic siege is Homer's *Iliad*. For centuries, it was thought to be more legend than fact. Then, in the 1870s, Heinrich Schliemann, the controversial treasure hunter and archeologist, discovered historical evidence (since disputed) of Troy's existence at a dig in Turkey.

According to Homer, the siege came about as the result of the goddess Aphrodite winning the beauty contest for which Paris, prince of Troy, was the judge. Aphrodite had promised Paris the most beautiful woman in the world if she won. That woman was Helen but unfortunately she was married. When Paris made off with the willing Helen, Menelaus, Helen's husband, told his brother Agamemnon, king of Mycenae. Together they called together a bunch of fellow Greek monarchs and led an expedition to Troy to get Menelaus' wife back. After many years of fighting, in which lots of men and heroes were killed, the Greeks won through treachery. They destroyed the city, Menelaus got Helen back, and the Greeks returned home.

The Greeks did believe the Trojan War was an historical event and that Troy was probably located in the vicinity of the Dardanelles Strait. The real reason for the conflict was almost certainly less romantic than Homer's version. Some historians theorize the Trojan War was a battle between two different civilizations for economic and/or political hegemony in the region. Another version suggests it was a "squaring of accounts" over a series of back-and-forth pirate raids. In this interpretation, the tipping point was an official visit by the Trojans, led by Paris, to the rulers of Sparta that turned into a pirate raid avenging an earlier such incident perpetrated on Troy. This incident then led to retaliation that turned into a siege and sack of the city.

The truth of what actually happened at Troy in the twelfth or thirteenth century B.C. may never be known. Regardless, the historical event inspired one of the greatest works of literature from the ancient world.

The death of Achilles, the hero of the Trojan War, who was said to have conquered 11 cities

Battle of Marathon

Greek victory that gave birth to Western culture

Darius I of Persia attempted to conquer the Greek city-states. With Athens as his first target, he landed an army on the plains of the nearby city of Marathon in 490 B.C.

Despite the positive experience at Salamis, the individual Greek city-states continued to be so stubbornly independent that not even the threat of conquest by the Persians could cause them to band together against a common foe. Some Greeks hated Athens so much that they chose to ally themselves with the Persians.

The original Athenian plan of defense called for their army to be commanded by ten generals, or *strategoi*, and that they confront the Persian army at the city walls—an arrangement that could only result in defeat. Fortunately for the Greeks, the Athenian general Miltiades succeeded in convincing the Athenian leaders to let him command the army. He chose to confront the Persians on the coast.

Though no accurate figures exist, historians estimate that Miltiades fielded an army of about 11,000 hoplites. The Persian army ranged from 25,000 to almost 30,000 men, including highly maneuverable cavalry and light infantry. Miltiades compensated for his weaknesses by taking up position on heights overlooking the Persian camp. His right flank was supported by a tall hill and his left was secured by a small river. This restricted the amount of enemy troops that could face him and inhibited their ability to outflank him. Miltiades then significantly reinforced his own flanks by reducing the amount of men in his center.

Miltiades attacked first, with his center force. The Persian center held its ground, then began to push back the hoplites. Just when it appeared the Greek center would break, Miltiades ordered his flanks to attack the overstretched Persian middle.

The Persian army was crushed. An estimated 6,400 invaders were killed at a cost of only 192 Greeks. The threat of Persian invasion remained but it was years before the Persians returned.

The decisive battle at Marathon

HOPLITE

Ancient Greek infantryman who was pivotal in the Battle of Marathon

The most important member of the ancient Greek army was the citizen-soldier called a *hoplite.* In Greek city-states, only freemen (the aristocrats of their day) could become hoplites. As a citizen of his respective city-state, a hoplite was bound to perform lifelong military service when emergencies arose. A hoplite went to war supported by slaves who carried his bulky armor and weapons and his supplies and baggage. The slave responsible for his weapons did double duty as a forager.

The word *hoplite* comes from *hoplon,* which means an item of armor. A hoplite was a heavy infantryman who wore armor and fought with a spear (*doru*) and short sword (*xiphos*) and protected himself with a shield (*aspis*). The spear was up to 10 feet long and was the hoplite's primary weapon. The sword was used to cut and thrust in close quarters. The round shield was large enough to protect the hoplite's entire body when he was in a kneeling position. Greaves of metal plates sewed on leather, a bronze helmet, and a cuirass (breastplate) completed his armor. All told, the armor and weapons weighed about 70 pounds.

Hoplites were accorded great honor and respect, one of the few times in history where the infantry branch was given equal or greater credence than such glamorous branches as the cavalry. One reason for this was that because armor and weapons were expensive, only the wealthy and powerful members of society were able to afford to be hoplites.

Hoplite armor was individually customized, often with designs and symbols that identified the hoplite's family and city-state. Each city-state also had a distinctive design for its armor. Spartans used a scarlet robe to identify themselves. This became a flourish imitated by other Greek city-states.

Hoplites were the shock troops of their era. They went into battle using the phalanx, a tightly organized rectangular formation that took advantage of the hoplites' mass. Discipline was the key in the phalanx attack. With their spears bristling out of an interlocked shield wall, if the hoplites were able to maintain formation after contact with their enemy, the chances were strong that they would win the battle.

Ancient Greek Hoplite

Battle of Salamis

The world's first decisive naval engagement

The Persian Empire had coveted the Greek city-states for years. King Xerxes I of Persia embarked on a campaign to conquer the Greeks using his army to march from the north, and his navy to destroy the Greek fleet in the south.

In the ancient world, battles at sea largely reflected the tactics used on land. Oar-driven ships would get close and "grapple" until an opponent surrendered or was sunk. Ships' weapons included wooden rams sheathed in bronze or iron and a cat-head, a device designed to shear an opponent's oars as the attacker swept its side. Boarding another ship was usually a last resort.

The most common warship was the trireme, which had three banks of oars on each side. The Athenian trireme of the period was 140 feet long and had a 20-foot beam. Its crew consisted of 174 rowers, twenty sailors, and a small force of hoplites (heavy infantry), used as marines. The maximum crew was 225 men. It is worth noting that the rowers were all freemen and skilled at their task, not impressed slaves.

Jealousies and rivalries among the Greeks caused disagreements about how to stop the Persian army. However, they managed to overcome enough of their prejudices against each other to form a naval alliance of mutual defense, with Athens commanding the fleet.

News of Greek land operations was grim: The Persians annihilated a force of 300 Spartan hoplites at Thermopylae and the advancing Persian army was laying waste to any city that did not surrender. If Xerxes could destroy the Athenian-led fleet, the Greek world would fall into his lap.

The Greek fleet, roughly half the size of the Persian, managed to lure the unsuspecting Persian ships into the narrow strait of Salamis in September. The attack degenerated into a chaotic melee, as approximately a thousand ships fought in the restricted waters.

In the end, the Persians lost 200 ships and the Greeks lost only forty. More important, the Persian fleet was driven from Greek waters. Because the Greek mainland had too little food and forage to support his troops, Xerxes was forced to abandon his plans of invasion and retreat.

Greeks defeating Persians at Battle of Salamis

SUN TZU

Military theorist (ca. 400–330 B.C.)

Like Homer, author of the epic account of the siege of Troy, *The Illiad*, very little is known about the author Sun Tzu, author of the most important book on military theory and strategy, *Ping-fa* (*The Art of War*). *The Art of War* is a benchmark work not only used by generals but also by political strategists of all persuasions, as well as corporate executives. Some historians think Sun Tzu lived in the sixth century B.C., but evidence suggests he actually lived in the fourth century B.C., serving as a general for King He-lu of Wu and fought during the late Chou dynasty. One of the few stories that exist about the author is that he used hundreds of Wu's concubines as "soldiers" in drill and maneuver demonstrations.

Sun Tzu's texts were studied for centuries by Chinese, Mongolian, and Japanese military and political leaders. The Western world became exposed to *The Art of War* when the Jesuit missionary in Peking (Beijing) translated and published the book in Paris in 1722. But it was not properly translated until the twentieth century. Samuel B. Griffith's translation, first published in 1963, is the most highly regarded.

The primary reason *The Art of War* has survived the centuries is due to Sun Tzu's success in distilling the principles of strategy to their most basic and universal level. He examined every branch of warfare and paid particular attention to its subtleties. For him, finesse trumped brute force every time. His tenets fall into two categories: prepare defenses strong enough to repel any attack, and discover the right methods to defeat an enemy. Incorporated in both is an in-depth examination of the psychological principles needed to overcome a foe. One of the more striking injunctions is his insistence on defeating the enemy *without* resorting to a clash of arms. For Sun Tzu, combat was literally the last resort.

Five Union army officers studying *The Art of War* by Sun Tzu during the American Civil War

Battle of Gaugamela (Arbela)

Alexander the Great's victory that secured Persia

Alexander the Great

Alexander's campaign had, by 331 B.C., conquered Greece, Egypt, and the Levantine coast. Only Darius III and his Persian Empire remained.

Alexander had previously defeated Persian armies at Granicus and Issus. As the Macedonian and Persian armies assembled on the plains of Arbela near Gaugamela, both sides knew that only one army and empire would survive the outcome.

Of the two, Darius's army was the larger. Estimates vary from 188,000 to perhaps half a million men. Alexander's army was about 57,000 strong. In addition, Darius had chosen the battle site and had it leveled as smooth as a parade ground to make it suitable for his chariots. He also ordered sharp stakes planted at key locations on the flanks to hamper Alexander's cavalry.

Darius then formed his battle lines according to traditional Eastern tactics that emphasized the power of bulk. Alexander, meanwhile, divided his force into three battle groups designed to fight independently. Alexander chose to lead the Macedonian cavalry on the far right. Through a combination of initiative, cunning dispersal of force, and swift counterattacks, Alexander nullified the Persian advantage of numbers. Alexander struck first, delivering rapid and disorienting blows on the Persian left flank. The ranks of the slow-moving Persian infantry became intermingled to the point of confusion.

When the Persian chariots charged, the Macedonian center opened its ranks. The chariots raced through unopposed. When the Persian chariots attempted to regroup, they were individually surrounded and cut down. Even so, the situation was growing desperate for the Macedonian left flank, where its cavalry was under heavy attack. Then, at what he perceived to be the right moment, Alexander hurled the full weight of his right flank against the vulnerable Persian left flank.

The shock of fresh attack caused the Persian troops on the left to panic. The panic spread and soon the whole Persian army began to flee. The Macedonians pursued the Persians all night for 25 miles, inflicting a fearful slaughter. A few days later, Darius was assassinated.

When Alexander entered Babylon, the Persian Empire was no more.

331 B.C.

The Macedonian moment of victory at Gaugamela

ALEXANDER III, THE GREAT

Macedonian leader at the Battle of Gaugamela (356–323 B.C.)

Alexander was the first military commander to attempt to conquer the known world. An innovative genius, he was also the first military leader to fully incorporate infantry, cavalry, engineers, logistics, and intelligence. His empire ultimately stretched from Greece to the border of India and included Persia, which had been the greatest empire of the time. He was never defeated in battle, fought with an army often outnumbered, and achieved it all before the age of thirty-three.

Alexander was the son of Philip II, King of Macedonia, and Queen Olympias. His father taught him the art of war and the philosopher Aristotle taught him other disciplines. Alexander fought his first battle at age eighteen at Chaeronea in 338 B.C., a victory that extended Macedonian rule throughout Greece. Two years later, when Philip was assassinated, Alexander inherited the throne. In 334 B.C., Alexander embarked on the path to empire.

Standing in the way of his ambitions was the Persian Empire. Alexander took his army into Asia Minor. By 331 B.C., the eastern Mediterranean down to Egypt was his. Turning inland, Alexander crossed the Tigris River and overthrew the Persian dynasty with victory at Gaugamela. He advanced through what is now Iraq and into Persia, sweeping north and then south. In 326 B.C., he marched his army through Afghanistan and entered India via the Khyber Pass. Along the way, he founded cities, turned former enemies into allies, reformed local governments and institutions, and married. Not only did he wed a Persian princess but, in a move designed to further bind Persian East and Greek West, he also ordered 10,000 of his men to take Persian brides. In 327 B.C., poised to advance further into India, he was prevented by a revolt of his army that, after eight years of fighting, had finally had enough and wanted to return home.

Alexander never made it back to Macedonia. In 323 B.C., in Babylon, he died. Reasons for his death vary and include poison, heavy drinking, or a fatal relapse of malaria. Alexander left no heir and his generals, known as the *Diadochi*, divided his empire among themselves.

The family of Darius begging for mercy at the feet of Alexander

PYRRHUS OF EPIRUS

Greek king whose name is used to refer to costly victories (318–272 B.C.)

Pyrrhus was a handsome, brave, despotic but popular ruler and he traced his ancestry to Achilles. He appeared to be something of a healer as well, thought to be able to cure problems of the spleen by pressing his right foot on a subject's back. His name, however, has become the word for military victories that were so costly that they may have well been defeats.

Pyrrhus' opportunity for military glory presented itself when the Greek city of Tarentum in southern Italy appealed to him in 281 B.C. for help against an attack by Rome. Whereas the Tarentines simply wanted to check republican Roman aggrandizement, Pyrrhus took in the big picture—the really big picture. As Alexander (Pyrrhus's distant relative) had conquered Persia, he, Pyrrhus, would conquer the rising Rome. And the courage he would display in his campaign would silence those who doubted his ancestry.

In 281 B.C., he crossed the Adriatic Sea with about 25,000 troops, 3,000 cavalry, and twenty elephants. He met the Romans at Heraclea. And won. But his losses were so great, and his resources in men and materials had been so reduced, that when an aide complimented him on his victory, he replied that another such triumph would ruin him.

But Heracleia was just the beginning. Pyrrhus fought the Romans again, at Asculum. And again he achieved a near suicidal victory.

Pyrrhus took on the Carthaginians in Sicily in 278 B.C. in campaigns that lasted two years. Having enduring heavy losses, he left Sicily, allegedly remarking, "What a fine field of battle I leave here for Rome and Carthage."

Pyrrhus was defeated by the Romans at Beneventum in 275 B.C. and returned to Epirus. The philosopher Plutarch observed, "What he got by brave actions he lost again by vain hopes, and by new desires of what he had not, kept nothing of what he had."

Pyrrhus embarked on a fresh campaign in 272 B.C. but it ended the same year when, in Argos, he was killed in battle when he was hit in the head by a tile thrown from a rooftop by an old woman.

Roman armies defeating elephant troops of Pyrrhus during the Battle of Asculum

BATTLE OF CANNAE

The greatest tactical victory in history

Rome's struggle with Carthage for domination of the Mediterranean world was one of the great rivalries in history. It led to three Punic Wars (from the Latin for "Carthaginian"—*Punicus*) over the span of more than one hundred years. The Battle of Cannae, during the Second Punic War (218–201 B.C.), is probably the most famous.

Carthage's greatest general was Hannibal Barca. His strategy was to shatter the Roman republic's confederation by invading the Italian peninsula. Hannibal embarked from his base in the Iberian peninsula, traveled through Gaul, and across the Alps, gathering reinforcements along the way. He scored two victories against the Romans shortly after he arrived in the Italian peninsula.

Despite the subsequent success of delaying tactics by dictator Fabius, the Romans decided to force a battle. The Roman army sent to destroy Hannibal numbered 85,000 men, almost double the Carthaginian army. But, Roman military leadership suffered by a bifurcated command system composed of two consuls who commanded on alternating days. It was the legionnaires' misfortune to be commanded on the day of battle by the hotheaded consul Tarentius Varro instead of the prudent Aemilius Paullus.

On August 2, the Roman legions assembled in three rows on the plain of Cannae in the Apulia region of southeast Italy. There they confronted a motley agglomeration of Iberians, Gauls, Libyans, Numidians, and others, each with its distinctive attire (or lack thereof) whose center temptingly arched toward them in a convex half-circle. At Varro's command, the Romans bore down on the arch, forcing it back until it became a concave bowl that folded in on the legionnaires.

Just as the center appeared to break, Hannibal ordered his unengaged wings of infantry and light cavalry to attack the Roman flanks and close the trap.

The result was a slaughter. The killing lasted into the evening and continued the following morning. An estimated 70,000 Romans, including consul Paullus and at least eighty senators, died. The roughly 15,000 survivors included consul Varro, who was disgraced.

Cannae was the most brilliant tactical victory in history and it caused many provinces to revoke their allegiance to Rome. Even so, Hannibal's campaign in Italy ultimately failed, for Rome never capitulated.

Hannibal acclaimed in triumph by his troops

QUINTUS FABIUS MAXIMUS VERRUCOSUS

Roman strategist and general during the Second Punic War (ca. 275 B.C.–203 B.C.)

The Roman campaign to defeat the Carthaginian invader Hannibal and his army in Italy had resulted in Roman defeats at Trebia and Lake Trasimene. In an unusual move, the Roman Senate in 217 B.C. named Quintus Fabius Maximus Verrucosus the dictator responsible for stopping Hannibal.

Fabius had enormous respect for Hannibal and especially the deadly Carthaginian cavalry. He marched north, making sure to keep his legions in the hills and woods where Hannibal's cavalry would be ineffective. His intent was to stay close enough to the Carthaginian army to be a constant threat but far enough away to be beyond the reach of powerful attack.

For months, Fabius only conducted harassment raids and skirmishes—using his troops more like guerrillas and irregulars rather than battlefield troops. His "small war" tactics targeted stragglers, foraging parties, and vulnerable supply trains. To combat the attrition he was suffering, Hannibal laid ambushes and tried to corner Fabius into sites for open battle—but Fabius resisted him at every turn.

Fabius' tactics bought Rome valuable time to renew its morale and military strength. However, eventually, many Romans became dissatisfied with the dictator's methods, there being little glory in no battle. His name soon became a term of insult and he was derisively called the Cunctator (Delayer). Rivals and enemies within the Senate further slurred Fabius' reputation. When Fabius' period of dictatorship ended, Rome reverted to its regular practice of command and tactics.

When Rome suffered another military disaster at Cannae, Fabius' reputation was not only restored, but the pejorative "Cunctator" was transformed into an honorific. Fabius' tactics against Hannibal were resumed and used against the Carthaginian general throughout his campaigns in Italy. Fabius died before the Second Punic War ended.

Today, *Fabian strategy* is the term for military doctrine designed to wear down an enemy by avoiding set-piece confrontation.

FABIAN

Strategy of caution

A Fabian strategy is perhaps the most sublime in war—it seeks victory through *threatening* to do battle without actually resorting to decisive combat. In an amendment of the famous axiom, it could be expressed as: The army that chooses not to fight and stays away, lives to fight another day.

The tactics of a Fabian strategy involve the (usually defending) general keeping his army close enough to the army of his enemy so as to be a threat, while remaining far enough away so that a quick attack by the enemy is not possible. The naval counterpart of this strategy is the "fleet in being," in which the presence of an enemy fleet is sufficient to influence an opponent's strategy, even though that fleet rarely, if ever, leaves port. Imperial Germany used this strategy with its surface fleet in World War I and Fascist Italy used this strategy in the Mediterranean in World War II.

The two most effective land uses of this strategy occurred in the Second Punic War (218–201 B.C.) and the Napoleonic Wars (1800–1815). Roman consul Fabius Maximus (the strategy that bears his name) was the first to use it, which he did with great effect against the Carthaginian general, Hannibal. The other was Russian general Mikhail Kutuzov against Napoleon. One of the consequences of a Fabian strategy is that its avoidance of battle can prove frustrating not only to the enemy but also to the general's own leaders and public opinion. And, in both cases, Fabius and Kutuzov succumbed to pressure back home—the former being relieved of command and the latter forced to do battles he didn't want to do, like Borodino. Ultimately, subsequent circumstances redeemed their reputations.

Italian fleet that used a Fabian strategy during World War II to threaten the British Royal Navy

ROMAN LEGION

Basic unit of the Roman army used during the Second Punic War

The Roman legion was a formation so supple that military historian Lynn Montross compared it to the human hand, saying, "The legion was capable either of closing up solidly like a fist, or of feeling out the enemy's weaknesses with the effect of exploring fingers."

The size of a legion varied as Rome grew from republic to empire but the basic formation generally remained the same. In battle formation, it contained three battle lines of troops: the *hastati* were in the first, *principes* in the second, and *triarii* and *velites* in the third. Typically, the first two lines were composed of 20 maniples, a unit containing 120 legionaries each. In the third line, ten units of light infantry (containing 120 men each) alternated with as many units of reserves (each reserve unit containing 60 men). The *hastati* were young men aged twenty-five to thirty. The *principes* were seasoned troops ranging in ages from thirty to forty. In the third line, the *triarii* were veterans usually fighting in their last campaigns and the *velites* were the youngest, ages seventeen to twenty-five, who served as light infantry.

The basic units of a Roman legion were the *centuria*, or century (a group of 80 men), maniple (120 men), and cohort (480 men). The professional officers were called centurions. As they gained experience and seniority, they rose in command responsibility. Though the bulk of a Roman legion was composed of infantry, it included cavalry, archers, and other support units.

The basic weapons of the legionnaire were the *pilum*, a seven-foot throwing and thrusting spear, and the *gladius*, a cut-and-thrust sword with a broad blade. Made of steel, it was heavy and sharp enough to sever an opponent's arm or leg. The legionnaire was protected by body armor and carried a rectangular shield called a *scutum*. The scutum was designed so that the legionnaires could form a shield wall that, in the hands of an experienced legion, was impenetrable.

Each legion had a name, or number, and distinctive symbol and some of them became quite famous during the course of empire. Those that brought shame to the legions had their name or number struck from the rolls.

General Belisarius leading the Roman legions

SWORD

Infantry weapon used during the Second Punic War

The sword is an ancient weapon, though it developed later than the bow or the spear. It was not until metallurgy became sophisticated enough to separate metal from ore and create alloys that practical swords were created. The first swords appeared in the Bronze Age (which lasted from about 4000 to 1000 B.C.). Because of its low tensile strength, these swords were relatively short (about a foot). Longer swords useful in combat were not developed until the Iron Age (which began roughly around 1000 B.C.).

Like the bow, swords were fashioned and shaped according to cultural prejudices and specialized combat requirements. Cavalry troopers needed lightweight, narrow swords with a long reach suitable for slashing. They also tended to be single-edged. The infantry needed heavier two-edged swords that could do double duty as a slashing or thrusting weapon. Cultural variations included the Arabian scimitar, the Japanese katana and wakizashi (long and short swords), the Indian tulwar, East Indian kris, and European dueling swords such as the rapier and smallsword. Wasters, practice swords made of wood, were used in almost all cultures that had metal swords.

One of the most famous swords was the Roman legionnaire's gladius (the Latin word for "sword"). The gladius was a two-edged steel alloy sword that was 25–31 inches long, 1.5–3.1 inches wide, and weighed 2.6–3.5 pounds. It had a small, knobbed hilt and a solid grip to minimize slippage caused by bloodletting. The scabbard of the gladius was mounted on a belt or shoulder strap. It was used, with variants, throughout the history of the Roman Empire.

The Scottish claymore (Gaelic for "great sword") was a long two-handed, double-edged steel alloy sword widely used in the medieval period. At about 55 inches in length, with a 13-inch grip, a 42-inch tapering blade, and weighing an average of 5.5 pounds, it was one of the longer, heavier swords.

By the early nineteenth century, sword use in the infantry was confined to officers. The ranks used bayonets that enabled their muskets or rifles to become spear-like weapons. The cavalry continued to use swords well into the nineteenth century.

Today, military use of swords is confined to ceremonial purposes.

Detail of Jacques-Louis David's *The Oath of Horatii* showing the Roman gladius

Battle of Zama

The decisive Roman victory over Hannibal

Scipio was Rome's greatest general in the Second Punic War. He was one of the few Romans who realized that the surest way to drive Hannibal out of Italy was to first eliminate the Carthaginian general's logistical base in Spain, then attack Carthage itself. Scipio accomplished the first goal in a two-year campaign that began in 206 B.C. Despite this success, the Roman Senate at first refused Scipio's request to attack Carthage, as Hannibal and his army remained in Italy. Eventually Scipio overcame the Senate's resistance and landed a small army in northern Africa. Scipio's victories against Carthaginian forces in 203 B.C. resulted in a desperate recall of Hannibal and his army.

Estimates vary on the size of both armies, though historians agree that in sheer numbers, Hannibal's was the larger. Scipio's, however, was better trained. Historians have speculated that Hannibal knew his army could not win when, on the eve of battle, he requested a parley. Upon Scipio's refusal to amend the strict Roman terms for peace, Hannibal prepared for battle.

Hannibal formed three lines of infantry, with the third containing his veterans from the Italian campaign. Hannibal began with an attack of eighty elephants. The Carthaginian elephants were routed off the battlefield, hotly pursued by the Roman cavalry, perhaps as Hannibal intended.

But the low quality of the first two lines of Carthaginian infantry resulted in chaos and panic as soon as the better-trained Roman infantry struck them. Yet, Hannibal's third line held and might have snatched victory from the jaws of defeat had not Scipio's reorganized cavalry returned in time to deliver the coup de grâce.

Hannibal's cavalry had a reputation of being his most powerful and feared arm. But, at Zama, the Carthaginian cavalry proved mediocre and was decisively outmatched by the Roman horse. The Carthaginian infantry was of even worse quality—it contained only a few of Hannibal's veterans from the Italian campaign.

The Romans smashed the Carthaginian army. Hannibal escaped—barely—with perhaps a quarter of his men. Carthage was forced to sue for peace, ending the Second Punic War.

Elephants being used during the Battle of Zama

HANNIBAL BARCA

Carthaginian general and "Father of Strategy" (ca. 247–183 B.C.)

Many generals have struck terror in their enemies' hearts. Even so, when nations or empires formally declare war, it's almost always against their fellow nation-states because generals are servants of their country. But two generals achieved the distinction of having enemy nations identify them *individually,* and not their country, as the foe to be defeated. Napoleon I was one. Hannibal was the other. Military historians consider Hannibal the "Father of Strategy" because of his visionary fourteen-year campaign in the Italian peninsula during the Second Punic War (218–201 B.C.).

Hannibal was the son of Carthaginian general Hamilcar Barca who fought Rome in the First Punic War (264–241 B.C.). Following its conclusion, Hannibal's father established an autonomous province in Iberia (Spain). Hannibal learned from his father to hate Rome and promised Hamilcar he would dedicate his life to fighting the empire. When Hannibal completed the Iberian Peninsula's conquest in 219 B.C., Rome, fearing a resurgent Carthage, declared war. The end of the First Punic War left Carthage too weak militarily and economically to seriously challenge Rome. Thus, the Second Punic War was less a war between the rival empires of Carthage and Rome than a personal war between Hannibal and the Roman Empire.

The following year, Hannibal's army arrived in northern Italy. Hannibal's crossing of the Alps with his army and elephants in 218 B.C. is one of the ancient world's most famous epics. For fourteen years, Rome sent army after army against him. Hannibal defeated all that dared fight him. Some, notably those led by consul Fabius, did not. Hannibal's victory at Cannae was his greatest. Only after Rome attacked Carthage did Hannibal depart to defend his homeland. Finally, he was defeated at the battle of Zama and Carthage surrendered.

Hannibal was eventually forced into exile in Syria, where he continued to be a thorn in Rome's side. At age seventy, facing imminent capture, Hannibal committed suicide. According to legend, his last words were, "Let us release the Romans from their long anxiety, since they think it too long to wait for the death of an old man."

SIEGE OF CARTHAGE, THIRD PUNIC WAR (149–146 B.C.)

Destruction of Rome's greatest rival

Rome's struggle with Carthage finally ended with the annihilation of Carthage and the incorporation of what remained of its shrunken empire at the end of the Third Punic War in 146 B.C.

This last conflict was caused when Masinissa, King of Numidia and an ally of Rome, attempted to seize territory from Carthage. According to the harsh terms of the treaty with Rome that ended the Second Punic War, Carthage had to first petition Rome and receive its permission before declaring war on an aggressor. Initially Carthage had asked Rome to mediate and when Rome refused, a desperate Carthage sent an army against Masinissa to defend its territory.

This caused Rome, whose suspicions of Carthage were virtually pathological, to send a large army and fleet to Africa. A Carthaginian delegation rushed to Rome, pleaded its case, and threw itself on the mercy of the Senate. The new conditions were unbelievably harsh: the handover of all arms, burning of the fleet, and the complete destruction of the city. The seafaring Carthaginians would be allowed to build a new city, but it could not be constructed as another port—it had to be built at least ten miles inland. In effect, they'd have to become farmers.

Faced with what amounted to an economic death sentence, the Carthaginians chose to fight, though it was a battle they knew they could not win. The city held out against siege for more than two years. In the spring of 146 B.C., with the help of Carthaginian deserters, consul Publius Cornelius Scipio Aemilianus breached the three lines of fortifications. House-to-house fighting continued for a week, with neighborhoods being put to the torch. The 50,000 survivors were sold into slavery. Then, over a period lasting between ten and seventeen days, the Romans proceeded to systematically reduce the city to rubble. Finally, according to legend, the ground was sown with salt to ensure nothing would grow.

After the rest of the Carthaginian Empire was made a Roman province, Rome's great rival was finally eliminated.

Ruins of the Acropolis in Carthage

BATTLE OF ALESIA

Julius Caesar's victory that secured Gaul for Rome

Julius Caesar's conquest of Gaul established him as one of history's great generals. After numerous individual defeats, the Gaulish tribes finally united against Rome. They chose Vercingetorix, chief of the Averni, to command their combined armies. In early 52 B.C., Vercingetorix defeated Caesar at Gergovia. After several smaller indecisive battles, Vercingetorix decided to regroup at Alesia.

Alesia was a hilltop-fortified stronghold surrounded by river valleys. Julius Caesar arrived at Alesia in September with twelve legions and support units totaling almost 60,000 men. Inside Alesia, Vercingetorix's numbers were about equal in warriors. Caesar decided the easiest way to win was to begin a siege and starve Alesia into submission.

Vercingetorix, for his part, saw an opportunity to destroy Caesar. Before the contravallation wall that sealed off Alesia could be completed, he sent out messengers carrying appeals to the Gaulish tribes. While he held Caesar and his legions at Alesia, they would band together in a great army of a million warriors, come to Alesia, and destroy the Romans. An army of about 250,000, led by Commius, king of the Belgic Atrebates, responded but the army was intercepted and routed with terrific slaughter.

When this attack and several breakout attempts failed, Vercingetorix realized he had to capitulate or his people would starve. He clad himself in his finest armor, jumped on his horse that was covered in rich ornaments, and exited the gate in great ceremony. He rode up to Caesar and after riding around the Roman, dismounted, stripped his horse of its gold and silver trappings, took off his armor, and threw everything at Caesar's feet. Then he sat down beside his trophies, having uttered not a single word during the whole time.

Though there would some later fighting, Vercingetorix's surrender marked the end of organized resistance in Gaul against Rome. Vercingetorix was taken to Rome where he was held prisoner under conditions amounting to comfortable house arrest. Five years later, at the end of a triumph honoring Caesar's victory over the Gauls, Vercingetorix was strangled to death under Caesar's orders.

Vercingetorix surrendering to Julius Caesar

GAIUS JULIUS CAESAR

Roman general at the Battle of Alesia and dictator (100–44 B.C.)

Julius Caesar was one of Rome's greatest generals. His conquests laid the foundation for the Roman Empire and for the 500-year period of stability referred to as the Pax Romana. His achievements as general and statesman were so influential that the German and Russian names for their kings (*kaiser* and *czar,* respectively) are derived from his last name.

Caesar was born into a patrician family. During his early years, he devoted his life to politics. It was a time of decline in Rome's republican institutions and, in 59 B.C., together with Pompey and Crassus, he formed the ruling First Triumvirate. Caesar's administrative region included Gaul. It would be there that Caesar gained fame as one of history's great generals.

Beginning in 58 B.C., and for the next seven years, Caesar waged a campaign of conquest in Gaul, which at that time included what are now France, Belgium, and parts of Germany, Holland, and Switzerland. Though his legions were often outnumbered, they were the better-disciplined force. For the first three years, he advanced north, defeating tribes of Helvetii (Swiss), Germanic peoples under Ariovistus, and the Belgae and Nervii (Belgians). Upon reaching what is now the English Channel, he swept first west into Brittany and then east to the Rhine. In 55 B.C., he invaded England and within two years made it a part of the Roman Empire.

Returning to Gaul, he marched through the country, putting down one revolt after another. His victory over Vercingetorix and the Gauls at Alesia in 52 B.C. ended the revolution. His account of the campaigns, *Commentaries on the Gallic War,* is a classic of war literature.

In 50 B.C., civil war broke out with his rival Pompey, who had been a part of his ruling triumvirate. By 44 B.C., he had defeated Pompey and other challengers and become dictator for life. Caesar planned sweeping reforms of Roman law and governance but was assassinated on the Ides of March (March 15) 44 B.C. by reactionaries jealous of his power. A short civil war followed, won by his nephew Octavian who, as Augustus Caesar, would enact many of Julius Caesar's reforms.

BATTLE OF ACTIUM

Octavian's victory over Marc Antony that ended a century of Roman civil war

Following the assassination of Julius Caesar, the leadership of Rome was placed in the hands of the triumvirs Octavian (Caesar's nephew), Marc Antony (a general under Caesar), and Marcus Aemilius Lepidus (a supporter of Julius Caesar). Disagreements between Octavian and Marc Antony reached a breaking point when Octavian formally declared war on Cleopatra (the Egyptian queen and Marc Antony's wife) and stripped Marc Antony of his political authority.

Using Cleopatra's money, Marc Antony organized an army of 120,000 men and a fleet of about 360 ships based near Actium, Greece. Octavian fielded an army of about 92,000 men and a fleet of about 400 ships. Marc Antony's warships were decaremes and octoremes—large, heavy war galleys. Octavian's were lighter and more maneuverable liburnae (probably modified triremes). The battle began on land and Octavian successfully outmaneuvered Marc Antony, sealing off his logistical base and laid siege to his army. As Marc Antony's men began to starve, desertion rates rose. Desperate, Marc Antony realized he had to escape or face capture and certain death. One plan called for him to escape north through Macedonia. But Cleopatra, who was with him, preferred a faster and more direct sea route to Egypt.

Marc Antony's fleet attempted to smash its way through Octavian's on September 2. Instead of following traditional tactics of ramming and boarding, the two fleets began with missile attacks of flaming darts and other projectiles launched by hand and catapults.

Despite some initial setbacks, at one point it appeared Marc Antony had a chance of winning. But, what swung the battle against him was the sudden breakout of Cleopatra's squadron of sixty ships, containing the payroll for the army and navy. When Marc Antony saw this, he inexplicably abandoned the fight and his men and followed Cleopatra.

At first his sailors and soldiers refused to believe that he had deserted them and the fighting continued for several days. When the truth was known, they capitulated.

Marc Antony's reputation as a trustworthy general was shattered. Both Marc Antony and Cleopatra committed suicide the following year. The Roman civil war was over, with Octavian reigning as the master of Rome.

The defeat of Marc Antony's fleet at Actium

ANTONIVS APERTO
NAVALI PRÆLIO
A ROMANIS DEBELLATVR
ET FVGIT

BATTLE OF TEUTOBURG FOREST

Roman military disaster

Caesar Augustus had added large swaths of land to the Roman Empire during his reign. He intended to extend Roman rule in the north, beginning with a recently pacified region the Romans called Germania. Shortly after Publius Quinctilius Varus became governor of Germania, he received news of growing revolt in the Rhine River Valley region.

Arminius, chieftain of the Cherusci tribe and a Romanized Germanic prince and military leader, had sent a message, asking for Varus' aid to fight some rebellious Germanic tribes. Despite receiving warnings that Arminius was not to be trusted and was actually in league with the rebellious tribes, Varus agreed to help. Following a route suggested by Arminius, on September 9, Varus took his three legions, the Seventeenth, Eighteenth, and Nineteenth, and support units through the dense Teutoburg Forest to what was supposed to be their objective.

The forest trail was narrow and made muddy by a rainstorm. The troops were forced to break formation and travel in a column later estimated to be anywhere from nine to twelve miles long. Even though he was in a hostile region, Varus did not send ahead any scouting parties. Once the Romans were well within the forest, the Germanic tribes (estimates range from 10,000 to 18,000 warriors) sprang their ambush.

Arminius used his knowledge of Roman tactics against the legionnaires. The barbarians were able to break the column into many small groups and slaughter Romans in detail. Those legionnaires who succeeded in escaping the trap and setting up a fortified camp only delayed their fate. The following morning they attempted to make a breakout to safety but instead fell into a second trap. Of the 20,000–25,000 Roman troops involved, at least 15,000, and possibly as many as 20,000, were lost. Varus was one of those killed.

News of the disaster threw Augustus into a massive depression. The numbers of the legions annihilated at Teutoburg Forest were struck from the list of legions, never to be used again. The battle also ended further Roman expansion in the north.

Romans being massacred by the Germans

SIEGE OF MASADA

Battle that ended the Great Jewish Revolt

The Great Jewish Revolt (66–73 A.D.) was the first of three Jewish-Roman Wars in Judea that stretched over a seventy-year period beginning in 66 A.D. The first revolt was caused by mounting religious tension in the region between Greeks and Jews; it then involved the Romans as well. Roman garrisons were attacked and soon Judea was in the middle of rebellion. Emperor Nero sent Roman legions to crush the rebellion and restore order. Jerusalem was sacked and leveled, and many Jews were rounded up and sold into slavery and scattered throughout the empire. Mopping up operations commenced and the last stronghold remaining was Masada, a onetime fortress-palace built by King Herod on a mesa overlooking the Dead Sea.

In 72 A.D., Lucius Flavius Silva, Roman governor of Judea, led the X Fretensis Roman legion to Masada and lay siege to the fortress. When direct attacks failed to breach the fortress's walls, the Romans shifted to a prolonged siege and built a circumvallation wall to seal off Masada. A rampart built out of nearby bedrock and a scaling ramp were completed in the spring of 73 A.D. The Romans then brought up a battering ram and finally broke through the fortress wall.

When the legionnaires entered, they discovered all the buildings except the food storerooms were on fire. Yet they encountered no resistance. Further searching revealed 953 bodies. The inhabitants had committed mass suicide rather than suffer whatever fate the Romans had in store for them. According to the Jewish-Roman scholar Josephus, he received the account of Masada from two women who, together with five children, survived the suicide by hiding in a cistern.

The Great Revolt was over and peace would remain in the region for forty-two years until the second uprising.

The siege of the fortress at Masada

BATTLE OF CHALONS

Battle that stopped Hun invasion of Western Europe

Through a combination of terror and demands of tribute, the Huns had dominated Europe for decades. In 450, the Roman Emperor Valentinian's sister, Honoria, was offered in marriage to Hun leader Attila and he accepted. When the engagement was later broken, Attila used it as an excuse to launch a campaign against the Roman Empire. Instead of defending Rome, Valentinian went into exile, leaving the new emperor, Aetius, to deal with the impending Hun invasion.

Attila, his Huns and their allies, marched across present-day Germany and into northern France, sacking one city after another. The Hun advance reached as far west as Paris and Orleans before turning east. In the meantime, Aetius had gathered what army he could in Italy and marched north to Gaul. There he met the Visigoth king, Theodoric I, and succeeded in convincing him to join with the Romans to defeat Attila. Other Goth tribes were convinced to join as well.

On about June 20 (the generally accepted date), the Roman and Visigoth armies met Attila's on the Catalaunian Plains somewhere near Troyes, in northeastern France. Auguries performed by the Huns the morning before battle predicted the Huns would encounter disaster and that one of the enemy leaders would die.

A large ridge dominated the plains and served as the focus of battle. The Huns seized the right side and the Romans the left, with the high center unoccupied. When the Huns attempted to take the center, the Goth warriors drove them back in disorder. Attila attempted to rally his troops and hold their position. But the Goths pressed the advantage and Roman troops joined in the rush that drove the Huns back to their camp. When night fell and the fighting stopped, the situation was so confused that Aetius thought he had lost.

When morning came, survivors discovered bodies littering large tracts of the plain. One of the slain was Theodoric, apparently killed when leading the counterattack.

The two sides warily faced each other, with neither choosing to make the first move to fight. Attila ordered his army to break camp and return east. Aetius was content to let him go, not willing to crown victory with possible defeat. Two years later, Attila died, and the Hun threat to Western Europe was erased.

Hun troops in battle at Chalons

SACK OF ROME

Pivotal event in the fall of the Roman Empire

Rome had become a lesser city since the division of the empire by Diocletian in 286. However, it was still filled with treasure. Alaric I, king of the Visigoths, had sacked Rome in 410—the first time in almost 800 years that it had fallen. Even though the looting had lasted only three days, and there had been little murder and rape, it was still a profound shock to the city's citizens. Yet, Rome recovered. In 442, Emperor Valentinian III signed a peace treaty with Geiseric, chief of the Vandals, one of the many northern tribes that the much-weakened Rome now had to accommodate.

But Valentinian III proved incompetent and vindictive and, after only eleven weeks in power, was murdered by a Roman mob. Senator Petronius Maximus, known as an able administrator, mounted the throne. He married Valentinian's widow, Licinia Eudoxia, though she suspected him of complicity in her husband's murder. She appealed to help from Geiseric, whom she had come to know during Valentinian's negotiations. And her daughter, Eudocia, had been betrothed to Geiseric's son, before Petronius broke the union.

Geiseric announced that Valentinian's murder had invalidated the peace treaty and he set sail from Tunis with his army for Rome. Panic gripped the city. Petronius, more concerned about saving his own life, did nothing to organize the city's defenses. He attempted to escape on May 31 but was caught by an angry mob and killed.

On June 2, Geiseric and his army arrived at the gates of Rome. Pope Leo I met the Vandal chief and begged him not to destroy the city or murder its inhabitants. Geiseric agreed and the gates were thrown open for him and his men. Accounts vary in details, but all generally agree the Vandals looted Rome for two weeks, stripping it of treasure and gathering many of its citizens together for sale as slaves. When they left, Geiseric also took Licinia Eudoxia and her daughters, including Eudocia, who later married Geiseric's son, as previously intended.

This time, Rome's recovery was not like before. The sacking hastened the city's decline.

A Vandal attack on Rome

BATTLE OF BADR

Decisive battle in Muhammad's war

Two important trading centers on the Arabian Peninsula in the seventh century were Mecca and Medina. Following his revelations at age forty, Muhammad, the founder of Islam, began preaching to the tribes in Mecca. Though he gained followers, he also encountered hostility among the tribes including his own, the Quraish. To escape persecution, he took his followers to Medina on what became the historic event known as the Hijra. During his time in Medina, he united those tribes and gained more converts. In 624, Muhammad discovered that a caravan traveling from Syria to Mecca was funded by valuables left behind by his followers when they departed Mecca. This was done in mockery of the Muslims. Muhammad organized an army of 300–350 men to take back what had been stolen.

When the caravan leader learned of Muhammad's plan to ambush them, he sent word to the Quraish who responded with an army of 900–1,000 men to protect it. When the Muslims received news of the army's approach, Muhammad called a council of war. Though the Ansar (Helpers) were not obliged to fight, all pledged to join in battle. Following a forced march, the Muslims reached the valley of Badr, where wells used by travelers and caravans were located.

At midnight, on March 17, the Quraish army marched into the valley of Badr, a day after the Muslims. There they set up camp and scouts returned with the latest intelligence about the Muslims. On the March 18, the battle began with both sides shouting at each other and champions issuing challenges. One duel was fought, with the Muslims losing. When both armies began firing arrows at each other, Muhammad gave the order to charge, throwing a handful of pebbles at the Meccans. Though outnumbered roughly three to one as recounted in the Koran, the Muslims, aided by angels, bravely rushed the Meccan line. They routed the Meccans, killing at least fifty and capturing more than forty. Only fourteen Muslims were killed.

Ascribed to the will of Allah, the victory transformed Muhammad overnight from an outcast to an important leader and gave an immense boost to Islam.

Eighteenth-century illustration of Muslims journeying to Mecca

BATTLE OF TOURS

Victory by Charles Martel that stops Muslim expansion in France

Following Muhammad's death in 632, the caliphs, "successors" of the Prophet, began campaigns to spread the faith. By 638, Arabic armies had taken Jerusalem. Within three decades, they had swept east to India and west across Egypt and North Africa. In 711, they crossed the Strait of Gibraltar and conquered most of Spain. In 732, a Muslim army under the Umayyad Caliphate led by Abdul Rahman Al Ghafiqi took the next great step and crossed the Pyrenees Mountains.

The Muslim army marched north, deep into France, almost reaching the Loire River. In October, near Tours, advance elements were stunned to discover that an army of the Franks led by Charles Martel waited for them on high ground. Martel had achieved total surprise. For the next seven days, the two armies skirmished as both sides waited for reinforcements.

On October 11, with armies at full strength (exact figures are unknown, though the majority opinion is that Martel's army was greatly outnumbered), the battle commenced. Martel had been preparing for this moment for ten years. He knew if he lost this battle, the Muslim armies would be impossible to stop. During those preparatory years, he trained his men year-round, an unprecedented action possible only because it was funded by the pope. Which is why, when the feared Muslim cavalry charged, his infantry formations held, even though the ranks were broken in places.

As the main battle continued, Martel's scouts entered the Muslim camp and began freeing as many slaves as possible. The intent was to draw off part of the Umayyad cavalry—and it worked. The rest of the Muslim army misinterpreted the cavalry's action to protect their property as a full-scale retreat. The Muslim general tried to stem the retreat but was killed. Martel's army resumed formation and rested in place that night, expecting to do battle the next day.

When the Muslim army did not renew the attack, Martel was suspicious of an ambush. But reconnaissance patrols discovered the Muslims had decamped during the night and begun a retreat south. Charles Martel had achieved one of the greatest victories in history. Western Europe would remain Christian.

Charles Martel leading the Franks army at Tours

ALFRED THE GREAT

First King of the Anglo-Saxons (ca. 849–899)

One of the more important monarchs in the Middle Ages was Alfred the Great, one of only two English monarchs to be known as "the Great" (Canute is the other). His defense of his kingdom against Viking raiders, primarily Danes, earned him the enduring love of his people. In addition Alfred became famous for his love of learning and his just administration. So great was the esteem for him that a poll of 100 Greatest Britons published in 2002 listed Alfred at number fourteen.

Alfred was the youngest of four sons born to King Aethelwulf of Wessex (in southern England). At age five, he went to Rome where he had an audience with Pope Leo IV. He later accompanied his father on pilgrimages to Rome, at one point staying there for one year to study.

In other circumstances, Alfred might have entered the church, a typical career for a son in his position. But, the reigns of his two eldest brothers were short. When the third brother, Ethelred, became king, Alfred was formally recognized as the successor. In 871, Alfred began what was later called "Alfred's year of battles" in which he participated in nine major engagements against Danish raiders, a mixture of victories and defeats.

Upon Ethelred's death in 871, Alfred became king and inherited the full responsibility of defending his kingdom and people against the Danes. His battles against the cunning Danish Chief Guthrum initially met with more failure than success. This changed with the Battle of Edington in 878, where he defeated Guthrum and converted the pagans to Christians.

Alfred continued to travel across England to counter recurrent threats by the Danes. Through war, diplomacy, and bribery, he checked the worst of Danish depredations. When he was not fighting, he was importing scholars. Such was his love of learning that he mastered Latin when an adult and translated Roman texts. Administratively, he established a legal code called Deemings that was one of his greatest legacies. It was a combination of Anglo-Saxon customs, Celtic Law, and Mosaic Law that was built upon by his successors. The date of his death is uncertain, though thought to be 899.

Viking Longboat

Ship used by Danes against Alfred the Great

The Vikings would never have become the terror of Western Europe during the early Middle Ages, nor globe-spanning explorers, traders, and raiders had they not had their longboats. The longboats were better designed than the Greek and Roman vessels of the Mediterranean world, and they overcame water resistance to a degree not equaled until modern times. They were distinctively designed, with wide, shallow-draft single-decked hulls and carved prows and sterns that rose high out of the water. They were built for speed and seaworthiness at the sacrifice of size. The largest longboat held fewer than two hundred men.

The longboat was generally made of oak, though exceptions were made depending on availability of local timber. Longboat design was perfected by the ninth century and from that point on Vikings would range far and wide. Longboats were propelled by sail and oars and their shallow draft allowed for easy portage. Their travels took them as far west as Iceland, Greenland, and North America and as far east as the Volga River in Russia.

The longboat use declined after the Middle Ages; ships based on the longboat design were still in use in some parts of the world until the 1950s.

Viking sailors used the longboat to make the voyage across the Atlantic to America

BATTLE OF HASTINGS

Duke of Normandy's victory that allowed for the Norman conquest of England

Three men had legitimate claim to the throne of England in 1066: Earl Harold Godwinson of Wessex, Harald Hardrada of Norway, and William, Duke of Normandy (also known as William the Conquerer). After Harold of Wessex was crowned king, he prepared to fight his rivals. Harald, the Norwegian king, was the first to challenge him. He landed with his army in northern England in the middle of September. The English king raised an army, attacked his Norwegian rival on September 25, and soundly defeated the Norse army. The two remaining men to battle were English King Harold and William, Duke of Normandy.

At the same time of the fighting between the Norse and English, William had raised an army of about 5,000 men and landed on the southern coast of England near Hastings on September 28. News rapidly reached King Harold and his troops still in the north. Deciding to strike before William had a chance to establish himself, Harold led his men on a two-week, 250-mile forced march south.

Harold had hoped to take William and his army by surprise but scouts kept William informed of Harold's progress. By the time Harold arrived at Hastings on October 13, William's men were ready and waiting. Harold's men, in contrast, were exhausted. Yet Harold refused to pause. He was determined to attack the following morning.

The battle lines formed the morning of October 14. William took the initiative and attacked at about 9 A.M. The initial clash of troops soon turned into a brutal slugging match in which Norman arrow, lance, and sword sparred with the terrible battle-axes of Harold's Saxon infantry protected by a stout shield wall.

When it was clear that the battle had stalled, William deployed his cavalry in a series of feigning attacks that lured some Saxons out from behind their shield wall. But the stratagem failed and the opponents continued to fight throughout the day, with neither side gaining a clear advantage. Then, near dusk, King Harold fell dead from an arrow that struck him in the face. Resistance collapsed and the Normans fell upon the retreating Saxons.

Days later, William was crowned king. A new chapter in English history had opened.

Detail from a 1082 tapestry showing the Normans killing Harold's men

WILLIAM I, THE CONQUEROR

Anglo-Norman ruler and victor at the Battle of Hastings (ca. 1027–1087)

The man who would lead the last successful invasion of England in 1066 was born the illegitimate son of Duke Robert, the Devil of Normandy. While acknowledged as his father's successor following Robert's death on a pilgrimage to Jerusalem in 1034, William had to suppress a baronial rebellion in 1035. Only through the help and protection of French King Henry I was William able to crush it. He increased his holdings in France with the conquest of the bordering provinces of Maine and Brittany.

William's ambitions then turned north, to England. Based on the fact that his grandfather's sister was the mother of Edward, king of England, and that Edward was childless, William declared himself heir to the English throne. William convinced Edward to support his claim in 1051. William buttressed his claim when he secured the agreement of Edward's brother-in-law, Harold Godwin (or Godwinson), the Earl of Wessex. But when Edward died in 1066, Harold reneged, and declared himself King Harold II.

William was determined to make good on his royal claim through a combination of force and diplomacy. Using threats and cajolery, William gained the military support of his barons who were unenthusiastic about the venture. On the diplomatic side, he allied himself with Harold's brother, Tostig, and Harald Hardrada, king of Norway, who also had a claim to the English throne. He also secured the support of Pope Alexander II and the neutrality of Holy Roman Emperor Henry IV.

When Harold was killed in the Battle of Hastings, William's claim to the English throne was clear. He was crowned William I, King of England on December 25, 1066, in London. For the next five years, William brutally suppressed a series of rebellions in the country, replacing the Anglo-Saxon aristocracy with his Norman followers.

William's desire to properly govern his kingdom led to the integration of Anglo-Saxon and Norman customs and traditions in England. One of the most notable features of his rule was the Domesday Book, commissioned in 1086, a detailed record of people, land and property. William died in 1087 from fatal injuries suffered in a horse accident.

SIEGE OF ANTIOCH

Key early campaign in the First Crusade

In 1095, Pope Urban II made a speech at the council of Clermont calling for a crusade to free the Holy Land. Some of the most illustrious kings and aristocrats of Europe, including Raymond of Toulouse, Godfrey of Bouillon, and Bohemund of Taranto, responded, formed armies, and embarked on what became the First Crusade (1095–1099).

The Crusader armies of the three met their first great military challenge when they arrived at the gates of the Moslim-held city of Antioch. Located on the Orontes River and near the Mediterranean Sea just north of modern Syria, Antioch (today, Antakya, Turkey) was a strategic city. After an initial disagreement over whether to attack or lay siege, the group chose to put the city to siege because the city's fortifications were so strong. The armies deployed themselves around Antioch and the siege commenced on October 20, 1097.

But the siege was unskillfully conducted. The Crusaders did not have enough troops to maintain a siege line strong enough to prevent supplies from reaching the city. Attempts to bombard the city with siege engines were ineffective. Food and supplies for the Crusaders and pilgrims accompanying the armies ran out, even though the region was rich in agriculture. As winter approached, inclement weather added to the Crusaders' misery. Their tents and shelters provided inadequate protection to the cold and rain. For weeks on end, common soldiers and pilgrims lived literally up to their necks in water.

The siege dragged on under ever-worsening conditions. Some chose to leave but most remained. Though exhausted, sick, and depressed, the remaining Crusaders still had enough energy to repel a Turkish army sent to relieve the city.

Ultimately, the city was invaded on June 3, 1098 after a tower guard had been bribed. An indiscriminate massacre followed, in which about 10,000 defenders died. Shortly after they had taken the city, the besiegers themselves became the besieged when a new Turkish army arrived. The Crusaders defeated this army on June 28 and secured an important base for their march to Jerusalem.

Godfrey of Bouillon

TREBUCHET

Mechanical artillery used in the Siege of Antioch

The advancement of warfare could be likened to a cacophonic demonstration of Newton's Third Law of Motion: For every action there is an equal and opposite reaction. Therefore, as cities built walls to protect their wealth and citizens from armies, armies responded by creating siege warfare. An enormous variety of siege engines were designed and built over the millennia. Surprisingly, even relatively primitive civilizations constructed machines of destruction that were remarkable technological achievements. Even today, it is difficult to successfully recreate some.

To defeat the defensive wall, armies had three options: go over, under, or through. Before the advent of gunpowder and cannon, the "through" option was done by mechanical artillery. Mechanical artillery includes catapults, ballistae, and other devices designed to hurl stones or arrows of various sizes and weights. The trebuchet is a counterweight-operated war engine that was the most powerful piece of mechanical artillery ever invented. The trebuchet first appeared in the twelfth century and is based on the concept of the sling. It could hurl an object weighing on average 300 pounds, though massive trebuchets could throw projectiles weighing as much as 3,000 pounds.

Despite their power, mechanical artillery had limitations. They were inefficient weapons against stout city walls. The weapons themselves were heavy and bulky, and logistics could become a nightmare, particularly if a region lacked stones for ammunition. It was not until after gunpowder and large cannon were invented that efficient means of destroying large defensive barriers became possible. Yet, for all of its limitations, mechanical artillery, and the trebuchet, remained active in many armies' arsenals into the 1700s, well after accurate and powerful cannon and mortars had been built. The primary reason for this was that, until the invention of red-hot cannonballs, mechanical artillery was the only way to fire incendiaries.

The trebuchet was used during the siege of Antioch

SIEGE OF JERUSALEM

First Crusade victory that ends in massacre of the city's population

Ruins of Karak Castle in Jordan, a main Crusader stronghold

The First Crusade (1096–1099) was the result of arguably the greatest propaganda campaign in history. Pope Urban II's call in the late eleventh century to liberate the Holy Land and free persecuted Eastern Christians from Muslim rule contained enormous exaggerations and distortions of the facts. Muslim rule of the Holy Land was benign, had existed for about four centuries without prior complaint from Rome, and, unlike Christian kingdoms, was tolerant to Jews. But motivated by spiritual redemption, the army of the First Crusade marched to the Holy Land to free it.

When the army finally saw the Holy City of Jerusalem in the late spring of 1099, there was an explosion of delirious excitement throughout the ranks unequalled by any other army at any other time in history. Once their paroxysm of joy subsided, they got down to business. They were there to fight and to snatch the city from the infidel.

The siege began on June 7 and continued for one month and ten days. Heat and lack of drinking water ravaged the Crusaders. An assault launched on June 13 to breach the walls failed. The Muslim defenders denigrated the religious zeal that motivated the Crusaders. They shouted insults and displayed from the walls desecrated crosses taken from Jerusalem's churches. This inflamed Crusader passions to murderous levels.

At about midday on July 15, the walls of Jerusalem were both breached and stormed. No quarter or mercy was given. Such was the slaughter of Muslim troops that, according to one account, "our men were wading in blood up to their ankles." The Muslim governor and a small party managed to barricade themselves and obtain from the Count of Toulouse the promise of protection following his surrender. It was the only one kept.

For the next two days, the Crusaders, inspired beyond reason by religious frenzy, scoured the city and killed all who fell in their path—civilian men, women, children, and elderly, Muslim and Jew. At least 40,000 people were massacred. As historian Zoé Oldenbourg wrote, it was "among the greatest crimes of history."

Godfrey of Bouillon and other lords leading the Crusader army into Jerusalem

BATTLE OF HATTIN

Saladin's victory that leads to capture of Jerusalem

The Kingdom of Jerusalem, established by the Crusaders in 1099 during the First Crusade, was in a state of crisis in 1187. Guy of Lusignan had gained the crown after a dynastic struggle but was not secure in the throne. Petitions to the kingdoms of Europe for assistance proved fruitless. Most threatening of all, Saladin, the Moslem leader who had united the neighboring nations following a series of civil wars, had launched a campaign against the kingdom.

Saladin quickly conquered a number of outlying forts and laid siege to Tiberias, the capital of Galilee. Guy responded by forming an army of almost 20,000 men, containing 1,200 knights, and marched to relieve the city. Their path led through arid land lain waste by Saladin's troops. Saladin slowly fell back, letting the July heat act as his ally to weaken the enemy.

Harassed by Muslim skirmishers, and suffering from the heat, the troops and horses were parched by the evening of July 3. But Guy chose to encamp at Hattin rather than risk a march through the dark to water at the nearby Sea of Galilee. During the night, the Moslims set fire to the dry grass. Clouds of smoke and Moslim archers sporadically firing into the camp added to the army's misery.

When dawn broke on July 4, Guy's army was dehydrated and exhausted. Guy's foot soldiers said they had no strength left for battle. Most of the knights also refused to fight and pathetically huddled about the relics of the True Cross, brought along to inspire the army to victory. A group of men-at-arms deserted and Saladin let them pass unimpeded. Guy and those of his men who could and would fight attempted first to break through the Moslim lines to reach water at the Sea of Galilee. When that failed, they somehow managed the strength to repeatedly charge Saladin's positions. These ended in failure, as well. Then Saladin ordered his men to attack.

Guy was captured and was one of the few survivors. Saladin continued his campaign against the now defenseless kingdom. On October 2, 1187, he victoriously entered Jerusalem.

Fighting between the Crusaders and Muslims

e demoun   i prat teir

SALADIN

Moslim military leader during the Battle of Hattin (ca. 1138–1193)

Saladin's Arabic name, Salah al-Din Yusuf ibn Ayyub, means "honor of the faith." And, though he was a man of great ambition—he founded the Ayyubid dynasty and ruled over land from Egypt to Iraq—he also led a simple private life of great frugality and generosity. At a time when plunder of the vanquished to gain wealth was customary, he gave away everything he gained in war—to women and children, Moslim and Christian, and even those he had conquered. One biographer, Beha ed-Din (or Baha ad-Din), noted that at his death, "He left neither goods, or houses, furniture, gardens, village, nor plowed land, nor any kind of property." But he was also a brutal man, for he consistently executed, instead of ransomed, the knights of the military orders that were captured.

Saladin was a Kurd, born in Tikrit, Iraq, and educated in Damascus. Though the West knows him primarily for his success against the Crusaders, much of his career was fought against fellow Muslims. Only after two decades of leading armies in a civil war, and after he became Sultan of Egypt, did he turn his attention to the Kingdom of Jerusalem.

He began his campaign against the kingdom in 1187. Leading an army of about 60,000 troops, he captured one fortress after another. His victory over the army led by Guy of Lusignan, King of Jerusalem, led to the capitulation of Jerusalem. Unlike the Crusader occupation in 1099 that ended in a bloodbath that wiped out the city's population, Saladin treated the citizens with compassion. Saladin's successes in Palestine led to the Third Crusade (1189–1192) that was financed in part by a levy called the "Saladin tithe." Richard I of England (Richard the Lionhearted) was one of the leaders of the Crusade. The two rulers fought each other in a series of campaigns that ended in an armistice signed on September 2, 1192. It recognized Saladin's dominance of the region and rule over Jerusalem itself.

Saladin died in Damascus the following year and was buried there. His tomb is a popular attraction to this day.

Mounted Crusaders and Muslims facing one another in battle

GENGHIS KHAN

Mongol conqueror of China in 1215 (ca. 1167–1227)

At the height of his power, Temujin—Genghis Khan ("universal lord," "rightful lord," or "precious lord")—ruled the largest contiguous empire in history, stretching across Eurasia from Poland to Korea and from Vienna to the Arctic Circle in Russia.

He was born into a family of minor Mongol nobility. Because his father was murdered when he was nine years old, his mother taught him horseriding and archery skills. She also instructed him that, in their harsh nomadic world, allies were essential for survival. As he matured, he applied his mother's teachings of diplomacy to assemble a number of trustworthy individuals. By the time Temujin was twenty-five years old, he had united the Mongol tribes into a federation and assumed the title Genghis Khan. He then organized the federation into an army and embarked on conquest.

Because his army was composed entirely of cavalry, Genghis Khan had the most mobile army of the time. His offensives, with their bold, rapid movements and swift, sweeping envelopments, were the first known example of blitzkrieg (lightning war) operations. Genghis Khan arranged his army in escalating groups of ten: ten men to a squad, ten squads to a company, ten companies to a regiment, up to the largest grouping, "Tumens," of 10,000 men. The bulk of it was made up of heavy cavalry warriors who carried a lance and sword and wore a leather armor and breastplate. The light cavalry warriors were archers who wore just a leather helmet.

Another important reason for Genghis Khan's military success was his use of terror. His army rarely took prisoners and their slaughters of conquered cities and peoples made the "barbarian Mongol hordes" the scourge of civilizations unfortunate to be caught in their marauding path. However, he proved to be an enlightened ruler to the conquered peoples who survived his army's savagery. He respected local customs and installed equitable governments composed of local individuals.

By 1215, Genghis Khan had conquered China. By 1222, he was deep into Russia, and by 1226, he ruled from Poland to Korea. He was enroute to punish a rebellion in China when he died in 1227.

Mongol ruler Genghis Khan orders a prisoner to be flogged

BATTLE OF COURTRAI

First battle of the "infantry revolution"

The French king, Philip IV, also known as the Fair, had completed his conquest of Flanders (in modern Belgium) in 1300. Two years later, resentful of French rule, the Flemish threw out the French governor and put to siege the garrison at the castle of Courtrai. Philip's decision to crush the rebellion would result in a landmark battle that inspired a revolution in military organization and philosophy.

Philip dispatched to Flanders an army of about 8,000 men. The centerpiece of the army was the 2,500-man cavalry, composed of the flower of French nobility. The French army arrived at Courtrai in early July. Opposing them was a well-equipped and determined army of Flemish infantry of about 9,000 men. They were grouped in tight formation behind two brooks and a trap-filled marsh. It was a tactical situation that heavily favored the Flemish.

The French infantry made the initial attack, scoring some success against the Flemish. But the French commander, Count Robert II of Artois, recalled the commoners of the infantry. He wished his fellow nobles to have the honor of claiming victory. It was a disastrous decision. The advancing cavalry formations, threading through the retreating infantry, were put in disarray. When they charged, the inhospitable terrain further diluted the force of their attack. The Flemish infantry held its ground and fought with determination. Instead of commoners, it was the nobility who broke and began to retreat from the field. The Flemish infantry counterattacked. The cavalry, hemmed by the brooks, were slaughtered and, in the words of one chronicler, "the glory of French made into dung and worms."

More than 1,000 French nobles perished in the battle. The Flemish gathered their golden spurs—thus giving the engagement its other name, the Battle of the Golden Spurs—which were hung in display in the Church of Our Lady in Kortrijk.

Flanders regained its freedom. The guilds, whose members formed the bulk of the infantry, rose to political prominence. Historians identified the Battle of Courtrai as the first battle in the "infantry revolution" that began the decline of cavalry use in war and the ascendancy of infantry.

The Courtrai Chest, which depicts the Flemish line during the Battle of the Golden Spurs, or Courtrai

BATTLE OF BANNOCKBURN

Scottish victory over England that preserved Scottish independence

Robert the Bruce statue at Stirling Castle

For years, England had waged campaigns of conquest in Scotland, with little success. The Scottish king, Robert the Bruce, had proved particularly adept at militarily stymieing England's ambitions in the north. Though Edward II had inherited the desire of previous English monarchs to possess Scotland, his military skills were not the equal of his ambitions. This would be proven on the battlefield at Bannockburn.

In 1314, Robert's brother, Edward, put the strategic English Stirling Castle to siege. As its loss would greatly embarrass England, King Edward gathered about him an army of about 20,000 men. He began the march north to lift the siege and destroy the Scottish army. Previously, Robert had used guerilla and skirmish tactics to drive out the English. This time, though, he decided to engage the English army in open battle, even though the English forces was more than three times his own. He was only able to field an army of about 6,500 men.

In June, Robert organized his army at Torwood, a forested region with broken ground that provided excellent cover for maneuver. Such was his command over his infantry of independent Scots that he was able to keep them in disciplined formation. As it turned out, it was the English cavalry who proved ill disciplined. Edward was unable to control the powerful nobles in his army. The vanguard of knights led a premature charge on the Scottish position in a disorderly and ragged formation. The infantry held its position and the English horses were impaled on the pikes of the Scots.

Robert's infantry then advanced. The broken ground helped the Scots and hindered the British. At the height of the fighting, Robert signaled his reserves to make a flanking attack. Upon seeing fresh Scottish troops smash into his embattled army, Edward was forced to retreat or be killed in the melee. His men began to panic. Many were pinned on the banks of the River Forth. Thousands were slaughtered—accounts say casualties were as high as 9,000.

England never again challenged Robert's rule.

1314

ROBERTVS I REX · SCOTORVM

M.CCCVI ANNO DOM

Pub.^d Novr 1 1797 by I Herbert.

E Harding Sc.

Battle of Crécy

The battle that heralded the end of the Age of Chivalry

The Hundred Years' War between England and France was seven years old when Edward III crossed the English Channel in 1346. He landed at the French port of Cherbourg in Normandy with his army. He was determined to settle his dynastic claim to France by forcing the French King Philip VI to do battle so he could "make an end to the war."

Edward's army was anywhere from 8,000 to 12,000 strong (accounts vary), with the bulk of it being archers armed with the English, or Welsh, longbow. Beginning in Cherbourg, Edward embarked on a great *chevauchée* (literally, ride) of destruction that started in Cherbourg and continued east along the coast until it reached Crécy-en-Ponthieu, near Calais. There it came face-to-face with the 80,000-man army led by Philip himself.

The bulk of the French army was composed of cavalry, which meant that the majority of French nobility was on the field that day. Their greater numbers and more distinguished bloodlines made the French equestrians arrogant and overconfident. The battle on August 26 opened with an exchange between archers, with the English longbowmen easily defeating the mercenary crossbowmen of the French army.

Impetuously, and prematurely, the French cavalry charged, riding over the hapless mercenaries. The knights rode to their doom. The combination of longbowmen firing one arrow an average of every five seconds and shellfire from primitive cannon that Edward had recently added to his arsenal, wrought fearful carnage. Amazingly, the French charged sixteen times, trying to break the English lines. Each time they were repulsed, leaving more dead and dying on the broken field.

As dusk began to settle, Philip, who had been wounded, ordered his army to retreat. It was a stunning defeat; as many as 3,000 French nobles had been killed. But, before Edward could complete his conquest, the Black Death plague struck. France received a respite, of sorts, from war. In the Treaty of Brétigny (1360) that ended the first phase of the Hundred Years' War, Edward had to settle for sovereignty of about one-third of France.

King Edward III fighting French knights at the Battle of Crécy

GUNPOWDER

Explosive compound used in early cannon in the Battle of Crécy

Broadly speaking, the "first generation" of weapons, such as spears and knives, was muscle powered. The "second generation" of weapons, such as catapults, was mechanical powered. "Third generation" firearms used a chemical process, namely, exploding gunpowder.

Gunpowder is the term used to describe a compound of sulfur, charcoal, and potassium nitrate that, when properly blended, creates an explosive mixture. It is generally agreed that Chinese alchemists in the ninth century were the first to create gunpowder. Its first use was in pyrotechnic displays for celebration—as in colorful fireworks. Accounts of gunpowder use in war began to appear in the thirteenth century in different parts of the world. The English friar Roger Bacon, in 1249, was one of the first to make mention of gunpowder. "Guns with powder" began to appear in Europe in the early fourteenth century and they included such weapons as the French *pots de fer* ("pots of iron").

Gunpowder was initially used to make bombs and similar exploding objects. As gunpowder was refined and weapons technology advanced, it found utility in a wide variety of weapons. Gunpowder, itself, also evolved. "Black gunpowder" had a high charcoal content and produced huge clouds of smoke when it burned. "Smokeless gunpowder" was introduced in the late nineteenth century and refinements of it are used today.

An early cannon used at the Battle of Crécy in France during the Hundred Years War

Bow

Archery weapon used in the Battle of Agincourt

The origin of the bow predates recorded history, as does its use in warfare. The first bows were made of a simple shaft of wood. Some archeologists and military historians have suggested that the rise of the use of chariots in warfare coincided with, or was followed by, the creation of the compound bow.

The compound bow was a technological breakthrough of enormous importance. In his book, *Technology and War*, the military historian Martin van Creveld wrote, "Made of wood, sinew, and horn glued together, with each material carefully coordinated with all the others so as to yield the optimum combination of strength and flexibility, the composite bow represented as great an advance over its simple predecessor as did the breech-loading rifle over the muzzle-loading flintlock musket." Depending on the type and size of the bow, and skills of the archer, a compound bow could fire an arrow 300 yards or more and its power and effectiveness remained unsurpassed for thousands of years.

The shape and size of a compound bow depended on the culture that used it. Nomads and cavalry used light and small bows. Longbows, like the English or Welsh styles, were more than 6 feet long and were the heavy artillery of archery. These bows were hard to draw—but in the hands of a skilled archer, an arrow shot by a longbow could penetrate armor. They proved to be the decisive weapon for the English in their victory at the Battle of Agincourt.

The crossbow is a smaller, mechanical variant of the bow. Crossbows, in which the bow is mounted on a stock and the bowstring is released by a trigger, required less skill to master.

With the advent of accurate repeating rifled firearms in the mid- to late-nineteenth century, the use of bows in warfare declined sharply. By the early twentieth century, they were used almost exclusively in hunting and sport. Modern compound bows are made of metal or synthetic materials and utilize a levering system of cables and pulleys to enhance the driving force of the arrow.

A Middle Ages battle scene that involves attackers using a moveable siege tower to gain entry to a fortified castle, while archers on the ground below fire over the wall

BATTLE OF AGINCOURT

The English victory immortalized by Shakespeare

Henry V's campaign in northern France in 1415 began poorly with an ill-conceived siege to seize the channel port of Honfleur. After several weeks, Henry abandoned the attempt and turned his attention inland. He embarked on an armed raid across northern France to the English-controlled port of Calais. He was hampered by the French scorched-earth policy that denied his army food, fodder, and shelter. Heavy rains, cold weather, and disease contributed further to his army's misery.

Then, near Agincourt, things suddenly got worse. On October 25, Henry found himself facing a French army of about 20,000 men, including more than 10,000 knights and men-at-arms. It appeared that the English faced certain defeat.

But Henry succeeded in placing his army on high ground in a clearing between two forests. This limited the number of French troops that could attack him at one time. And it denied the French cavalry the room to maneuver to strike his flanks. Henry held another advantage: unity of command. He was the clear and undisputed leader of the English army. But, on the French side, no such unity existed. Charles d'Albret, Constable of France, and Marshal Boucicaut held nominal command; at least seven members of royalty (including the crown price, or dauphin) and high nobility were on the field, each jealous of his prerogatives.

Marshal Boucicaut drew up a plan of attack that, had it been carried out, probably would have succeeded. But his plan fell apart shortly after the order to advance was issued. Mounted royalty, nobility, and knights, each seeking glory, jostled with foot soldiers and archers, throwing the ranks of commoner and chivalry into disarray. The French attack degenerated into a mob rush.

Fighting with better discipline, the English casualties remained at just a few hundred, though they included Henry's cousin, the Duke of York. French casualties, on the other hand, were enormous: 10,000 men, including Charles d'Albret, were estimated to have fallen.

France signed the Treaty of Troyes (1420) that recognized Henry V as regent of France upon the death of King Charles VI, among other terms that cemented his claim.

King Henry V at the Battle of Agincourt

HALBERD

The first practical multiple-use weapon employed in the Battle of Agincourt

The halberd, created some time during the 1300s, was one of many weapons that came to prominence in the Middle Ages. The halberd was an infantry weapon that replaced the battle ax. The basic halberd is a long shaft topped by a heavy steel head that has the blade of an ax, the point of a spear, and a hook designed to pull a rider out of a saddle. Halberds were effective in both offense and defense. A halberd in the hands of one skilled in its use could block thrusts, disarm opponents, and kill or disable armored infantry or cavalry in quick succession.

The Swiss were the first to use the halberd, in 1315 in the Battle of Morgarten, against Austrian knights. The halberd went on to become the national weapon of the Swiss. The deadliness of the halberd was so effectively demonstrated in the Battle of Sempach in 1386—an Austrian invasion of Switzerland where half the Austrian army was slain—that Switzerland's independence was never again seriously threatened. And, as is the case with success, halberds soon began appearing in armies throughout Europe.

Use of the halberd as the infantry's main heavy arms weapon was relatively short, less than three hundred years. As firearms developed in sophistication, reliability, and accuracy, the use of edged weapons by infantry waned; the halberd was the first weapon to be discarded in favor of firearms. It does, however, remain the ceremonial weapon of the Swiss Guards in the Vatican.

Italian soldier with halberd

SIEGE OF ORLÉANS

Turning point in Hundred Years' War

Statue of Joan of Arc

The on-and-off Hundred Years' War was in its ninety-first year in 1428. England, together with its allies, the powerful dukes of Burgundy, held northern France, including Paris. Charles the Dauphin, the disinherited French heir to the throne, had his court in Chinon, about 200 miles southeast. Strategically placed between these two capitals was the walled city of Orléans. Still in French hands, Orléans had come to hold great symbolic and strategic importance. If England could seize it, the way south would be open for conquest. On October 12, 1428, the English army arrived and put Orléans to siege.

Siege warfare usually involves long waiting periods with relatively little action by most of the combatants; in this case, four months passed. The first pitched battle did not occur until February 12, 1429, when a French army attempted to intercept an English supply column. Called the Battle of the Herrings, after the salted fish the convoy was carrying, it ended in French failure.

Then, French fortunes seemed to change. A peasant girl from Lorraine arrived at Orléans at the head of a relief army that successfully entered the city on April 29. She claimed to be the much-rumored maid of prophecy who would drive out the English and bring victory to France. The girl, Joan, wrote to the English army at Orléans, calling on them to quit the siege and, together with their countrymen, leave France entirely. If they did not, she would raise a "war cry against them that would last forever."

The battle for Orléans then began in earnest. A key moment came on May 7, with a French assault of the important Les Tourelles fortified gateway that the British had seized. Joan led the attack, shouting her war cry, "He who loves me, follow me!" The fighting was bitter and lasted most of the day. At one point, she was wounded but in the end the French had taken Les Tourelles. It proved to be a decisive moment, for two days later the English decamped and left.

Joan became a hero, the Maid of Orléans. Thousands rallied to the French cause. The fortunes of the Dauphin had finally turned for the better.

The French valiantly resisting the siege

JOAN OF ARC

French heroine during the Siege of Orléans (1412–1431)

Emperor Napoleon I said, "The moral is to the material as three to one." No greater example of the triumph of moral ascendancy in battle is Joan of Arc, one of the most unusual military leaders in history. Her gender, military ignorance, career of less than a year, and violent death at age nineteen made her unique. She appeared like a shooting star, flashed brilliantly, and then was gone, leaving the French an inspirational memory.

Joan of Arc was born to a pious peasant family from Domrémy in Lorraine during the 116-year dynastic struggle between England and France known as the Hundred Years' War. At age thirteen, Joan began hearing voices from saints. In 1429, she approached militia captain Robert de Baudricourt. She told him of her visions and that God had made her responsible for freeing France from England. She somehow convinced him to take her to the Dauphin (crown prince), Charles.

Charles was in the middle of an unsuccessful military campaign against the English when he met Joan of Arc. Afterward, he asked church leaders to interview her. Up to this time, even though the experienced French armies were materially superior in numbers, guns, and supplies, the English were winning. Ironically, Joan of Arc's innocence of military affairs was seen as a virtue. Troops and citizens rallied to her.

In 1429, clad in white armor, Joan of Arc lead an army to Orléans, then under siege. She was able to lift it in just nine days—an incredible achievement. French spirits soared over the news. Joan then opened the roads to Rheims where, on July 17, Charles was crowned king.

After that, her military career went downhill. An attack at Compiègne in 1430 failed and she was captured. She was unjustly tried as a heretic in January 1431. After a recantation of a confession, she was charged as a "relapsed heretic" and burned at the stake on May 30. Her death inspired the French to action. Within five years, the English were driven out of the country. She was canonized Saint Joan of Arc on May 16, 1920, by Pope Benedict XV.

FALL OF TENOCHTITLAN

Capture of the Aztec Empire capital by Conquistadors

Skulls of Aztec
enemies

Hernándo Cortés observed, "We Spaniards suffer from a disease that only gold can cure." As the conquistador who toppled the Aztec Empire and later became governor general of New Spain, his was arguably the voice of experience.

After a career as a planter and chief magistrate in Cuba, Cortés became inspired by tales of Aztec wealth. In 1519, with the sponsorship of the governor of Cuba, Cortés set off to conquer the "kingdom to the west." He and about 450 conquistadors landed on the coast of Mexico at a place he named Vera Cruz. Cortés and his troops, including Indian allies, entered the Aztec capital, Tenochtitlan, on November 8, 1519. They met Montezuma, the Aztec king, captured him and held him hostage. Cortés, believing that Montezuma held the same unquestioned authority as that possessed by the absolute monarchs of Europe, attempted to control the Aztecs through orders issued by Montezuma. But Aztec ruling society was more complex and independent. When the Aztecs realized what had happened, they revolted. The Spaniards killed Montezuma, escaped the capital, and commenced to wage war on the Aztecs.

Fighting between the conquistadors and Aztecs continued for the next year and a half. Cortés received reinforcements from Cuba. Though still greatly outnumbered, the superior weaponry of the Spaniards turned the tide against the Aztecs. In May 1521, Cortés was once again at the outskirts of the Aztec capital. He proceeded to put the city to siege. Initial attacks cut off the causeway system that fed water to the city. As the weeks passed, the situation became desperate for both sides. Within the city, the Aztecs were running out of food and water. As the Spaniards had less than 2,000 troops, they feared that a prolonged siege would cause them to lose the Indian allies they desperately needed (who numbered as many as 200,000 warriors).

The walls were breached and bitter fighting continued throughout the city. Finally, on August 13, 1521, the exhausted Aztecs capitulated. An estimated 240,000 Aztecs were killed, including almost all of the Aztec nobility. Cortés had conquered the Aztec empire.

Mural depicting the great city of Tenochtitlan

HERNANDO CORTÉS

Spanish conquistador and victor at Tenochtitlan (1485–1547)

With just a few hundred men and a handful of horses and cannon, Cortés conquered an empire of more than five million people. His success, and his vision of Spanish opportunities in the New World, made him arguably the ablest and most resourceful of the conquistadors.

Cortés was born into a Spanish family of minor nobility. At age nineteen, he went to the New World to seek his fortune. He began as a gentleman farmer in Hispaniola. In 1511, he was part of the military campaign that captured Cuba. Under the patronage of his father-in-law, the governor of Cuba, Cortés led an expedition to Mexico in 1519.

After burning his ships to make sure his men would not desert, he embarked on the campaign that would make him famous. He exploited the Aztec myth that he was the white-skinned, bearded god-king Quetzalcoatl and met with Montezuma, the Aztec ruler. Through a brilliant combination of bluff, brinkmanship, battle, and bribery over the next few years, Cortés not only conquered the Aztecs but he also avoided being arrested by the Spanish.

At one point during his campaign in Mexico, he discovered that he had come under arrest for charges that he had exceeded the conditions of his expedition. After his conquest of the Aztecs, Cortés cunningly packed a ship full of treasure and sent it to the King of Spain, claiming that all of what he had done had been in service of the king and not for personal gain. The king pardoned him.

Cortés became governor of the region he conquered. He led new expeditions, but growing jealousy by rivals of his ambitions caused him to be recalled to Spain several times. In 1539, he left the New World for good. He lived luxuriously in an estate near Seville until his death in 1547.

BATTLE OF PANIPAT

Battle that began the Mughal Empire

The Khyber Pass between modern Afghanistan and Pakistan and the small town of Panipat in northern India have long played a role in the history of civilizations and empire on the Indian subcontinent. The rulers of the Delhi sultanate in northern India had, out of necessity, formed large and well-trained armies for defense. Though raiders came often through the Khyber Pass, they rarely remained long. Zahir ud-Din Muhammad Babur was one such raider. But unlike in years past, when he took his army of about 15,000 across the Khyber Pass in 1526, it was different. He had brought with him matchlock firearms and cannon. He had come to stay—and conquer.

The Delhi Sultan Ibrahim Lodhi had gathered an army of about 30,000 warriors and at least 100 war elephants and advanced toward Panipat to stop the invader. Babur, meanwhile, had his men build trenches, barricades, and other fortifications anchored by the town of Panipat. The battle began on April 21, with Babur's matchlocks and cannon firing into the ranks of the Delhi sultan's army. The noise of the gunfire panicked the war elephants, who wreaked havoc among the sultan's army. Then, into this chaos swept Babur's cavalry. Ibrahim Lodhi was killed and his army routed.

Babur became the new master of Delhi. His victory at Panipat marked the beginning of the Mughal Empire in India.

Seventeenth-century illustration of a Mughal emperor astride an elephant

ZAHIR UD-DIN MUHAMMAD BABUR

Founder of the Mughal Empire and victor of the Battle of Panipat (1483–1530)

Babur was a Chagatai Turk from Central Asia. His father died when he was twelve, and Babur inherited a band of cavalry and some disputed land rights. For twenty years, he lead a feast-or-famine life filled with extremes. One year he might be the lord of Samarkand, the next, so poor he barely had sufficient fodder for his horses. Yet, his men loyally stayed with him throughout those years. He was charismatic, an excellent fighter, and he was willing to share everything with his men.

Babur's troops, armored horse cavalry, were among the deadliest archers in the world. They were also equally dangerous as infantry with sword and battle-ax. Babur developed fighting tactics so effective that he used them throughout his campaigns with only minor modification, even after the Mughal Empire was founded. These tactics generally consisted of a frontal charge with the cavalry firing arrows as they closed on the enemy line. Then, once they had breached the enemy line, they leaped off their horses and fought as infantry. Babur's only real change came after he had formed his empire and incorporated artillery in his assaults of walled cities. Previously, his men would use scaling ladders.

Babur began raiding the Indian plains in the early sixteenth century with just a few hundred troops. By 1529, he had conquered much of northern India and created an empire that would last for more than 300 years.

Siege of Vienna

Ottoman Empire hegemony in Central Europe is checked

Vienna's geographic position on the Danube River in south central Europe made it an historic gateway for barbarians and civilized peoples, both hostile and pacific. In 1137, it became an important "border city" between the Holy Roman Empire in the north and the Ottoman Empire in the southeast.

In 1526, the Turks, under Suleiman I, had conquered Hungary. Three years later, in September 1529, Suleiman returned to the region, leading an army of about 250,000 men and a fleet of four hundred ships. Their objective: the capture of Vienna, gateway to the north. When they arrived, Suleiman demanded the city surrender, or face the consequences. His demand was refused and the siege commenced on September 27.

To breach the thick city walls, Suleiman's engineers dug tunnels under them. Explosives were to be set and detonated to topple a section the wall, creating large gaps for attacking troops. The defenders had heard the digging and an underground war was fought as defending engineers conducted countermining operations.

On October 12, the Turkish leaders met in council. Though a relief army for the city had failed to arrive, Vienna was stubbornly continuing to resist. In the Turkish army, supplies were becoming low, troop morale was sagging, and the air held a chill that portended an early winter. Options were discussed, among them a lifting of the siege and retreat. The decision was made for a final attempt to invest Vienna.

On October 14, two mines blew up beneath the city's outer wall. Turkish troops rushed through the two gaps. For two hours, the two sides fought in an increasingly desperate struggle. Seeing that further fighting would be too costly, Suleiman decided to end the siege. He gave the signal to retreat. The next day the Turks struck their tents and began the march home.

Historians later speculated that Suleiman didn't really want to take Vienna; he only wanted to intimidate the Holy Roman Empire so it wouldn't try and seize Hungary. Regardless of the real reason, the siege spelled the northernmost limit of Ottoman expansion.

A sixteenth-century map of Vienna during the time of the first Turkish siege

SULEIMAN I

Ottoman Empire ruler defeated at the Siege of Vienna (1494–1566)

Suleiman I, known to his subjects as "the Lawgiver" and "the Magnificent," was one of the greatest military leaders in the sixteenth century. At a time when Spain was reaping enormous wealth from its New World colonies and conquests, and France was the most powerful nation in the west, Suleiman turned the Ottoman Empire into the most powerful nation in the world.

Suleiman was the tenth sultan of the Ottomans. He learned the art of war as a youth in first his grandfather's and then his father's army. He inherited the throne at age twenty-six. While his able and trusted vizier, Ibrahim Pasha, oversaw civil administration, Suleiman embarked on campaigns to expand the Ottoman Empire.

Suleiman was fortunate to have inherited an army that was the largest and best trained in the world. Suleiman first struck west, advancing as far north as Hungary where in 1526 he defeated the Hungarians at the Battle of Mohács. Three years later, he attempted to invest Vienna but was forced to stop by the onset of an early winter.

After a third campaign in Hungary (1532), he turned his full attention eastward to fight the Persians with whom he had been warring for a decade. From that point on, he alternated campaigns east and west. He concluded an alliance with France against the Holy Roman Empire. His admiral, a former pirate named Barbarossa, made his fleets the dominant navy in the Mediterranean. Suleiman died on September 5, 1566, in the middle of another campaign in Austria.

Suleiman was a brilliant, remarkable individual. A patron of the arts, a fine administrator and great general, he also was smart enough to surround himself with competent, trustworthy individuals. Under his reign, the Ottoman Empire rose to the peak of its glory.

Battle of Cajamarca

Conquistador attack on Inca rulers

Inca ruins of Machu Pichu near Cusco, Peru

When Pizarro and his 162 conquistadors landed in Peru in 1532, all Pizarro knew of the Incas was that they possessed fabulous wealth. His twin objectives were to loot the Incan empire and subjugate its people to Christianity and Spanish rule.

He soon learned that the empire was in civil war, the result of a dynastic struggle between the half-brothers Atahualpa and Huáscar for the Incan throne. Atahualpa got the upper hand and brutally slaughtered all members of the royal family except Huáscar, whom he imprisoned.

Meanwhile, when Pizarro and his men arrived in Peru in their exotic panoply of attire, weaponry, and horses, Pizarro was hailed as a son of their white-skinned god Viracocha. Since Viracocha also controlled the thunder, the Spaniard fired demonstrating shots from cannon and muskets, adding credence to their belief. Pizarro brutally exploited Incan credulity and he and his conquistadors plundered their way through the country, meeting almost no resistance.

When word of the Conquistadors' conduct reached Atahualpa at Cajamarca, the Incan king ordered the Conquistadors to return what they had stolen. In November, Pizarro and his small band entered the city. Though the group was greatly outnumbered by Incan warriors, Pizarro refused to be intimidated. He boldly had a priest, Brother Vicente, attempt to convert Atahualpa. But Atahualpa contemptuously threw the Bible on the floor. Then, according to an account written by Huaman Poma, a member of the Inca nobility, Pizarro shouted orders to his men, "telling them to attack these Indians who rejected God and the Emperor. The Spaniards began to fire their muskets and charged upon the Indians, killing them like ants." Atahualpa was taken captive.

Pizarro announced to the Incas that he would free their ruler if they gave him enough gold and silver to fill a room. But Pizarro had no intention of releasing Atahualpa. Though the room was filled twice, Pizarro convicted Atahualpa in a mock trial and offered him the choice of being burned alive as a heathen or strangled as a Christian. Atahualpa chose the latter, was baptized Juan de Atahualpa, tied to a stake and garroted. Now leaderless, the Incas were helpless to stop Pizarro's conquest.

Francisco Pizarro taking Atahualpa captive

STIRRUP

Invention used by Pizarro's cavalry at Cajamarca

The stirrup is regarded as one of the most significant non-lethal inventions in the history of warfare. It greatly enhanced the stability and leverage power of the rider, as well as his ability to fight. The stirrup is basically a ring with a flat bottom on which the foot rests. It is attached to the saddle with an adjustable leather strap.

As with many early inventions, the origin of the stirrup is unknown. It did not make its appearance until relatively late in history. Stirrups were used in China possibly as early as the fourth century. Not until the sixth century did widespread evidence of it exist, beginning with the nomadic peoples of the central Asian steppes. By the eighth century, stirrups were in use throughout Europe.

The combined use of the stirrup, high-backed saddle, and the metal horseshoe made it possible for cavalry to become the pre-eminent fighting arm during the Middle Ages. Though horse cavalry would begin to decline in importance in the fourteenth century, it would not lose its place in armies until the end of the nineteenth century.

Battle between the forces of Persia and Turan

Francisco Pizarro

Spanish conqueror of the Incas and victor at Cajamarca (ca. 1471–1541)

The conquistador who would become famous for toppling the Inca Empire was born the illegitimate son of a professional Spanish soldier. Pizarro joined the army when he was twelve. Though he remained illiterate throughout his life, and never received formal military training, he learned quickly about the art of making war.

Pizarro arrived in Hispaniola in 1502, and in 1513 participated in Vasco de Balboa's expedition to Panama. He remained in Panama until 1523, serving in government posts that made him wealthy. Inspired by reports of the wealth gained by Cortés in his expeditions in the north against the Aztecs, Pizarro decided to seek greater fortune also. Upon hearing of an Incan civilization possessing vast wealth, Pizarro, after receiving permission from the governor, took a ship and sailed south.

The first voyage ended in hardship. The second voyage (1526–1528), though full of travails, ended better. According to legend, on the second voyage Pizarro drew a line in the sand with his sword and invited those who desired "wealth and glory" to step across the line and join him. Only thirteen did so. They succeeded in returning with much wealth. However, it was not until 1531 that Pizarro was able to mount a full expedition with 200 soldiers and about 65 horses. It was with these men that he would achieve wealth, glory, and immortality.

Pizarro conquered the Inca Empire that included most of present-day Peru, Ecuador, and parts of Chile and Bolivia. He established Lima as a port to exploit his gains. However, he did not live long enough to enjoy his new wealth. A falling out with a former partner escalated to murder and Pizarro was killed.

SIEGE OF KAZAN

Pivotal battle in Russo-Kazan War

The Kazan khanate was a large Tatar state in central Asia that stretched roughly from the Volga River to modern Tatarstan. The khanate's relationship with the growing Muscovite Russia Empire in the north was a complex one, with pro- and anti-Moscow factions jockeying for power. In 1545, a revolt broke out and the pro-Moscow nobles succeeded in placing one of their own on the Russian throne.

Shortly after the revolt, Ivan IV, later known as Ivan the Terrible, began a series of intermittent campaigns in the region. They were designed to show his support for the new regime and expand his control in the region, but little of substance was accomplished. Finally, in 1551, Ivan decided to invade Kazan and seize it outright.

Ivan led a 150,000-man army into the khanate in June 1552. By August 30, he was at the walls of Kazan. Shortly thereafter, the siege commenced. For the next month, siege cannon pounded the city walls and his troops and cavalry fought off forces sent to relieve the city. Ivan's sappers dug tunnels and blew up the city's source for drinking water.

On October 2, sappers blew up a large section of the city wall and Russian soldiers poured into the city. The civilian population joined with the defenders to fight the Russian troops. It was a desperate battle in which no quarter was given. When it was over, the civilian population was massacred. Estimates put the deaths at about 110,000 soldiers and civilians killed. The few civilians who survived were later sold into slavery. Ivan then sacked the city and used the loot to pay his soldiers. As they prepared to leave, Ivan ordered the city to be burned to the ground. When the Russians left, all that remained of the city was ashes.

The Kazan Khanate was destroyed and Ivan added its territory to his growing empire.

A rebuilt section of Kazan

BATTLE OF OKEHAZAMA

Pivotal battle in Oda Nobunaga's unification of Japan

Born into a daimyo family in Owari province (near Nagoya), Oda Nobunaga had ambitions to unify Japan. His quest began in 1557. For the next three years, he established uncontested authority in the province. In spring 1560, he learned the powerful rival, Yoshimoto Imagawa, had formed an alliance with the Takeda and the Hojo clans. Yoshimoto then claimed that he was marching with an army to the Japanese capital at Kyoto to support the frail Ashikaga shogunate. Yet Yoshimoto's path would take him through Oda's land, which, in truth, he planned to invade.

Just before his march, Yoshimoto, whose army numbered about 25,000 men, publicly announced that he was leading an army of 40,000 warriors. This exaggeration was designed to cow any fence-sitting factions. Oda, meanwhile, had assembled an army of 2,000 men. Oda did not believe Yoshimoto's exaggerated claim. Even so, Oda's force was outnumbered more than ten to one.

When Yoshimoto entered Oda's land, he initially destroyed two outpost castles, Wazashi and Marune. Oda found Yoshimoto's army camped in a gorge by the village of Okehazama. Overconfident, the army was in the midst of a celebration. Oda boldly decided upon a surprise attack. Using his intimate knowledge of the terrain, he set an ambush using dummy troops and false banners to give the impression his army was larger than it was. Once the decoys were ready, he secretly marched his army around to his enemy's rear.

June 19 began with stifling heat that, around mid-day, broke into a thundershower that drove Yoshimoto's men to shelter. As soon as the storm ended, Oda attacked. Yoshimoto and his men were taken completely by surprise. Initially, Yoshimoto thought that his men had begun arguing with each other. It was only when he was set upon by Oda's samurai that he realized, too late, the truth.

Yoshimoto's death at Okehazama ended the power of his faction. Oda's victory was acclaimed as a miracle and proved to be the pivotal event in his goal of unifying Japan. By the end of the decade, Oda Nobunaga was the most powerful and feared warlord in Japan.

A Japanese warrior on horseback

Battle of Lepanto

Battle that checked Ottoman Empire expansion in Europe

The Ottoman Empire had been a threat to the Christian nations of Europe for a number of decades. In 1570, it launched a powerful expedition to seize Cyprus, then under rule by Venice, and another to conquer Tunis, a Spanish protectorate. The following year, Venice and Spain signed an alliance with the papacy, called the Holy League. Among the major allies were the Republic of Genoa, the Duchy of Savoy, and the Knights of Malta who provided ships and troops to form a Grand Fleet created to fight the Ottomans. Commanding the more than 200 galleys was Don John of Austria, the illegitimate son of Austrian emperor Charles V and half-brother of the king of Spain. Ali Pasha led the Ottoman fleet of almost 300 ships, including 230 galleys.

The Grand Fleet intercepted the Ottoman fleet in the Gulf of Lepanto in western Greece. Shortly before the battle was joined, Ali Pasha reportedly informed his Christian galley slaves, "If I win the battle, I promise you your liberty. If the day is yours, then God has given it to you."

The ships closed and the fighting commenced on October 7, with galleys from both sides soon becoming intermingled. Ships were boarded and desperate fighting broke out between elite Ottoman Janissaries and Christian troops and mercenaries. But the Holy League had the decisive advantage in cannon: 1,815 against its adversary's 750. The outgunned Ottoman galleys took tremendous pounding. When action broke off late afternoon, the Turks had lost about 200 galleys and 20,000 to 30,000 men (accounts vary).

The Battle of Lepanto was the largest naval engagement of the time. It was a crushing defeat for the Turks, who had not lost a major sea battle in more than one hundred years. News of the Christian victory inspired uprisings in Greece and Albania against their Turkish rulers.

But, it was not a decisive blow. As a Turkish minister later explained to the Venetians, "You have shaved our beard, but it will soon grow again." The following year, the Turks had rebuilt their fleet. By 1577, the Ottoman Empire had regained all it had lost in 1571.

The Christian and Ottoman fleets in action at Lepanto

BATTLE OF NAGASHINO

The first modern battle in Japanese history

The Takeda was the most powerful clan in sixteenth-century Japan. In 1573, it began a campaign to eliminate is rivals and achieve total hegemony of the country. On June 17, 1575, Takeda Katsuyori began a siege of the Nagashino Castle in the Mikawa province, whose position threatened his supply lines. The castle was defended by Okudaira Sadamasa, a vassal of Katsuyori's rival, Tokugawa Ieyasu. In addition to a relief force from Ieyasu, Oda Nobunaga also agreed to lead his troops to raise the siege. Nobunaga also brought with him about 1,500 soldiers trained to use the new arquebusier firearm. Earlier, arquebusiers had performed only a minor supporting role in a few battles. This time his gunpowder weapons would be the major force in the upcoming fight.

The combined army of Oda Nobunaga and Tokugawa Ieyasu was about 38,000 men. They faced an army less than half that size but Takeda Katsuyori's army, led by his cavalry, was at the height of its reputation.

After the combined army had taken up position near Nagashino castle, Nobunaga constructed fortifications and positioned his army behind them, with his arquebus troops in the vanguard. The battle began the morning of June 29. Katsuyori's cavalry was tricked into repeated charges and its ranks were savaged each time by deadly arquebus fire. Those that were not killed by gunfire were cut down by spear- and sword- wielding infantry. By mid-afternoon, Katsuyori's army broke and began to flee, hotly pursued by Nobunaga and Ieyasu's men. Though estimates vary on how many men Katsuyori lost, there is complete agreement on the Battle of Nagashino's impact. The power of the Takeda clan was irreparably broken. A new era of warfare in Japan had begun, and Oda Nobunaga and Tokugawa Ieyasu would go on to become some of the most famous warlords in Japan.

A Japanese samurai warrior, who was no match for the arquebus

ARQUEBUS

Early firearm used in the Battle of Nagashino

The development of gunpowder and firearms introduced a fundamental change in warfare, though many nations were slow to accept them. The earliest record of the use of firearms occurred in the early fourteenth century. By the fifteenth century, a variety of firearms including handguns of various designs, shoulder weapons including muzzleloaders and crude breechloaders, and even a pushcart-driven repeating gun (ribaldequin) existed. Around the start of the sixteenth century, the arquebus, or harquebus, became the dominant firearm.

The arquebus ("hooked tube") got its name from the shape of the butt of the barrel which was attached to the stock. It fit snugly to the human anatomy in the manner that became typical of all shoulder arms. This heavy butt made it possible for the arquebus to have a barrel longer than its contemporaries, which had the additional advantage of giving it greater accuracy and power.

An arquebus was a large-bore muzzleloader fired by first a matchlock and then a wheel-lock mechanism. Portuguese traders introduced the arquebus to the Japanese in 1543 and by the mid-sixteenth century they were in widespread use in Japan. The arquebus was succeeded in the latter years of the seventeenth century by the musket that, though smaller than the arquebus, was both lighter and easier to use.

European arquebusier of the sixteenth century

Spanish Armada

Spanish defeat that was cornerstone of the British Empire

Sir Francis Drake

The might and glory of King Philip II's Spanish Empire were at their zenith in the mid-sixteenth century. But England had persistently challenged his hegemony. In 1588, Philip formed an armada under the Duke of Medina Sidonia to invade England.

Though the Spanish fleet had a glorious reputation, there were important strategic differences that gave an edge to the British. The Spanish fleet was philosophically a continuation of the ancient Greek and Roman fleets—floating fortresses designed for close combat. The nascent English fleet, with its smaller, maneuverable ships and long-range cannon, was created for war at sea.

A battle between the two was like a boxer trying to fight a wrestler. Should the boxer strike enough long-armed blows, he had a chance to win. But if the wrestler succeeded in embracing his foe in a death-grip, the boxer was doomed.

Fighting commenced in July 1588, with the armada forcing its way up the English Channel. Its goal was to rendezvous with the Duke of Parma's army in Flanders, take them aboard, and then invade England. Sir Francis Drake and the other English commanders had learned much about the armada from these Channel skirmishes. On August 8, off Gravelines near Calais, they launched their main attack.

The superiority of English seamanship, gunnery, tactics, and ships quickly showed. The Spanish were fair-weather sailors and their cannon were designed for medium- and short-range fire. Their lumbering ships could not exploit wind and current like the English vessels. The troops on the Spanish ships, used for boarding, were useless. Eleven Spanish ships were sunk or damaged. The rendezvous with Parma's army was cancelled.

Wind from the south caused Medina Sidonia to take his armada northward, charting a course for Spain that would take him around Great Britain. After the fleet rounded Scotland, it ran into deadly North Atlantic gales that drove many ships onto the rocky shores of Scotland and Ireland. When the fleet reached Spain, Medina Sidonia had lost half his ships, mostly due to storms.

The threat of invasion was over. Britain had become the world's new sea power.

The English fleet's flag ship

Battle of Sekigahara

Battle that established the Tokugawa shogunate of Japan

Tokugawa Ieyasu was one of the important leaders in the wars of Japanese unification. Through unshakeable will, battlefield skill, and diplomacy, he slowly built his clan into one of the major forces in Japan.

Tokugawa Ieyasu was one of five regents for Hideyori, son of the powerful Toyotomi Hideyoshi, who had died in 1598. War broke out between him and a coalition of anti-Tokugawa lords of southern and western Honshu. Ieyasu seized the initiative and, after taking the strategic area around Sekigahara, managed to entice the coalition to do battle against him on ground of his choosing. His enemies readily took his bait and marched toward Sekigahara.

Ieyasu was in a difficult tactical position, his enemies were approaching him from three sides and their combined force far outnumbered his. But Ieyasu, having gained much *realpolitik* experience over the previous years, played his diplomacy card to its fullest. Though inducements of land and leniency, he convinced a number of daimyo (lords) approaching from the west to either switch sides or not participate in the upcoming battle. Ieyasu's effort in successfully driving a wedge in the coalition against him would prove decisive.

The Battle of Sekigahara took place on October 21. The combined armies totaled about 160,000 men, making it the largest battle on Japanese soil. It was a bloody daylong affair that became more melee than battle. As evening approached and the battle became more intense, it appeared that Ieyasu would lose. Then, at a critical moment, Kobayakawa Hideaki, one of the daimyos Ieyasu had attempted to enlist, threw his hand in favor of Ieyasu. It proved to be the decisive move that swung the battle in Ieyasu's favor. The coalition army was crushed. Though it would take three more years for him to consolidate his control over Japan, Ieyasu had reached the pinnacle of his power.

The Tokugawa would be the last shogunate to rule Japan.

Helmet from Japanese samurai suit

GUSTAVUS ADOLPHUS

Swedish king and "Father of Modern Warfare" (1594–1632)

Gustavus Adolphus was one of the most brilliant and innovative strategist and generals of his time. He was also one of the bravest and most foolhardy. He was often found in the thick of combat. Ultimately, he was killed in battle, at Lützen in 1632, his last victory.

Gustavus displayed an interest in the military at an early age. By the time of the Thirty Years' War, he had already gained experience in war making. He was the first to completely integrate the different branches of infantry, cavalry, artillery, and support units. By the time of his death, he had made Sweden the dominant power of the Baltic, a position it would hold for about a century.

Gustavus Adolphus's fame came as a result of his victories in the Thirty Years' War (1618–1648). Germany was the battleground for a religious conflict between Catholic and Protestant nations that also had dynastic overtones. Sweden was a Protestant nation, and Gustavus Adolphus entered the fray in the summer of 1630, when he arrived in northern Germany with just 4,000 troops. When allies deserted him, he still scored victories against enemies whose armies were larger than his. By the end of 1631, Gustavus had secured northern Germany for the Protestant cause. During the winter, he made plans for a campaign against the Holy Roman Empire in the south.

Gustavus invaded Bavaria in March 1632. His campaign, including the victory in the Battle of Lech (also known as the Battle of Rain) in April, secured the safety of Protestant Saxony. However, his death at the Battle of Lützen deprived the Protestant cause of its unifying champion. His army took his body back to Sweden and his country thereafter remained mostly on the sidelines. The Thirty Years' War would continue for another sixteen years.

Gustavus' strategic and tactical innovations were copied during his lifetime. Napoleon Bonaparte was the most famous of his many disciples.

BATTLE OF ROCROI

Watershed battle that ended the aura of Spanish military invincibility

Though France's greatest rivalry was with England, it also had a long, though lesser-known, conflict-ridden history with Spain. One of the major events in the power struggle between the two nations was the Franco-Spanish War (1653–1659).

France in the mid-seventeenth century was hemmed between Spain and its dynastic possession in the north, the Spanish Netherlands. In the spring of 1643, Spanish Governor Francisco de Melo led an army of about 20,000–25,000 troops (accounts vary) south from the Spanish Netherlands into France and proceeded to besiege the strategic French fortress at Rocroi in eastern France.

A young Louis II de Condé, Duc d'Enghien arrived near Rocroi in early May at the head of an army of approximately 23,000 troops. The Spanish army was regarded as the most formidable fighting force of the time. Though the two sides were close to being numerically matched, the Spanish army had the clear upper hand with regard to reputation.

D'Enghien organized his battle lines and attacked in the morning of May 19. Leading his cavalry on the right flank, he overcame the Spanish horse before him. But, as this was happening, his own cavalry on the left flank were being defeated. He would soon be in danger of attack by Spanish cavalry swinging around and rushing up from behind.

In a stunning turning of the tables, d'Enghien ordered his cavalry into an enveloping gallop. They succeeded in reaching the rear of the Spanish cavalry and delivered on them a swift, surprising defeat. The Spanish infantry, though they put up a valiant defense, were defeated in detail.

For the first time in a century, Spanish troops had lost a major battle. Spanish reputation on the field and in diplomacy would swiftly decline. D'Enghien would go on to become one of France's greatest generals, the Great Condé. And France would become the predominant military power on the continent.

French map of Rocroi

CARTE
DE
ROCROY
Ech. 50

BATTLE OF BLENHEIM

The battle that shifted the European balance of power away from France

Blenheim Palace

The French Sun King, Louis XIV, was at the height of his glory when the Spanish throne became vacant. He trumped his rival claimants, the Hapsburgs of the Holy Roman Empire, to obtain the throne for his grandson in 1700. In so doing, he ignited the War of the Spanish Succession (1701–1714), a dynastic chess game that involved practically all of Europe. It pitted the Grand Alliance, led by England and the Holy Roman Empire, against France, whose king was the *bête noir* of European monarchs in the late seventeenth and early eighteenth centuries.

France's only important ally was Bavaria (Spain remained neutral). Louis XIV's plan in the opening stage of the war was to have his army, under the Duc de Tallard, link up with the Elector of Bavaria's army under Ferdinand de Marsin and capture Vienna, capital of the Hapsburgs. John Churchill, Duke of Marlborough (and an ancestor of Winston Churchill's), leader of the Anglo-Dutch army, was determined to save Vienna. In a brilliant maneuver, Marlborough marched his men night and day from Holland to the Danube—a distance of about 250 miles—and linked up with the Imperial army under Eugene of Savoy.

Tallard and Marsin were stunned to discover that Marlborough had eluded the French blocking force meant to keep him in Holland. Now on the banks of the Danube, near the city of Blenheim, was an Alliance army almost numerically their equal.

The attack commenced on August 13. Marlborough's superior cavalry overwhelmed French fortifications and drove Tallard's army into Blenheim, where Tallard and 12,000 troops surrendered. Then Marlborough's cavalry rushed to assist Eugene's hard-pressed army. Together they forced Marsin's troops to retreat.

Though the war continued off and on for ten more years, the balance of power had shifted. As one historian noted, "The decisive blow struck at Blenheim resounded through every part of Europe. It at once destroyed the vast fabric of power which it had taken Louis XIV, aided by the talents of Turenne and the genius of Vauban, so long to construct."

John Churchill, Duke of Marlborough

FORTIFICATIONS

Man-made defense barriers used during the Battle of Blenheim

A *fortification* is any sort of temporary (field) or permanent construction designed to prohibit or restrict attack or movement by an opponent. A "wall" is the fortification that comes to mind most often, the most famous being China's Great Wall, used to keep out the Mongols. However, fortifications can be as simple as stakes in the ground such as the ones used by the Persians at Gaugamela.

The first town to encircle itself with a complete belt of permanent stone fortifications is thought to have been Jericho, the earliest construction dating to 8000 B.C. and the latest about 5000 B.C. Evidence of fortifications dating from 2500 B.C. to 1500 B.C. have been discovered at archeological sites in Egypt, Sumer, and Palestine. Relics of walls, and siege engines used to overcome them, were discovered and dated to as early as 1300 B.C.

Military historian Martin Van Creveld noted that primitive fortifications do not mean they are ineffective (the example of Gaugamela to the contrary). In *Technology and War*, he wrote, "At the right time and place, field fortifications however simple could present a formidable obstacle, since they force the enemy to divide his attention between dealing with them and protecting himself." English archers at Crécy and Agincourt used stakes in the ground that successfully protected themselves from attack by mounted knights.

Gunpowder weapons created a different need for protection and spurred a revolution in fortifications. At one extreme are the stout fortress walls. At the other end are the trenches and barbed wire supported by machine guns and artillery of World War I's Western Front.

The artificial satellite literally raised the art of fortifications to a new level. One example is the undeployed Strategic Defense Initiative or "Star Wars" program. Satellites have now created a "virtual wall" in which the barrier that inhibits and influences enemy military movement is no longer made of wood, stone, or metal. Rather, the fortification is composed of information.

A medieval fortress in Iran

SÉBASTIEN LE PRESTRE DE VAUBAN

Greatest military engineer in history (1633–1707)

Had it not been for Vauban's engineering genius, King Louis XIV of France would never have been able to conduct his many wars of aggression. Vauban's skill in building fortresses was unparalleled; equally amazing was his genius in devising strategies for investing them. It was argued that only Vauban was capable of tearing down something that he had built. Many of his fortresses are still in existence and are studied by students of the military disciplines.

Vauban was born into a Burgundian family of petty nobility. In 1651, he began his military career serving under the famous French general, the Great Condé. Later he participated in the Fronde rebellion during Louis XIV's regency. In 1653, he switched sides and aligned himself with the king.

He began to make his mark as an engineer in a war against Spain that ended in 1659. When Louis XIV officially began his reign in 1661, Vauban had laid the foundation of a close relationship with his king that would last most of his life. Though Vauban brought considerable talent to the construction and destruction of fortifications, historian Paul Sonnino noted that what separated Vauban from all the rest was his ability to give the king what he wanted, "a method of waging war elegantly and with a minimum of bloodshed."

Vauban's method used massive geometric fortifications, bastions, and outworks for defense. For attack, it was an elaborate weaving of trenches, circumvallation, and mines. With fortresses already achieving a high level of design by the Italians and the Dutch, it was less *what* Vauban built than *how* he built it that set him apart.

Vauban received many honors from the grateful King Louis XIV, including the title of marshal. He was made an honorary member of the French Academy of Sciences. He died in Paris of an inflammation of the lungs in 1707, eight years prior to the death of the king whom he had loyally, and indispensably, served.

HERMANN MAURICE, COMTE DE SAXE

Marshal general of France (1696–1750)

The future *Comte de Saxe* (French for Count of Saxony) was the first of 354 acknowledged illegitimate children fathered by the man named (appropriately enough) Augustus the Strong. Augustus was the elector of Saxony and later the king of Poland.

Though Saxe's bastardry did not bar him from society, he had to make his own way in the world. At age twelve, he enlisted in the Saxon army. He fought for the allied Dutch and Austrian armies against the French in 1709 at Malpaquet in the War of the Spanish Succession. Though the allies won, it was a victory dearly bought. The lessons of that Pyrrhic victory would influence Saxe for the rest of his life. At the conclusion of that war, he was commander of a cavalry regiment.

Saxe then began a career of what might be called a mercenary general in assorted dynastic struggles. His fortunes rose and fell during periods of war and peace. Saxe's reputation as one of the greatest soldiers of his time was established during the War of the Austrian Succession (1740–1748). Now a general in French King Louis XV's army, Saxe was promoted to marshal of France following for his capture of Prague, a *coup de main* that made him famous. Saxe's great victory was the Battle of Fontenoy (May 11, 1745). He commanded French troops from a litter while sick from dropsy (edema). The grateful Louis XV conferred to him the beautiful Chateau de Chambord for life.

After the war, Saxe wrote *Mes Reveries* (*My Dreams*), published after his death. It became a classic of military philosophy that had great influence on Napoleon. In it he wrote, "It is not the big armies that win battles; it is the good ones."

Saxe died on November 20, 1750, shortly after a troupe of actresses visited him. His doctor ruled Saxe's death the result of "*un excès de femmes*," what one biographer observed was "an end only a shade less glorious to a Frenchman than death in action."

Battle of Fontenoy, a victory for the Count de Saxe

Battle of Leuthen

Frederick the Great's victory that saved Prussia

The Seven Years' War began as a conflict between England and France that soon involved most of the nations of Europe. The small Germanic kingdom of Prussia had the misfortune of allying itself with England. All its larger and more powerful neighbors, Austria, Russia, Sweden, and Saxony, were French allies.

The summer of 1757 was particularly grim for Frederick, king of Prussia. His army, regarded as one of the best in Europe, had suffered a number of reverses that placed the future of Prussia in great peril. The situation was partially restored when Frederick scored an important victory against the French at the Battle of Rossbach (November 5).

But with the Austrian army at Leuthen, he faced a more difficult challenge. He was outnumbered almost 2 to 1 (35,000 versus 65,000) in men and the Austrians had a numerical advantage in cannon, as well. But the Austrian commander, Prince Charles of Lorraine, had his army on land that had been used as a training ground for the Prussian army. This gave Frederick an advantage of intimate knowledge of the terrain.

Frederick chose to attack first. He began by maneuvering his forces into strong tactical positions, some of which were hidden from his enemy. Then he launched a feint on the Austrian right flank that fooled the Austrians into thinking that was the main attack. They drew forces from their left flank for reinforcements. Frederick then launched a powerful assault on the weakened Austrian left and smashed it.

Charles managed to recover enough to form a new defensive line anchored on the village of Leuthen. Bitter fighting ensued, with the disciplined Prussian infantry and cavalry pressing their advantage to the fullest. The Austrian line eventually broke due to confusion and a desperate retreat followed.

Leuthen was later acclaimed as one of Frederick's greatest victories. It saved Prussia. Austria's defeat caused them to abandon Silesia, which they had seized from Prussia. Though the battle did not end Austria's participation in the war, its later campaigns were more cautious and timid. Prussia was never again seriously threatened by Austria.

The Prussian assault at Leuthen

FREDERICK II, THE GREAT

King of Prussia and victor of the Battle of Leuthen (1712–1786)

The monarch who would become one of the great generals of his time began life as a child terrorized by his dictatorial father. At the age of eighteen he attempted to run away from home. For this, and other rebellious acts, his father brutally punished him, even placing the young man under a suspended sentence of death. The year 1740 was a watershed for Frederick: He inherited the throne and began a lifelong correspondence with the philosopher Voltaire, who would have an immense influence on Frederick's life; and Maria Theresa became the empress of the rival Hapsburg Empire.

Prussia at the time was a small German kingdom. It had few natural barriers, no continuous border to unite dynastic holdings scattered throughout the region, and was surrounded on three sides by the great powers of France, Austria-Hungary, and Russia. When Maria Theresa ascended the throne, he knew that Prussia would be caught in the middle of a new round of dynastic struggles for hegemony in Europe. Unless he fought back, Prussia would be destroyed in the crossfire.

Frederick began to make Prussia's army the best, and most feared, in the world. Soldiers were enlisted practically for life. Training was a brutal regimen, with the goal of producing living automatons. Frederick incorporated all aspects of Prussian life and industry to service the needs of his army. He became so effective in his transformation of his army and realm that Voltaire later commented, "Prussia is not a country which has an army, but an army which has a country."

When his army was ready, Frederick surprised his neighbors by attacking. Between 1741 and 1745, he became central Europe's master. In 1756, France, Russia, and Austria formed a grand alliance to crush the upstart nation and the Seven Years' War began. Frederick scored dramatic victories at Rossbach and Leuthen but suffered enough defeats that he faced the very real danger of being crushed. Then one of his greatest enemies, Czarina Catherine of Russia, died and Russia quit the alliance. A treaty signed in 1763 between the warring powers recognized Prussia's new position as a major European power.

BATTLE OF PLASSEY

Clive's victory that began British dominance in India

In the mid-eighteenth century, business interests of the rival European powers, chiefly England and France, were locked in a high-stakes power grab within the crumbling Mughal Empire of India. These trading companies, which acted like independent nations outside their home country borders, sought—and often fought—to obtain economic contracts and concessions that would be worth millions to their companies and investors. The stakes were raised even higher when England and France became locked in the Seven Years' War. The Province of Bengal in eastern India had broken free of the declining Mughal Empire in the 1720s. In 1756, Siraj Ud Daulah, the new nawab of Bengal, began an ambitious plan to reduce the influence of the Europeans. He particularly focused on the British East India Company that had greatly interfered in Bengal's internal affairs.

When the nawab's army captured the British garrison at Calcutta, the British East India Company in Madras, about 800 miles south, organized a rescue operation of less than 1,000 European troops and a little more than 2,000 native sepoys under the command of Colonel Robert Clive. Against him, the nawab had an army of about 50,000 men and was advised by the French.

Clive and his men were encamped in a grove of mango trees where they were attacked on the morning of June 23 by the nawab's troops. A heavy rainstorm at about noon caused the fighting to stop. The rain stopped at about mid-afternoon, and Clive seized the opportunity to counterattack. Because the nawab's troops, unlike the British, had neglected to protect their gunpowder from the rain, they were helpless before the British cannon and musket fire. The nawab's army fled in panic, with losses of about 500 men. Clive lost only 72.

Siraj Ud Daulah was soon deposed and a nawab more sympathetic to British trade interests was installed. British trading privileges were restored and within ten years, the British had complete control of Bengal. The wealth obtained from Bengal would be used to fund the British armies that later conquered the rest of India.

Robert Clive leading his army into battle

ROBERT CLIVE

British general and victor of the Battle of Plassey (1725–1774)

Robert Clive was one of the greatest natural generals of all time. Despite a total lack of formal military education, he would conquer for England "the brightest jewel in the British crown"—India.

Clive came from a respectable family and his father had been a member of Parliament. Clive was an unruly child who was expelled from numerous schools. At age eighteen, his family enrolled him as a bookkeeper clerk in the East India Company and he was packed off to India.

India at that time was in a state of political flux. The Mughal Empire was disintegrating and France and Britain were rivals in the subcontinent's hegemony. Government proxies in this rivalry were the French Compagnie des Indes and the British East India Company. Three years after Clive arrived, this rivalry erupted into a clash of arms, a ripple effect of the War of the Austrian Succession in Europe. Clive joined the army in India and finally found his calling.

By 1751, France and England were locked in a full-scale war in India and Clive was in the thick of it. His courage, leadership, and tactical genius caused him to rise quickly through the ranks. In a series of brilliant campaigns, Clive victoriously led a small force (always outnumbered, sometimes as much as 20 to 1) that shattered French power in India.

When he returned to England in 1753, at age twenty-eight, Prime Minister William Pitt hailed him as a "heaven-born general." Pitt returned to India in 1755 and more campaigns. His stunning victory at Plassey in 1757 established British supremacy in Bengal and paved the way for eventual British mastery of the subcontinent.

Clive's later life was marked with both success and scandal. He was awarded the title Baron of Plassey and received other honors. He was involved in financial scandals but successfully defended himself against all charges. He died by suicide on November 22, 1774.

BROWN BESS MUSKET

Smoothbore shoulderarm used at Battle of Plassey

The British Land Pattern Musket, better known by its nickname "Brown Bess," is one of the most famous smoothbore firearms. Muskets differ from rifles in that the barrels of muskets do not have grooves that impart a spin to the bullet that allows for greater accuracy and range. But, for more than 400 years, those disadvantages were outweighed by the advantages of low-cost manufacture and ease of operation.

The Land Pattern Musket was adopted as the standard firearm of the British army at a time of expansion during the British Empire. As such, it served troops around the world and became one of the ubiquitous symbols of the empire. The origins of the nickname "Brown Bess" are unknown. The word *brown* is thought to refer to the color of the musket's stock or to the color of the barrel. The origins of *Bess* range from a reference to Elizabeth I ("Good Queen Bess") to a derivative from firearms predecessors arquebus or blunderbuss. Another suggestion is that it is the Anglicizing of the German *brawn buss* ("strong gun") or *braun buss* ("brown gun") because King George I, who commissioned the Brown Bess, was from Germany.

Because it was a smoothbore, its accuracy even at close range was poor. Thus explaining why at Bunker Hill General Israel Putnam (or Colonel William Prescott) phrased his order, "Don't shoot until you see the whites of their eyes!" Musket fire was more noted for its shock value in volley fire. Typically, infantry would approach an enemy in line formation of two or three rows, stop at close range (usually 50 yards, sometimes less) whereupon the first row would drop to one knee and fire in unison. Then the first line would step to the rear and reload, the second row would drop down and fire, and the process would be repeated, or a bayonet charge would be ordered, depending on circumstance.

The Brown Bess remained in service into the middle of the nineteenth century. It was phased out following the Crimean War (1853–1856).

The Battle of Bunker Hill, where the Brown Bess musket was used

BATTLE OF QUEBEC

Pivotal battle in the French and Indian War

The taking of
Quebec by
English forces

The Battle of Quebec, also known as the Battle of the Plains of Abraham, was fought during the French and Indian War. This was the North American counterpart to the Seven Years' War, which was between England and France and fought in Europe. In 1759, after three years of fighting, the British sought to attain a decisive advantage over the French in Canada with a campaign up the St. Lawrence River.

The British began a siege of Quebec City, strategically located on the St. Lawrence River, in June. The British army, led by Major General James Wolfe, totaled about 9,000 men and was supported by a fleet of war and support ships commanded by Admiral Charles Saunders. General Louis-Joseph, Marquis de Montcalm, commanded about 4,000 troops, composed of regulars and militia, stationed in Quebec City.

The siege proved frustrating for the British. They did not have sufficient troops for the siege, even with bombardment help from the warships. To break the deadlock, Wolfe decided on an aggressive move. A reconnaissance patrol had found a small trail up the steep cliffs along the riverbank leading up to the Plains of Abraham southwest of the city.

On the night of September 12–13, he led a force of about 4,000 men (accounts vary) up the cliff. When dawn broke on September 13, Montcalm saw a British army lined up to do battle on the Plains of Abraham. Deciding that the western walls of his fortifications were too weak to resist a concerted attack, Montcalm accepted the challenge of battle.

After getting organized, the French opened fire first. Their cannon savaged the advancing British ranks with grapeshot. The well-disciplined British troops got to within 40 yards of the French when Wolfe gave the order to open fire. Volley after volley tore into the French lines. The battle became a melee in which both Wolfe and Montcalm were shot and killed. Surviving French troops escaped back into Quebec City. Five days later, the dispirited defenders surrendered. Though expulsion of the French from North America would not come for several more years, the British victory at Quebec heralded the downfall of French rule in Canada.

The death of General Wolfe

INVASION OF CANADA

Unsuccessful Continental Army attempt to capture Quebec

In the opening days of the American Revolution, General George Washington approved a plan to invade Canada. Its capture would deprive the British of a base from which they could conduct offensive operations against New York and New England. The key to achieving this goal was the seizure of the strategically important fortress of Quebec located at the confluence of the St. Lawrence and St. Charles Rivers.

Two armies were assigned to the task. One, starting in September from Fort Ticonderoga and initially led by Major General Philip Schuyler and later by Brigadier General Richard Montgomery, traveled north mostly along waterways. The second army, also leaving in September and led by Colonel Benedict Arnold, took an extraordinary overland route through the Maine wilderness. After a horrific march, Arnold and less than 700 starving members of his army rendezvoused with Montgomery and his men near Quebec in November.

General Guy Carleton was the commander of the Quebec fortress. He was an experienced and talented officer with steady nerves. However, his garrison was a mixed force of few soldiers and many irregulars, some of questionable reliability. The defenses of the fortress were strong and he was confident he could resist any siege the Continental Army might conduct.

Montgomery and Arnold, after having rested their men and performed reconnaissance, decided to launch a two-pronged attack. At 4:00 A.M. on New Year's Eve 1775, in the middle of a howling blizzard, a rocket signaled the beginning of their attack. Montgomery was at the head of one column. He and his men got within a few feet of a fortified house when the British defenders opened fire. Montgomery was killed instantly, as were many of his men. The survivors were routed.

Arnold's attack fared no better. When the fighting ended that evening, the Americans had lost, with 60 men killed or wounded and 426 captured. The British had only 5 men killed and 13 wounded. Arnold gathered up the other survivors and began a long retreat south. The Continental Army's invasion of Canada was over.

The death of General Montgomery in battle

BATTLE OF TRENTON

General George Washington's victory during the War for Independence

Crossing the
Delaware River

The year 1776 had not been a good one for George Washington and the cause for American independence from Britain. His army had suffered one defeat after another. It had lost New York City and northern New Jersey and been forced to retreat into eastern Pennsylvania. His only good fortune was that December began. The British, following the custom of the time, ceased offensive operations, and put up in winter quarters for the season. However, that reprieve was undercut by the fact that the enlistments for many of Washington's men were due to expire on December 31. If he didn't use his small army before then, he would find himself to be a general without any soldiers. The best way to keep his army intact and to encourage additional enlistments was to achieve a dramatic victory.

Washington chose to attack the strong, but somewhat isolated, Hessian garrison under Colonel Johann Rall, encamped in Trenton. His plan was to have three divisions secretly cross the Delaware River on Christmas Day and attack the Hessians on the December 26. Bad weather dogged his army's advance, and of the three divisions, only one, led by Washington himself, managed to cross the river and assemble for battle. Undaunted, he decided to continue and divided his division into two crops, one attacking from the south, the other from the north.

The attack commenced at about 8 A.M. the morning of December 26. The Hessians, groggy and drunk from celebrating the holiday, were lulled into a false sense of security by the inclement weather. They were surprised by the attack and stumbled into the streets in confusion. Resistance was sporadic and uncoordinated. During a withdrawal to regroup, Colonel Rall was shot and mortally wounded. Within an hour and a half, the fighting was over.

Washington made good use of his victory by quickly retreating back to Pennsylvania with his prisoners and captured arms before British troops in nearby Princeton could respond.

General George Washington after Battle of Trenton

GEORGE WASHINGTON

American general, victor of the Battle of Trenton, and U.S. president (1732–1799)

George Washington was a respected Virginia plantation owner who began his military career as an officer in the Virginia militia. In 1754, Lt. Colonel Washington was ordered to lead an armed force to Fort Duquesne (modern Pittsburgh), where the French had taken over a fort, and deliver a message stating that the French were trespassing on land claimed by England and that they had to leave. A skirmish erupted in which a French diplomat was killed, creating an international incident that touched off the French and Indian War. He participated in a number of campaigns during the conflict, most notably with the disastrous 1755 expedition against Fort Duquesne led by British general Edward Braddock.

Following the end of the French and Indian War in 1763, Washington entered Virginia politics. He was a delegate from Virginia in the First Continental Congress and a member of the Second Continental Congress. On June 15, 1775, Congress named him commander in chief of continental forces. As commander of the Continental Army during the American Revolution, he conducted a military campaign that had the distinction of handing the British Empire one of the few decisive defeats in its history.

The path to victory was not an easy one. In the beginning, Washington lost more battles than he won. Part of the problem was that many troops under his command were untrained militia whose enlistments were of short duration. Throughout the war, Washington was never sure of the strength of his armies or how long he might have them.

The year 1777 was the low point for Washington. Winter quarters at Valley Forge became a symbol of dedication to the cause of independence. Washington also had to squash the notorious Conway Cabal that sought to replace him with General Horatio Gates, the hero of the Battle of Saratoga.

With the help of such subordinates as drillmaster Baron von Steuben, the Marquis de Lafayette, General Nathanael Greene, and others, Washington began to prevail against the British. His victory at Yorktown in 1781 effectively secured independence for the Thirteen Colonies. Washington was elected unanimously as the United States' first president and served two terms. He died in 1799.

BATTLE OF SARATOGA

Battle that secured French alliance with America

The troops
assembled at
Saratoga

The British employed a divide-and-conquer strategy in the northern colonies. In 1777, this called for Major General Sir John Burgoyne and his army to advance south from Canada down the Hudson River and link with General Sir Henry Clinton's army traveling up the river from New York City. But poor communications (a chronic problem), vagueness of orders from British Commander-in-Chief General Sir William Howe, and assorted delays resulted in an uncoordinated and greatly weakened campaign.

Major General Horatio Gates had recently assumed command of the continental forces in New York, with Major General Benedict Arnold and Colonel Daniel Morgan his main lieutenants. Gates's forces were strongly entrenched at Beemis Heights. Under the urging of Arnold, Gates ordered Morgan on September 19 to take his men and reconnoiter British advance positions at Freeman's Farm. A seesaw battle quickly erupted that lasted for several hours and was reinforced by both sides.

Though Burgoyne's men successfully held the battlefield, the victory was more apparent than real. Casualties were heavy, troops were exhausted, and unlike the British, most of the American troops had not been committed. Instead of retreating, Burgoyne chose to remain, believing he would soon receive reinforcements from General Clinton.

But it was Gates who received decisive reinforcements. In addition, he used the pause to strengthen even further his fortifications. On October 7, Burgoyne chose to attack the Americans at Beemis Heights. The Americans responded with heavy fire and counterattacks on both British flanks. The heroes of the battle were Colonel Morgan and General Arnold. By most accounts, Gates never left the safety and comfort of his headquarters. At the end of the day, though the British still held their positions, it was clear they had been decisively defeated.

At first unable to face facts, Burgoyne delayed the inevitable for several days, finally surrendering his army to Gates on October 17. But Gates's terms were so generous that Congress later repudiated most of them. Even so, the victory held enormous strategic value, for it convinced the French government to officially provide aid to the rebellious colonies.

The surrender by Major General Sir John Burgoyne

BENEDICT ARNOLD

American general, hero in the Battle of Saratoga, and traitor (1741–1801)

Benedict Arnold was born into a distinguished Connecticut family in 1741. During the French and Indian War, he served briefly in the militia. He was a successful businessman when the American Revolution broke out. He entered militia service as a captain and assisted in the siege of Boston in 1775. Promoted to colonel, he led a unit of Massachusetts militia and, with Ethan Allen and his men, captured Fort Ticonderoga in May of that year.

Arnold was instrumental in forestalling British offensives in the northern colonies in the early years of the war. Though Arnold had earned the respect and admiration of the men under his command, his relationship with his superiors and Congress was tempestuous. He was hot tempered and inclined to take offense over any perceived slight. He and Major General Horatio Gates were barely on speaking terms at Saratoga. It's telling that Arnold's success in that battle came because he was insubordinate. Washington was Arnold's only admirer.

Arnold was wounded at Saratoga. Because his wound prevented him from serving in combat, Arnold, now a major general, was placed in command of Philadelphia in May 1778.

Philadelphia was the seat of Congress and the state government and was divided into pro-British and pro-Independence factions. He met and married Peggy Shippen, a British sympathizer, in 1779. During this period, he became involved in a financial scandal and was court-martialed. Washington reduced the punishment to a mild letter of reprimand. The court-martial proved the breaking point to the cash-strapped Arnold. He entered into treasonous correspondence with the British and promised to deliver the important fort at West Point once he became its commander. When Major John André was captured carrying correspondence that revealed Arnold's treachery, Arnold escaped to British lines.

Arnold became a brigadier general in the British army. But the British did not trust him, and he was never given any important responsibility in military affairs. In 1781, he went to live in London. He died in 1801, with his name synonymous with treason in the land of his birth, and as an outcast in the country to which he had sold his reputation.

Siege of Yorktown

War-winning American victory

The fierce battle that led to surrender

British lieutenant general Charles Cornwallis's campaign of conquest in the south had not worked out. Retreating north to Virginia, he led his army of about 7,500 men to the port of Yorktown. Here it took up defensive positions against Washington and his combined Franco-American army of about 16,000 troops. Cornwallis knew that his situation was not strong enough to withstand a long siege. His hope was that the Royal Navy would arrive in time with sufficient supplies and reinforcements to enable him to break out.

But what Cornwallis did not know at the time was that a French fleet had intercepted the relieving British fleet. In the Battle off the Chesapeake Capes on September 5, the British were defeated and forced to return to New York City. The French fleet then took up a blockade position. Washington kept up the pressure on the British with regular artillery barrages and forays against the British positions. When Washington's troops captured an outer ring of defenses, Cornwallis knew surrender was inevitable unless he could escape. On the night of October 16, Cornwallis attempted to escape across the mouth of the York River to Gloucester with his men. But a combination of too-few boats and a sudden storm forced him to abandon that effort.

On October 17, Cornwallis made an offer to surrender. Two days later, his army laid down its arms. Cornwallis was too embarrassed to surrender personally. Instead, he remained in his tent and sent an aide who attempted to offer his sword to the French general, the Comte de Rochambeau. Rochambeau declined and pointed to Washington.

The violation of protocol merely emphasized the enormity of the American victory. The former colonists had challenged one of the mightiest empires in Europe—and won.

The British surrender at Yorktown

BATTLE OF VALMY

Battle that saved the French Revolution

A poster celebrating the French victory

Afraid that the revolution in France that had deposed King Luis XVI might spread, the monarchs of Austria and Prussia in 1792 formed the First Coalition. This was the first of ultimately seven alliances created to fight first republican, and later imperial, France under Napoleon I.

The leaders of the new French republic raised armies of citizen soldiers to defend their nation from the Austro-Prussian invaders—but spirit and passion proved poor substitutes for training and discipline. French armies broke and ran before the experienced army led by Karl Wilhelm Ferdinand, the Duke of Brunswick.

When the duke's army captured Longwy and Verdun, panic seized the citizens of Paris. Only a small force of ill-disciplined troops that had never before seen battle stood between the city and the invaders. The rag-tag force was led by General Charles Dumouriez. In early September, he threw up a blockade along the invaders' line of communications. This caused the duke to stop his advance and decide to smash the "rabble" opposing him. Then he would continue to Paris and free the imprisoned French king.

Meanwhile, Dumouriez was reinforced by a 36,000-man army led by General Francois-Christophe de Kellerman. Even though the French army now totaled about 52,000 men and 40 cannon, the Duke of Brunswick was so confident of victory he believed a detachment of 34,000 men and 36 cannon was sufficient to overcome the French. The Prussian attack on September 20 managed to fight through the French blockade line. But they were stopped by Kellerman's artillery at Valmy. The fighting abruptly ended at about 4 P.M. when a severe thundershower forced both sides to seek shelter.

In truth, fighting had been so light that the outcome itself was inconclusive. But the duke unaccountably decided to leave the field and take his army back to Germany. This was a time when victory was usually decided by which army still held the battlefield. Because the French did, French propagandists were able to declare a great victory. Morale of the citizens of the new republic soared. The French Revolution had survived.

The French fighting the Austrian troops lead by the Duke of Brunswick

Battle of Aboukir Bay

Pivotal battle establishing Royal Navy dominance of the seas

Republican France had become a threat to England. General Napoleon decided to sunder British dominance by seizing Egypt. British admiral Horatio Nelson failed to intercept Admiral François-Paul Brueys d'Aigalliers's French fleet before his ships, filled with General Napoleon Bonaparte's troops, reached Egypt. Napoleon, aware of Nelson's proximity, ordered Brueys to set sail for Corfu as soon as he had finished unloading and to take extra care to elude the British fleet. Brueys was delayed by bad weather and anchored his ships in Aboukir Bay to wait out the storm. Brueys's fleet had thirteen powerful ships-of-the-line and four frigates and he had taken up what he believed was a strong defensive position, flanked by shoals and a fortress. Thus, Brueys was confident he could repel British attack when Nelson's fleet of fourteen ships-of-the-line and one sloop appeared on the horizon on August 1.

Because Nelson's fleet arrived late in the day, Brueys began to leisurely prepare for action he thought would commence on August 2. He refused to believe that Nelson would dare risk his deep-draft ships-of-the-line with a night attack in the shallow, shoal-filled waters. But Nelson surprised him. Splitting his fleet into two so it could attack the line of French ships from both sides simultaneously, he ordered an attack as the sun was beginning to set. Though the two fleets were evenly matched on paper, the morale of the poorly trained French crews was low. The British crews had superior discipline, seamanship, and courage. Nelson's ships raked the French vessels, meting out fearful punishment. Nelson, on the *Bellerophon*, was slightly wounded in the head and had to go below to have his wound dressed. When he returned, at about 10 P.M., he saw Brueys's flagship, the 120-gun *l'Orient*, blow up, killing almost everyone aboard, including the admiral. The tremendous explosion stunned everyone and there was a brief pause in the battle. When it resumed, the French fleet was all but destroyed. Only four ships managed to escape.

Napoleon would continue to campaign in Egypt and also conquer much of Syria. But the British victory established their naval superiority for the remainder of the French Revolutionary Wars.

Warships in Aboukir Bay

NAPOLEON I

French Emperor and victor of the Battle of Austerlitz (1769–1821)

The man who became the most feared and admired European leader in the early nineteenth century was born in Ajaccio, Corsica. Napoleon attended military school in France. Had it not been for the French Revolution, Napoleon would have remained a gifted, but anonymous, junior officer of artillery in the army of the *ancien regime*. But the revolution opened the door to advancement for the ambitious Corsican who rapidly rose through the ranks. In 1795, he suppressed a Royalist uprising. In gratitude, Napoleon was given his first field command, as general leading the Army of Italy. His brilliant campaign in Italy in 1796–1797 was a foretaste of what was to come in Europe for the next two decades.

Having achieved fame in Italy, Napoleon then took an army to Egypt to disrupt England's trade with India. This campaign ultimately proved fruitless and he quickly returned. In 1799, he led a successful coup against the government and became First Consul. From that point on, Napoleon was involved in one war after another with the nations of Europe.

In 1803, needing money to finance his war against Great Britain, he sold to the young United States territory later called the Louisiana Purchase. In 1804, he crowned himself Emperor of the French. At the height of his power, Napoleon I dominated through direct rule or various alliances Europe from the Iberian Peninsula to Moscow. Many of his battles have become classics of study in the art of maneuver and concentration of attack.

Napoleon's genius was not limited to the art of war. His Napoleonic Code reorganized and simplified laws in France and established many civil and educational institutions. It proved such a remarkable achievement that parts of it remain in existence today.

Napoleon's invasion of the Iberian Peninsula in 1808 marked the beginning of his decline. His ill-fated invasion of Russia in 1812 hastened it. He was forced to abdicate in 1814. In 1815, he returned to France from exile on the island of Elba. His defeat at Waterloo later that year led to a second abdication, and exile to the remote island of St. Helena, where he died in 1821.

Battle of Austerlitz

Napoleon's tactical masterpiece

Napoleon at
Austerlitz

Austria, Russia, and Sweden and some minor German principalities joined Great Britain in the Third Coalition alliance designed to stop Napoleon's aggrandizement in Europe. Napoleon responded with a plan to invade England. But, after a few weeks, it was shelved and replaced with a campaign against the Third Coalition continental allies.

Napoleon I was thirty-six years old and at the height of his ability. His *Grande Armée* was one of the best armies in the world when he led it across the Rhine River near Strausbourg at the end of September 1805. In the weeks that followed, Napoleon racked up one victory after another.

Even though Napoleon seized the Austrian capital of Vienna, Emperor Francis I refused to capitulate. Instead, the remnants of the Austrian army joined the Russian army under General Mikhail Kutuzov. Accompanying it were both the Austrian emperor and the Russian czar, Alexander I. The meddling presence of the two monarchs created command conflicts that Kutuzov, the nominal tactical commander, could not overcome. Despite Kutuzov's protests, the emperors agreed on a plan to reinforce their army's right wing and use it to attack and outflank the French left wing.

Napoleon anticipated such a move by his enemy. When the Russians began their attack on the morning of December 2, his right wing gave way slowly, drawing the Russo-Austrian forces further away from the center. Napoleon had also organized his troops to further deceive the Russo-Austrian attack, making it appear that they had a more decisive numerical advantage. The "bait" of Napoleon's right wing performed its role well. The French troops slowly fell back, pulling with them the attackers and reinforcements from the Russo-Austrian center who were eager to "finish off" the French. When his enemy had stripped its center of all but a skeleton force, Napoleon ordered a smashing counterattack.

When the battle concluded, Napoleon had won what would later be acclaimed as his most brilliant tactical victory. The Russian army retreated back to Poland. A few days later, the Austrian emperor sued for peace. The Third Coalition was finished.

Napoleon at his camp on the eve of the battle

Battle of Trafalgar

Decisive British naval victory in the Napoleonic Wars

Nelson's Ship,
the HMS *Victory*

Napoleon's greatest foe during his reign was Great Britain. In 1805, he decided to invade his troublesome enemy. As he was drawing up his plans, Napoleon I wanted the French fleet to draw the Royal Navy fleet under Admiral Horatio Nelson away from the invasion sites. The result was a naval version of cat-and-mouse that covered half the globe. The only battle of any consequence during this time occurred off Cape Finisterre on the northwest coast of Spain on July 25, 1805. Though the battle was not important, it resulted in the French fleet under Admiral Pierre de Villeneuve seeking refuge in the harbor of Cadiz, about 80 miles west of the British base at Gibraltar. There it was blockaded by a British fleet.

In the meantime, Nelson devised a battle plan should the French fleet at Cadiz choose to run the blockade. At first, it appeared the French fleet would not. But Napoleon was furious with his admiral. He fired off a stinging reprimand to Villeneuve, accusing him of cowardice and ordering him to set sail and attack the British fleet. Despite reservations, Villeneuve obeyed.

Nelson sighted Villeneuve's combined French and Spanish fleet of thirty-three ships on the morning of October 21, off Cape Trafalgar about 30 miles southeast of Cadiz. When Villeneuve saw Nelson's fleet, he attempted to reverse course and return to Cadiz. But Nelson's ships proved faster. As the British ships closed on the enemy, Nelson's flagship the *Victory* hoisted the signal, "England expects that every man will do his duty."

Attacking in two columns, Nelson's thrusts splintered of the Franco-Spanish fleet into three parts. From that point on, the battle became a melee in which superior British seamanship and gunnery proved decisive. The British were on the cusp of victory when, at about 1:15 P.M., a French sharpshooter shot and fatally wounded Admiral Nelson. Nelson lived for three hours, long enough to learn that his fleet had won and that Admiral Villeneuve had been captured.

It was England's greatest naval victory in the Napoleonic war. Napoleon never again attempted to seriously challenge the Royal Navy's supremacy of the seas.

The fighting aboard the *Victory*

HORATIO NELSON

British admiral and victor of the Battle of Trafalgar (1758–1805)

Great Britain's most famous admiral, and one of the most influential admirals in history, was the son of a clergyman. He entered the Royal Navy in 1770 as a midshipman. In 1777, he received his first promotion and for the next several years he served on a variety of ships and commands in the West Indies. When war broke out with Revolutionary France, Nelson transferred to the British Mediterranean Fleet, where he was repeatedly in the thick of action. He lost an eye in an amphibious operation in 1794. During this time, he also met Emma Lady Hamilton, wife of the British ambassador to Naples, who became his mistress and an influential presence at court and in the government on his behalf. While Nelson would have achieved fame for his victories, Lady Hamilton's advocacy added a luster that helped elevate him to the level of immortality.

In 1798, Nelson was victorious against the French fleet supporting Napoleon's invasion of Egypt, causing him to abandon Egypt. Nelson's next important fleet action was in 1801. Now a vice admiral, he joined Sir Hyde Parker in a fleet action against Denmark to discourage them from aiding Napoleon. Nelson boldly led a squadron of twelve ships into Copenhagen Harbor. In the heat of battle, Parker signaled Nelson to retire. In an anecdote that became famous, Nelson placed his telescope against his blind eye and said he couldn't see the signal, remarking, "I have only one eye—I have a right to be blind sometimes." At the end of the day, Nelson had won the battle. In recognition, he was made a viscount.

Nelson's most famous battle occurred of the coast of Spain, at Trafalgar. At the height of the battle, Nelson, who had a habit of wearing his dress uniform complete with medals and badges, was shot and mortally wounded by a French sharpshooter. Nelson lived long enough to learn his fleet had won. His last words were, "Now I am satisfied. Thank God, I have done my duty."

Nelson's body was preserved in a barrel of brandy or wine (accounts vary) and taken to London for a state funeral.

BATTLE OF FRIEDLAND

Napoleon's victory that ends Fourth Coalition alliance

Statue of Napoleon

Napoleon was in a precarious position when the year 1807 began. Years of warfare had made France weary of fighting and conscripts he was receiving were no longer had the same high quality found in earlier campaigns. His Continental System, an economic blockade of England, was backfiring. And at Eylau (February 1807), the Russian and Prussian armies of the Third Coalition (Prussia, Russia, Austria, Naples, and Great Britain) claimed to have scored a victory. In reality, the laurels belonged to France but it was a Pyrrhic victory. To reverse his sagging fortunes, Napoleon needed to score a clear-cut decisive battlefield victory—and quickly.

General Levin August, Count von Bennigsen, Napoleon's adversary at Eylau, was en route for a rendezvous at the fortress of Königsberg. He stopped to rest his 60,000-man army at the Prussian city of Friedland, on the Alle River, roughly 20 miles from Napoleon's camp. At 3:00 A.M. on June 14, Bennigsen's troops were stunned awake by the sound of French cannon fire. His army was under attack by an advance corps led by one of Napoleon's marshals, Jean Lannes, whose reconnaissance parties had discovered Bennigsen's location the previous day.

Bennigsen's Russian troops rallied and counterattacked. They might have won the day but Napoleon and the rest of his army arrived by noon. In a series of brilliant maneuvers that demonstrated that his plodding at Eylau had been a fluke, Napoleon outflanked the Russian army. He drove its shattered ranks across the Alle River, where many of the troops drowned. Survivors fled in panic to Tilsit where Czar Alexander I had his headquarters.

Napoleon's crushing victory over the only large Russian army in the region caused Alexander to contact Napoleon and sue for peace. The Third Coalition was finished. On July 7, on a raft in the middle of the Niemen River, the two emperors met and signed the Treaty of Tilsit that ended the war between Russia and France and began an alliance between the two empires. It was the high water mark of Napoleon's reign.

BATTLE OF TALAVERA

The British victory in which Wellesley becomes Wellington

Napoleon had deposed the Spanish monarchy and installed his brother Joseph as Spain's new king. Even though the previous rulers had been inept and its government brutal and corrupt, the Spaniards united in revolt against their new, imposed ruler. And when French armies marched into Portugal, that nation rebelled, too. Napoleon's venture into the Iberian Peninsula would ultimately prove to be a major reason for his eventual downfall.

The Battle of Talavera, located about 70 miles southwest of Madrid, began with a series of missteps that would have been comedic were not the circumstances so serious. General Arthur Wellesley and General Gregorio de la Cuesta had an Anglo-Spanish army with a combined strength of more than 55,000 men. Relations between the groups were strained. Wellesley had discovered that the Spanish were not entirely reliable and subsequent experience at Talavera would only add to the mistrust.

The allied army had surprised a French corps under the combined leadership of Marshals Claude Victor, Jean-Baptiste Jourdan, and King Joseph Bonaparte on Sunday, July 25. But the corps was allowed to escape untouched to defenses at Talavera because Cuesta told Wellesley the Spanish would not fight on Sunday. The following day, Monday, saw Cuesta fling his army in a wild attack that was fought off. A French counterattack turned the Spanish retreat into such a precipitous rout that Wellesley was almost captured by French cavalry. That evening, a mounted French patrol so rattled the Spanish troops that 10,000 of them fired a thunderous volley into the night. Unnerved by their own gunfire, the Spaniards ran away in panic.

The British found themselves almost alone and outnumbered roughly 2 to 1 when the set-piece battle began on July 27. Fighting turned into a brutal slugging match that lasted for two days under a scorching sun. At one point, fighting was halted for a couple hours so both sides could collect their wounded. Late afternoon on July 28, the French had had enough.

Though casualties had been heavy, the British held the field and were able to declare victory. In appreciation, Arthur Wellesley was made viscount Wellington.

The Duke of Wellington

BATTLE OF BORODINO

Largest and bloodiest single-day battle in the Napoleonic Wars

Within five years, the harmony of Tilsit between Napoleon and Alexander had soured. A disagreement over the fate of Poland caused the breach, but a parting of ways, and war, was inevitable. When he led his *Grande Armée* of about 130,000 men into Russia in the summer of 1812, Napoleon began a campaign that would become the opening chapter in the downfall of his reign.

Czar Alexander proclaimed a Patriotic War. After Prince Mikhail Barclay de Tolly proved unable to stop the French army advance, he appointed the experienced General Mikhail Kutuzov as commander of the Russian armies. But, instead of leading his troops into battle as Barclay de Tolly had (with disastrous results), Kutuzov chose a Fabian strategy. Suddenly Napoleon found himself frustrated by the proximity of a large Russian army that remained tantalizingly close but refused to fight. That situation changed about 70 miles west of Moscow. Borodino is a small village on the banks of the Kolocha River. It was there that Kutuzov's army, 112,000 strong, would stand and fight.

When he saw Kutuzov's army, Napoleon was filled with joy; finally, battle was at hand. On September 6, both sides prepared for combat. Napoleon issued a proclamation exhorting victory. Kutuzov ordered priests to carry sacred icons through the Russian camp.

The battle was joined on September 7. The two sides were almost evenly matched in men and cannon. Both sides fought with such heroism and tenacity it was as if each combatant knew that the destiny of Europe depended on the outcome. The tide of battle swept from one side to the other. Brave men who achieved fame in earlier campaigns, such as Peter Bagration of Russia and Auguste de Caulaincourt of France, died in valiant charges. Others, like Marshal Michel Ney, repeatedly stared death in the face and survived to be covered in more glory.

When night fell, the Russians slowly retreated, leaving the French masters of the battlefield. But Napoleon knew he had not delivered the decisive blow he intended. On September 15, he and his army entered Moscow, a defeat disguised as victory.

The Battle of Borodino

BATTLE OF LEIPZIG

The largest battle in the Napoleonic Wars

The Germans called it the *Völkerschlacht*—literally the "Slaughter"—of Leipzig. Others came to call it the Battle of Six Nations. The Battle of Leipzig was the largest assemblage of illustrious generals the world had yet seen. On Napoleon's side were nine of his greatest marshals. On the allies, there was an impressive array that included the Prussian von Blücher, as well as Jean-Baptist Bernadotte, once a marshal of Napoleon's and now King of Sweden and Napoleon's enemy. It was the climactic battle in Napoleon's Campaign of 1813. The allies had formed the Sixth Coalition and, this time, was determined not to stop until Napoleon was crushed.

Napoleon's campaign in Germany was rapidly turning against him. He found himself being pursued from different sides by the armies of Austria, Bavaria, Sweden, Russia, and England. Napoleon stationed his army in Leipzig. Approaching from the north were Prussian and Swedish armies, from the east, the Russian army, and from the south, Austrian and German armies.

The attack began from the south on October 16 but it was poorly organized and Napoleon was able to throw it back. The attack from the north, though better organized and more serious, was also blunted. The next day held little serious fighting and Napoleon used the day to reposition his troops. He commanded about 195,000 men. But allied troop strength, initially 257,000, now numbered 365,000 men. On October 18, the allies launched a coordinated concentric offensive against all sectors of the French line. Incredibly, the French troops held their positions for nine hours. Napoleon began a phased withdrawal west. Though the allies kept up the pressure, at no time did Napoleon lose control of his men. His evacuation of Leipzig against tremendous odds ended in success.

Though Napoleon had saved his army, an armistice that would save France and his throne was no longer possible. In November, Napoleon was in Paris. In December, the allies crossed the Rhine and entered France. In March, they had taken Paris, and in April, Napoleon was forced to abdicate.

The battle of nations near Leipzig

BATTLE OF WATERLOO

The battle that ended the Napoleonic Wars

Napoleon during his last battle

The leaders of Europe participating in the Congress of Vienna had almost completed their redrawing of the map of Europe when they received stunning news. Napoleon I had escaped from exile on Elba and returned to power in France. The leaders immediately formed the Seventh Coalition, declared Napoleon an outlaw, and raised an army to defeat him once and for all.

Napoleon decided to attack before the allies could assemble their armies into an irresistible host. Napoleon launched his campaign on June 15. His purpose was to drive a wedge between the English and Prussian armies, led by the Duke of Wellington and Field Marshal Gebhard von Blücher, respectively. He hoped to defeat each individually before they were reinforced by the approaching Russian and Austrian armies.

Napoleon defeated the Prussians at Ligny. But he was unable to finish them off, thanks to timely support from the Duke of Wellington. On June 17, Napoleon split his force. While part would pursue the retreating Prussians, he would lead the rest and smash Wellington's army.

Wellington, meanwhile, had taken up defensive positions near Waterloo. He sent a message to von Blücher promising to fight Napoleon at Waterloo if von Blücher could reinforce him with a corps. Von Blücher promised to send two.

Napoleon's plan was to make a diversionary attack on Wellington's right flank. Then, after he had taken the bait, launch his main attack on what he hoped would be Wellington's weakened center. Heavy rain on June 17 delayed Napoleon's approach and disposition of troops. He was not able to initiate his feint until 11:30 A.M. on June 18. But Napoleon's enemies had long ago learned his stratagems. When the attack occurred, Wellington was not fooled.

The main attack by the French commenced at 1:30 P.M. and it proved poorly organized. Meanwhile, von Blücher delivered upon his promise. Both corps arrived at crucial moments in the battle. Even so, as Wellington said later, "It was a near run thing." At the end of the day, Napoleon's army was defeated. Within weeks, he would be once again sent to exile, this time for good on St. Helena.

The French retreat at Waterloo

Carl Philipp Gottlieb von Clausewitz

Prussian military theorist who fought in the Napoleonic Wars (1780–1831)

Clausewitz and General Antoine-Henri Jomini were contemporaries who fought in the Napoleonic Wars and whose writings were heavily influenced by their experiences. Jomini's texts have since fallen by the wayside. Historian Lynn Montross observed that the reason for this "may be explained by the fact that Jomini produced a system of war, Clausewitz a philosophy. The one has been outdated by new weapons, the other still influences the strategy behind those weapons."

Clausewitz was the son of a disabled Prussian officer. He joined the Prussian army as a sub-lieutenant at the age of twelve. Clausewitz was taken prisoner at the battle of Jena in 1806, and spent two years in France before being repatriated to Prussia. During the Battle of Waterloo he was a member of Marshal von Blücher's staff, acting as liaison between the Russian and Prussian armies. In 1818, he was promoted major general and appointed Director of the Berlin War Academy, a post he held until just before his death of cholera in 1831.

Clausewitz is known for his book, *Vom Kriege* (*On War*). Begun in 1819, it was an attempt to distill and systematize his observations on strategy and the conduct of war. *On War* was published posthumously by his widow in 1832.

Clausewitz used a dialectical method to make his points, leaving his arguments susceptible to misinterpretation. The most important example is the much quoted, and much misused, line: "War is merely a continuation of politics." This is an oversimplified statement that is an excerpt from a complex synthesis of thought. Clausewitz expressed many war concepts for the first time in words. *Fog of war*, to describe the chaos that occurs as soon as a battle is joined, is just one of many.

Acclaim over Clausewitz's theories caused even generals to fall prey to the cult surrounding "the High Priest of Strategy," as he became known in his country. Of this acclaim, General Hans von Seeckt, chief of the German army after World War I, said, "He should be praised less and read more."

BARON ANTOINE-HENRI JOMINI

Swiss-French general and military theorist during Napoleonic Wars (1779–1869)

Though his work is almost unknown now, Jomini was one of the foremost military theorists of the nineteenth century. He entered the Swiss army at age nineteen and was promoted to major two years later. He began his writing career at about the same time and his first four military histories caught the eye of French field marshal Michel Ney. Ney was so impressed, he made Jomini a member of his staff. He later joined the staff of Napoleon and became a general.

Vain and pompous, Jomini had a falling out with Napoleon's marshals and joined the staff of Russian emperor Alexander I in 1813. After the Napoleonic wars, he served in a variety of advisory roles in Russia before moving to Brussels where he wrote his most famous and influential work, *Précis de l'art de la guerre* (*Summary of the Art of War*), published in 1838. Jomini continued to serve the court of the Russian czar before retiring to the French Alps in 1859, dying there ten years later.

During his lifetime, Jomini was vilified for deserting Napoleon to join the czar against the emperor. That criticism became muted following the publication of *Précis*, which made him famous, respectable, and wealthy. Jomini's success was in his timing. He wrote the first popular books that analyzed Napoleon's art of war in a systematic manner. He brought to the military lexicon the phrases *theater of conflict* and *lines of direction*, among other terms still in use. His ideas emphasized the reduction of the conduct of war to a few immutable guiding principles. His approach was that of a military scientist seeking to condense his observations into a workable formula for other soldiers. It also helped that he was able to accurately critique Napoleon's failings on the battlefield. Jomini commented, "One might say that [Napoleon] was sent into the world to teach generals and statesmen what they ought to avoid."

With new technologies that made many of his observations obsolete, Jomini's books began falling out of favor. By the mid-twentieth century, his works were read only in military academies.

Battle of Eylau, where Jomini received the Legion of Honor

BATTLE OF NEW ORLEANS

American victory occurring after the end of the War of 1812

Andrew Jackson

In late 1814, the British and Americans had entered into negotiations in Ghent, Belgium, to end the war that had been waging for three years. In an attempt to strengthen their bargaining position, the British leaders ordered Major General Sir Edward Pakenham and his army of 5,300 troops, supported by naval forces under Vice Admiral Sir Alexander Cochrane, to capture the port of New Orleans. Opposing them was Major General Andrew Jackson, commanding a motley army of about 4,700 men composed of army regulars, Creoles from New Orleans, militia sharpshooters from Kentucky, Tennessee, and Louisiana, and pirates led by Jean Laffite.

By the time Pakenham's army arrived on December 25, Jackson had built a strong defensive position south of New Orleans. Pakenham probed Jackson's line with reconnaissance attacks and what proved to be ineffectual artillery barrages on December 28 and January 1. Because the barrages exhausted his supply of cannon shot and shells, Pakenham was forced to delay his main attack for a week in order to replenish his artillery ammunition.

On January 8, Pakenham launched his main attack on Jackson's right flank. A secondary attack on the west bank of the Mississippi River designed to draw away some of Jackson's men started late and did not help the main attack.

Morning fog hid the advancing lines of British troops. When the fog lifted, the British found themselves facing the strongest part of Jackson's line. American artillery and rifle fire erupted. The British continued to advance but accurate American fire decimated their ranks. Pakenham was killed. His subordinate, Major General John Lamberet, took over command and ordered a retreat. The British suffered 300 killed, 1,262 wounded, and 484 captured. American casualties were just 70 men, including 6 killed.

Though neither side knew it, the Treaty of Ghent, ending the war, had been signed on December 24. In real terms, the battle was only a symbolic American victory. But it was a powerful one. The reputation of American citizen soldiers had been enhanced, and Jackson became a national hero.

Rifle

Grooved-barrel firearm used in the Battle of New Orleans

The rifling technique creates a set of helical grooves cut into the walls of a weapon's barrel. Rifling itself is used in sidearms, shoulder arms, and cannon, but the word *rifle* applies only to the shoulder arm. The purpose of rifling is to impart a spin on a projectile, increasing its accuracy and range.

It is not known exactly when rifling was first used in weaponry. The principle of rifling was known even in ancient times. War engine armorers made attempts to impart spinning motions to spears shot from their ballista. Experiments in rifling began in Europe during the early 1400s and the first examples of true rifled weapons appeared in the mid-fifteenth century. However, the advantages of rifling were offset by the slow rate of fire, the clogging of the barrel with gunpowder residue, and the difficulty in making precision rifled firearms. Rifles would not become a significant factor on the battlefield until the American Revolution.

It was a backwoods invention that helped make the muzzle-loading rifle a practical weapon in war. Some unknown genius in the American frontier in the eighteenth century discovered that a "greased patch" could be placed over the muzzle as a temporary wrapping for a ball driven home by a few light strokes of the ramrod. The piece of lubricated linen had the additional advantage of cleaning out the barrel and trapping explosive gasses behind the bullet, producing more driving power. A smoothbore musket of the period, like the British Brown Bess, had an accuracy rate of about 40 percent at 100 yards. An American frontier rifle from the same period, such as the long rifle or Kentucky long rifle, had an accuracy rate of 50 percent at 300 yards, greater if the shooter were an expert marksman.

As technology progressed and muzzleloaders were replaced with breech-loading firearms, accuracy and reliability increased. By the end of the nineteenth century, they had completely replaced smoothbores as standard weapons in national arsenals.

A soldier firing an M-16 assault rifle

Battle of Gqokli Hill

Pivotal battle in the Zulu Civil War

Tensions had been growing between the Ndwandwe and Zulu nations for some time. It was becoming obvious that only war would resolve the differences between the two. Zwide, chief of the Ndwandwe, recognizing the growing strength of the Zulus under its new chief, Shaka, chose to launch a pre-emptive offensive campaign to defeat the Zulus before they became too powerful. An army (accounts vary, one estimate has it at around 7,000 warriors), under the command of Nomahlanjana, was assembled and invaded the land of the Zulu some time in March-April 1818.

When Shaka learned of the Ndwandwe invasion, he prepared for what would be the first important battle of his reign. He assembled an army (again, accounts vary, but general agreement is that Shaka's force was outnumbered 2 to 1) and took up a defensive position at Gqokli Hill. The key feature of the hill is a large depression in its summit, and it was there Shaka hid the bulk of his troops. The summit had an additional advantage: it was the only source of drinking water in the immediate area. Shaka then arrayed warriors in a series of defensive rings, perhaps as many as five, around the hill.

Shaka used a third force to create a diversion by escorting Zulu cattle away from the battlefield. This diversion was successful, for Nomahlanjana dispatched a large force to capture the cattle.

The main battle began in the morning, with the Ndwandwe making a series of probing attacks at different locations of the Zulu lines. Though casualties were inflicted, the Zulu lines held. The Ndwandwe attacks continued throughout the day. As the afternoon progressed, the Ndwandwe, who had suffered numerous casualties, began to tire. Thirst was also becoming a factor and a number of warriors left in search of water.

Nomahlanjana then concentrated his warriors into a tight column for a final attack to drive through the Zulu lines. Shaka responded by sending down his reserves and the column was destroyed. The defeated Ndwandwe army retreated back to its land.

Shaka would crush the Ndwandwe the following year.

Zulu warriors crossing a river

SHAKA

Zulu chief and king of the Zulu nation (ca. 1787–1828)

The dominance of the Zulu nation during the nineteenth century is largely the work of its greatest chief, Shaka. He turned the small Zulu clan into a warrior nation that dominated the southern tip of Africa for most of the 1800s.

Shaka was the illegitimate son of a Zulu chief and a woman of a lower-class clan. Because of this, Shaka suffered much abuse during his childhood. When he was sixteen, he joined the warrior force of a nearby tribe. It was there, under the tutelage of the chief Dingiswayo, that he began his military education. When his father died in 1816, Shaka returned to his tribe and became its military leader. Among his first acts was to exact revenge against those who had abused him and his mother when he was young.

Once in power, the ambitious Shaka reorganized the Zulus into a powerful warrior society. Prior to Shaka, combat generally took the form of a mass charge. Once they got within range, they would throw their spears and await the results. Shaka literally rewrote the rules of warfare in the region.

He instituted a regimental system similar to what he had learned under Dingiswayo. Shaka forbade his warriors from wearing sandals, and drilled them in their bare feet to toughen their soles. Forced marches and other conditioning drills were common. He replaced their standard weapon, the assegais (light throwing javelin), with the iklwa, a heavy, bladed thrusting spear. He added a heavy cowhide shield as well and introduced innovative drills and tactics. These included the "buffalo horns" formation in which the center closed with the enemy while the flanks conducted an enveloping maneuver. After he had defeated an enemy, Shaka offered the survivors a choice: become a Zulu or be killed. As a result, he was able to rapidly increase his army's ranks.

At the time of his death in 1828, the Zulu nation dominated the southeast tip of Africa. Shaka's legacy proved so strong the Zulus would continue to be a force almost to the end of the century.

A Zulu warrior in full war dress

BATTLE OF MAIPÚ

Pivotal battle in the Chilean War of Independence

Argentine General José de San Martín crossed the Andes with his army in 1817 and promptly began his campaign to liberate Chile. He scored early victories at Cacabuco and Chalchuapa and succeeded in capturing Santiago from the Spanish royalists. But a royalist army under General Mariano Osorio defeated him at Cancha Rayada in March 1818, forcing San Martín to fall back and regroup at Santiago. The following month, San Martín led his army out of the city and into the Andes for a showdown with Osorio and his army.

Instead of following up on his advantage against the rebels, Osorio abandoned the offensive campaign and took up defensive positions in Loma Blanca, near the Maipú River. When San Martín arrived and saw how Osorio had arranged his troops, he reportedly said, "Osorio is clumsier than I thought. Today's triumph is ours. The sun as witness!" What San Martín had seen was that, even though royalist troops were in place along a commanding ridge, Osorio's left flank was vulnerable, being dangerously separated from the main body.

Both sides were evenly matched, each having about 5,000 troops. San Martín commenced his attack late in the morning of April 5. He quickly isolated and defeated the royalist left flank. He then turned and launched an assault against the royalist center that was initially rebuffed. The royalists then launched a counterattack that San Martín broke up with accurate artillery fire. When he saw his counterattack fail, General Osorio lost his nerve and deserted his troops, leaving one of his colonels in command. When San Martín threw in his reserves, the royalist lines were overwhelmed. The survivors soon surrendered.

San Martín's victory at Maipú was the crowning achievement in the liberation of Chile. He followed this up with a campaign in the north that led to the liberation of Peru.

Statue of José de San Martín and Simon Bolívar

José de San Martín

Argentine general, liberator, and victor of the Battle of Maipú (1778–1850)

José de San Martín was the most important general and patriot in the wars of liberation in the southern part of South America. He was born into a poor Creole family and was sent to Spain where he received a military education. He became an officer in the Spanish army at age sixteen and fought against Napoleon's armies in the Peninsular Campaign, rising to the rank of lieutenant colonel. When the independence movement broke out in the United Provinces of South America (present-day Argentina), he returned to join the cause.

After an early victory at the Battle of San Lorenzo (1813) and an initial foray leading a revolutionary force of irregulars into Upper Peru (Bolivia), San Martín decided that the fastest way to gain independence for his country was to turn the men he led into a trained army. He went to Mendoza, a remote frontier town in the Argentine foothills of the Andes, and there, with the aid of volunteer officers from Europe and the United States, established facilities for training his raw recruits. Two years later, he had a small army of about 3,000 infantry, 1,000 Gaucho cavalry, and some artillery.

In January 1817, he crossed the Andes into Chile and won a victory against royalist forces at Chacabuco. The following year, in April, he achieved a decisive victory at Maipú, near Santiago, that secured the liberation of Chile. San Martín then consolidated his gains and reorganized his army. He embarked on a campaign north in Peru and by 1821 had secured its independence from Spain. He was installed as the new country's first president on July 28.

The following year, on July 22–23, he met his fellow liberator, Simón Bolívar, in Guayaquil, Ecuador. No record exists of what was discussed. But following the meeting's conclusion, San Martín resigned from the army and retired, leaving Bolívar the sole military leader in the independence movement. After his wife died in 1824, San Martín moved with his daughter to Europe, where he remained for the rest of his life, dying impoverished in France in 1850.

Dedication of the San Martín statue in Washington D.C.

Battle of Carabobo

Pivotal victory that achieved Venezuela's independence

A statue of Bolívar in Paris

The conclusion of the Napoleonic wars in 1815 proved to be a boon for the independence movements in South America. Suddenly surplus weapons of all kinds were available at rock-bottom prices. In addition, scores of troops had been discharged and remained unemployed in the new, depressed peace economy in Europe. Though Spain was now free to send its own armies to South America to crush the rebellion, out-of-work veterans and weapons significantly began to strengthen the rebels' armies. In 1821, Simón Bolívar took advantage of this windfall to launch a campaign to liberate Venezuela.

Bolívar's army of about 6,500 men included a "British Legion" of about 900 Irish, Welsh, and English riflemen and 1,500 *llaneros*, considered among the best irregular cavalry in the world. Royalist General Miguel de la Torre commanded an army of perhaps as many as 5,500 troops (accounts vary), mostly native Venezuelans. Aware that Bolívar's army was taking the road from Valencia to Puerto Cabello, de la Torre had his men take up defensive positions on the high ground overlooking the road.

When Bolívar saw the royalist positions, he divided his force and sent half, including the British Legion and the *llaneros* through the rough country in an attempt to outflank the royalists. De la Torre responded by detaching part of his army to counter the maneuver.

De la Torre's artillery and volley fire routed Bolívar's main force of patriots. The royalist general then brought the full weight of his army to bear on the threat to his flank. The 900 British troops formed into a defensive square and held off de la Torre's army for about an hour. They had lost about one-third of their men and were literally down to their last bullets when the *llanero* cavalry came to the rescue. De la Torre's infantry, shattered by the cavalry attack, soon surrendered.

Bolívar's victory at Carabobo eliminated the main royalist force in the region and secured independence for Venezuela.

Simón Bolívar in battle

Simón Bolívar

Venezuelan revolutionary, liberator, and victor of the Battle of Carabobo (1783–1830)

Simón Bolívar was born to a wealthy Creole family in Caracas, Venezuela. He was orphaned at age six and raised by an uncle. Trips to Europe in the early 1800s brought Bolívar in contact with the writings of Rousseau, Montesquieu, and Voltaire. He was also deeply impressed with the Napoleonic Empire. When he returned to Caracas, he dedicated his life to rebellion and liberation. He received his opportunity to achieve his dream as a liberator when Napoleon deposed the Spanish royal family in 1808.

Commanding armies never larger than 10,000 men, Bolívar had his share of setbacks and successes. Some came about due to his ignorance in military operations, and because of his impetuous temperament. But even after a string of failures, he continued inspire and unite men to follow him. He won a surprise victory at Boyacá in 1819, after a remarkable and grim crossing of the high Andes. Two years later, his victory at Carabobo liberated Venezuela. By 1824, he had also liberated Peru, Colombia, Panama, and Ecuador and his trusted lieutenant, General Antonio José de Sucre, had liberated Upper Peru (Bolivia).

Bolívar met his fellow liberator José de San Martín for two days, July 26–27, 1822, at Guayaquil, Ecuador. There were no witnesses or records. It is believed they discussed strategy on how to overcome the Spanish forces remaining on the continent. Apparently, the two were unable to reach an agreement. All that is known is that San Martín gave command of his army to Bolívar and retired to civilian life in Buenos Aires.

Bolívar proved unequal to the challenges of governing following the end of the war of liberation. His harsh autocratic rule led to strife and his "Grand Colombia" separated into the nations of Colombia (then including Panama), Venezuela, Ecuador, and parts of Costa Rica, Peru, Brazil, and Guyana. In 1830, he died of tuberculosis at age forty-seven.

...U RECUERDA LOS HECHOS HEROICOS VENERANDO A SU LIBERTADO...

THE ALAMO

Rallying point in the Texas war for independence

The Alamo

Mexican leader General Antonio López de Santa Anna feared the growing numbers of Americans settling in the Mexican province of Texas. In 1835, he ended further American settlement, dissolved the provincial government, and enforced the Mexican prohibition of slavery. The 30,000 Americans already in Texas, together with their Tejano allies, revolted. With General Sam Houston as their leader, they declared an independent Texas republic and prepared to defend themselves.

A group of Texans in San Antonio kicked out Santa Anna's cousin, General Martin Perfecto de Cós, and fortified the Franciscan mission, the Alamo. Determined to exact revenge, Santa Anna organized an army of 5,000 men and marched on the mission. Though General Houston had ordered the Alamo to be abandoned and destroyed, Colonel James Bowie, commander of the Texan volunteers at the Alamo, chose to fight. He was reinforced with a small band of Texans that included Colonel William Travis, Davy Crockett, and Tejano leader Juan Nepomucno Seguín.

Santa Anna's army arrived at San Antonio on February 23. After announcing that no quarter would be given to the defenders, he ordered his army to lay siege to the Alamo. Seguín, under orders from Travis, managed to slip some of his Tejanos through the Mexican lines with messages asking for reinforcements. Only thirty-two volunteers were able to sneak into the Alamo. The defenders were outnumbered more than 20 to 1.

Santa Anna began his assault of the Alamo on March 6. The defenders fought off the first two attacks but the third one breached the north wall. Hand-to-hand fighting raged for the next hour and did not stop until all the defenders were killed. Word of the defeat quickly spread. But instead of demoralizing the Texans and causing them to abandon their cause, the massacre at San Antonio inspired them to greater efforts at independence. "Remember the Alamo!" became a rallying cry for the Texas army.

The battle of the Alamo

BATTLE OF SAN JACINTO

The battle that secured Texas independence from Mexico

Immediately after his victory at the Alamo, Mexican leader General Santa Anna began a campaign to capture the leaders of the Texan rebellion. Leading a small force of 600 soldiers, he caught up to General Sam Houston and his army of about 900 men just east of present-day Houston, where the Buffalo Bayou joins the San Jacinto River and flows into Galveston Bay. There, Santa Anna paused to await the arrival of his cousin, General Cós, leading an army of 1,200 troops. When that army arrived on April 20, Santa Anna felt that he had more than enough men to overwhelm the Texans.

The proud Santa Anna thought of himself as the Napoleon of Mexico. Unfortunately for his country, he possessed little of Napoleon's skill and less of that great general's prudence and instincts. He neglected to build fortifications around his camp and he was lax about posting sentries.

Meanwhile, a copy of Santa Anna's plan of attack fell into Houston's hands. He decided to stage an attack when the Mexicans would least expect it, late in the day of April 21. He formed his infantry into a line of battle supported on the right by artillery and cavalry. The troops advanced quietly. They got within 200 yards of the Mexican camp when they were spotted. They promptly began rushing the Mexican camp, shouting their battle cry, "Remember the Alamo!" Hastily constructed breastworks were easily knocked aside. Within eight minutes, the fighting was over.

Among Sam Houston's men, only nine were killed and thirty were wounded. Houston, himself, was one of those wounded. Mexican casualties totaled 630 killed, 208 wounded, and 730 captured. Among the prisoners was Santa Anna.

Houston promptly took advantage of this opportunity and forced him to sign a treaty that recognized Texas's independence. The Mexican Government later unsuccessfully tried to repudiate the treaty and restore its authority over Texas. Texas would remain an independent nation for nine years, until it was annexed by the United States in 1845. But the dispute about sovereignty over Texas would not end until after the Mexican-American War concluded in 1848.

Sam Houston

Battle of Chapultepec

The climactic battle of the Mexican-American War

The attack on Chapultepec

General Winfield Scott's campaign to capture Mexico City and end the Mexican-American War began in mid-August 1847. To stop him, Mexican leader Santa Anna had organized an army of 25,000 men, composed mostly of hastily trained recruits and national militia. Only a few thousand were trained regulars. Scott advanced from his base at Veracruz on Mexico's Gulf Coast. Victories at Cerro Gordo, Contrearas, Churubusco, and Molino del Rey brought Scott and his 10,000-man army to within sight of the Mexican capital.

After consulting with his staff, Scott decided to make his final attack on the western gates of the city. But this meant he had to overcome the strategic fortified castle on the hill at Chapultepec. The 200-foot slope presented a challenge to any frontal assault. But the castle was weakly defended, containing only a few cannon and about nine hundred troops, including fifty-one cadets from the Mexican Military Academy. Late in the afternoon of September 12, Scott began his attack with an artillery barrage on the castle's western slope. At dawn on September 13 he ordered a two-pronged attack from the east and south. Both thrusts managed to breach outer defenses and reach the castle walls. There, the attacks bogged down because scaling ladders had been left behind. Reinforcements carrying the ladders were rushed forward. By 9:30 A.M., the castle's defenders had surrendered.

Scott immediately advanced on Mexico City. Santa Anna desperately tried to stop the attack but the American troops overcame one obstacle after another. By the end of the day, Santa Anna and the remnants of his army were in full retreat and Scott's troops were entering the city.

Scott officially entered Mexico City on September 14. Sporadic fighting in the city continued for a few days but the war was effectively over. Throughout his campaign, Scott had displayed great sensitivity and diplomacy to the Mexicans. This continued with the signing of the peace treaty, which are typically named after the cities in which they are signed. To avoid humiliating the Mexicans by signing it in their capital, he had the peace treaty signed in the nearby city of Guadaloupe Hidalgo.

General Scott entering Mexico City

SIEGE OF FORT SUMTER

The battle that started the Civil War

Fort Sumter after
the battle

By the spring of 1861, seven southern states—South Carolina, Georgia, Florida, Mississippi, Alabama, Louisiana, and Texas—had seceded from the Union and created the Confederate States of America. Governor Francis Pickens of South Carolina ordered that all federal property be turned over to the states. President Abraham Lincoln refused, saying that free passage should be granted to supply ships sailing to Fort Sumter in Charleston harbor because they were not carrying weapons or ammunition. The stage was set for confrontation—but which side would fire the first shot?

Time worked against the Confederacy. Though Provisional President Jefferson Davis wanted the Union to be known as the aggressor nation by shooting first, he was even more determined that the supply ships not be allowed to provision Fort Sumter. Upon receiving approval from his cabinet, on April 10, he ordered General Pierre G. T. Beauregard, commander of the Confederate forces in Charleston, to deliver an ultimatum to Major Robert Anderson, the fort's commander: Evacuate or prepare to be attacked.

Anderson was a southerner from Kentucky, and though he sympathized with the South, chose to remain loyal to the Union, whose uniform he had worn for thirty-five years. Low on food, water, and ammunition, Anderson replied that he would evacuate Fort Sumter by noon, April 15, unless attacked or unless he received supplies or other instructions from Washington. Knowing that supplies were en route and that he had to act promptly, Beauregard responded by stating that he would open fire at 4:20 A.M. on April 12.

For thirty-four hours, Confederate mortars and cannon bombarded the pentagon-shaped brick fort with about 4,000 rounds, which started fires and inflicted minor damage. On April 14, Major Anderson surrendered. At noon, the federal garrison boarded a steamer for New York City. The only federal fatalities occurred during the cannon salute at the surrender ceremony. Private Daniel Hough was killed during an accidental explosion of powder and two others were wounded, one fatally. Hough is considered the first fatality in the Civil War.

The bombardment of Fort Sumter

First Battle of Manassas (Bull Run)

First major battle of the Civil War that pointed out deficiencies on both sides

Soldiers beside damaged railroad in Manassas Junction

War fever swept both the North and South following the fall of Fort Sumter. Virginia, Arkansas, North Carolina, and Tennessee seceded and joined the Confederacy. Almost everyone believed the war would be short. In communities everywhere, volunteers were forming militia units or enlisting in the army.

Union general Irvin McDowell had reservations about the fighting ability of his army because most of the men under his command were barely trained. However, he knew that if he did not use his army soon, it would literally walk out on him because the law at the time limited federal enlistments to a maximum of ninety days. On July 1, with bystanders shouting, "On to Richmond!," McDowell led his army of 30,600 men into Virginia in the first offensive campaign of the war. They were followed by reporters, congressmen, and assorted curiosity seekers who packed picnic lunches.

McDowell's objective was the railroad center at Manassas Junction, which led to the Shenandoah Valley, the breadbasket of Virginia and the South. Opposing him was the Confederate hero of Fort Sumter, General Beauregard, and an army of 20,000 men in defensive positions near Bull Run Creek, north of Manassas Junction.

On the morning of July 21, 1861, McDowell launched an attack against the Confederate positions. Because troops on both sides were green and untrained, confusion inherent in combat was compounded, threatening to make the battle completely unmanageable. McDowell's original plan of attack was sound and, despite his men's inexperience, it looked like the tiring Union army would win. Then, at about 3:30 P.M., fresh reinforcements from General Joseph E. Johnston's army and other nearby units arrived and attacked the exposed Union right flank. Beauregard promptly ordered his engaged troops to counterattack.

The exhausted Union troops began a retreat that turned into a rout. Their path took them straight through the civilians who had assembled on a hill two miles away to watch. The Confederacy took the first major victory in the war and had a new hero: Brigadier General Thomas Jackson, who earned the nickname "Stonewall" for his successful defense during the battle.

Union troops heading into battle

Thomas Jonathan "Stonewall" Jackson

Confederate general and hero of the First Battle of Manassas (1824–1863)

Jackson was born in the poor hill country of what is now West Virginia. When he entered West Point in 1842, he was an orphan, ill educated, and socially awkward. Yet through hard work, he graduated seventeenth in a class of fifty-nine cadets.

The custom of awarding medals was not common at the time. Instead, individuals who performed their duty with distinction were honored with brevets (promotion, but without concomitant pay) and mentions in official dispatches. Jackson served with distinction in the Mexican-American War, earning two brevets. He resigned from the army in 1852 and became an instructor at Virginia Military Institute.

When Virginia seceded, Jackson joined the Confederate Army. He was commissioned brigadier general in June 1861. In October of that year, he was promoted to major general. A year later, he was promoted to lieutenant general.

Jackson was arguably the most eccentric general in American history. He was deeply devout and he had unusual personal habits and diet. Yet when it came to waging war, Jackson knew how to fight. In his book, *Lee's Lieutenants*, Douglas Southall Freeman wrote, "He lives by the New Testament and fights by the Old."

Jackson's Shenandoah Valley Campaign in 1862 is regarded as one of the greatest feats in the art of military maneuver. Through a series of swift countermarches, Jackson blunted or halted the attacks and offensive maneuvers of three Union armies. After the campaign, his footsore men nicknamed themselves, "Jackson's foot cavalry."

As a corps commander in the Army of Northern Virginia, Jackson became, in General Robert E. Lee's words, "my strong right arm." During the Battle of Chancellorsville in early May 1863, Jackson once again demonstrated his ability to swiftly move large units of men long distances in order to make decisive surprise attacks. During the night of May 2, while conducting reconnaissance, Jackson was accidentally shot by friendly fire. His left arm had to be amputated. While convalescing, Jackson contracted pneumonia and died on May 10, 1863.

John Singleton Mosby

Confederate partisan ranger who fought at First Manassas (1833–1916)

Mosby was a successful lawyer in Virginia at the outbreak of the Civil War. He enlisted with the 1st Virginia Cavalry as a private and fought at First Manassas. In February 1862, he was commissioned a first lieutenant and served under Jeb Stuart. He participated in Stuart's celebrated ride around Union General George McClellan's Army of the Potomac in the Peninsular Campaign.

In January 1863, he received permission to organize a band of partisan rangers in the Loudoun Valley in northern Virginia. Beginning with only 100 men, Mosby conducted one of the greatest guerilla campaigns in military history. In one of his raids, he captured Union Brigadier General Edwin Stoughton. According to legend, Mosby found the general asleep in bed and awoke him with a slap to the backside with the flat of his sword.

Mosby's constant disruption of Union supply lines, interception of couriers, and destruction of military property proved so effective that, at one point out of frustration, General Ulysses Grant ordered that if any of Mosby's men were caught, they were to be hanged. This death sentence, with Mosby responding in kind, lasted for a about two months before both sides resumed treating prisoners humanely.

The constant success of Mosby's activity, and the support he received from the local populace, caused the region where he and his men roamed to become known as "Mosby's Confederacy."

By December 1864, he had been promoted to colonel and his command, now more than 200 strong, was formally incorporated into the Confederate Army as the 43rd Battalion of the Virginia Cavalry. Mosby has the distinction of having never surrendered. Instead, shortly after Lee's surrender at Appomattox and when he saw that the Confederacy would not survive, Mosby disbanded his unit on April 20, 1865, and returned to his law practice.

After the war, he became a controversial figure in Virginia because of his support of the Republicans and Reconstruction policy. He worked for Grant's presidential election campaign and became a close friend. When death threats made living in Virginia dangerous, Mosby was appointed consul in Hong Kong. He held a number of government positions in the West and later wrote his memoirs. He died in 1916.

BATTLE OF FORT DONELSON

The battle that propelled Ulysses S. Grant to national attention.

Major General
Ulysses S. Grant,
hero of Fort
Donelson

Union strategy in the west was to divide the Confederacy by seizing control of the Mississippi River. The first stage was the capture of Fort Henry and Fort Donelson, strategic Confederate fortifications near the western border of Kentucky and Tennessee. Commander of the campaign was Brigadier General Ulysses S. Grant. Fort Henry fell to him after a brief fight on February 6. General Albert S. Johnston, the area Confederate commander, ordered the Fort Donelson commander, Brigadier General John B. Floyd, to hold the fort until his forces, in danger of being cut off north of the Cumberland River, were clear. As insurance, he sent reinforcements to help Floyd, bringing the garrison's strength to about 21,000 men.

Bad weather slowed Grant's advance. On February 12, his 15,000-man army reached Fort Donelson. Sporadic, but inconclusive, fighting broke out on February 13. Grant then received help from Flag Officer Andrew H. Foote's flotilla of four ironclad riverboats, mounting a total of twelve cannon and three unarmed gunboats. This force took up position along the Cumberland River. By February 14, Fort Donelson was surrounded.

The only hope now for the Confederate garrison was escape. General Gideon Pillow and Buckner led a breakout attempt on the morning of February 15. Grant, who had been conferring with Foote on the gunboats, quickly returned and rallied the Union troops. The Confederate effort almost succeeded. The Union line had been breached. But then, Floyd received what appeared to be contradictory reports from Buckner and Pillow. Floyd, an incompetent, took counsel of his fears, dithered, and then ordered a retreat. That evening, additional federal troops arrived bringing Union strength to 27,000 men. Confederate leaders, meanwhile, decided to on a second breakout attempt across the Cumberland. Under the cover of darkness, Floyd, Pillow, and about 5,000 troops, including Colonel Nathan Bedford Forrest's cavalry, escaped.

General Buckner chose to remain with the rest of the garrison. When Buckner requested surrender terms, Grant responded, "No terms except unconditional and immediate surrender can be accepted. I propose to move immediately upon your works." Bucker promptly capitulated and the Union had its first real hero: "Unconditional Surrender" Grant.

The capture of General Buckner at Fort Donelson

ULYSSES S. GRANT

U.S. general, victor at Fort Donelson, U.S. president (1822–1885)

Little in Grant's upbringing suggested that he would have great success in life. He was an average student at West Point who distinguished himself in two things: drill and horsemanship. In the former, he displayed a lack of rhythm that fellow cadets found painful to watch. But he was an outstanding horseman and won numerous competitions with records that stood for many years. Grant served with distinction as a junior officer in the Mexican-American War. Later, he was posted to California, where reports of chronic and excessive drunkenness caused him to resign.

Grant was a failure in civilian life. A claim could be made that if Grant saved the United States, it was because the Civil War saved Grant. When the South seceded, Grant attempted to rejoin the army but was rejected. He entered the war as a colonel of volunteers for an Illinois militia regiment.

Grant's success in capturing Forts Henry and Donelson and his demand of "unconditional surrender" propelled Grant to national prominence. He was promoted to major general of volunteers and commander of the Army of the Tennessee. His campaign on the Mississippi River included victories at Shiloh and Vicksburg. He was then given a promotion to major general in the regular army and command of the Military Division of the Mississippi. In this capacity, he lifted the Confederate siege of Chattanooga.

In March 1864, President Lincoln promoted him to lieutenant general and made him responsible for the entire military campaign against the Confederacy. Grant rewarded Lincoln's faith in him with a grand strategy campaign of unprecedented scope. From New Orleans to Virginia, all the Union armies attacked in a coordinated and unrelenting series of offensives designed to destroy the Confederacy's ability to defend itself. The hallmarks of this strategy resulted in General Sherman's march through Georgia and South Carolina and General Lee's surrender of the Army of Northern Virginia in 1865.

Following his service in uniform, Grant was elected president of the United States and served two terms. His autobiography, written while he was dying of throat cancer, is considered a classic work.

Nathan Bedford Forrest

Confederate cavalry general who fought at Fort Donelson (1821–1877)

Forrest was a wealthy businessman at the outbreak of the Civil War. In October 1861, he raised and mounted a battalion of cavalry at his own expense. Impressed, the Confederate government commissioned him a lieutenant colonel to command them. Forrest was at Fort Donelson at the time of General Grant's attack. Forrest succeeded in escaping with his command prior to the fort's surrender. During the Confederate retreat at Shiloh, Forrest effectively led the rear guard action that stymied Union pursuit.

On July 21, 1862, he was promoted to brigadier general and shortly thereafter began conducting the raids that made him famous (or infamous). Forrest's success in disrupting communications, rail lines, and harassment made him and his men the scourge of Union troops in the West.

Forrest was one of the most skilled cavalry leaders of the war. His raids, particularly his victory at Brice's Crossroads on June 10, 1864, were noteworthy demonstrations of the art of cavalry war. His consistent successes (he only began suffering defeats in the final months of the war) were even more amazing because he had no formal military training. When General William Sherman was conducting his Atlanta campaign, Forrest's cavalry was so effective in its harassment that Sherman was quoted to say that Forrest must be hunted down even if "its cost bankrupts the Federal treasury."

Forrest's campaigns have since become studies in major military academies. A number of his statements have become military aphorisms. The most famous is, "Get there first with the most men." It is usually, and erroneously, presented as "Git there fustest with the mostest." For all his success, Forrest's military career is overshadowed by the Fort Pillow Affair (April 12, 1864), in which captured African American Union soldiers and civilians were massacred.

In the final months of the war, Forrest was promoted to lieutenant general. Following the war, Forrest became a businessman. His name became associated with the white supremacist Ku Klux Klan movement, though he denied participation. He died in 1877.

GUERILLA

Strategy of insurrection used by Colonel Mosby

Guerilla wars ("little wars") are fought with one side, sometimes both sides, using irregular forces. Because these forces are not as well-equipped as their conventional force foes, their primary tactics are the hit-and-run raid and ambushes where they have numerical superiority. Guerillas seek to avoid set-piece battle confrontations where they will be defeated. Instead, they use mobility, camouflage, hidden sanctuaries, and the ability to blend in with the local population to maintain their combat capability.

Guerilla forces in combat have appeared throughout history. The North American Indians were unsurpassed experts in guerilla warfare. America's first special operations unit, Roger's Rangers in the French and Indian War, took many of its tactics from experience fighting the Indians.

World War II saw the most widespread use of guerilla warfare. Partisan groups appeared in almost all the countries occupied by the Axis forces. They were supported by the Allies through the Office of Strategic Services (OSS), the predecessor to the CIA, and such special operations units as the Jedburghs, the Carpetbaggers, and British Commandos.

During the Vietnam War, the Communist Viet Cong waged guerilla warfare in South Vietnam. Their attempt to overthrow the South Vietnamese government during the 1968 Tet Offensive ended in failure when they were crushed by American and South Vietnamese conventional warfare units.

Today, guerilla warfare is also known as Military Operations Other Than War (MOOTW) and is the situation that American troops encountered in Iraq following the conclusion of the conventional military campaign in Operation Iraqi Freedom in 2003.

Viet Cong guerrillas convey ammunition and supplies on bicycles through a forest in South Vietnam during the Vietnam war

BATTLE OF SHILOH

The bloodiest battle of the Civil War up to that time

The gunboats *Tyler* and *Lexington* supporting the Union troops

The capture of Forts Henry and Donelson opened the way for the next stage of the Union's campaign in the west. Grant, now a major general, steadily advanced his army of 42,000 men south along the Tennessee River. In early April, he established a base camp at Pittsburgh Landing, Tennessee, just 20 miles northeast of the Confederacy's most important rail junction in the region at Corinth, Mississippi. His orders were to wait for the 25,000-strong Army of the Ohio led by Major General Don Carlos Buell. The combined force would then continue south.

At Corinth were General Albert Syndey Johnston and his 44,000-man Army of Mississippi. Johnston's plan was to attack Grant's army before Buell's arrived. Not expecting an attack, Grant allowed his troops to set up camp without constructing proper defenses.

At dawn, Sunday, April 6, Johnston's army attacked federal lines near Shiloh Methodist Church. The Union troops were completely surprised and retreated in disarray. At least 5,000 Union soldiers fled in panic. The only real Union success that day came from troops at the Hornet's Nest, about 2 miles east of Shiloh Church, who fought off twelve Rebel attacks before falling back at about 5:30 P.M. It was also at Hornet's Nest that General Johnston was fatally wounded in the leg. General Beauregard, Johnston's subordinate, assumed command and continued the attack. When fighting concluded that evening, the Confederates held almost all of General Grant's camp and Beauregard thought the Yankees were beaten.

However, Grant had no intention of retreating. In fact, he was making plans for a counterattack even before the fighting had ended. A nightlong storm made conditions miserable for Grant and his troops. But also that night, Buell's army arrived. The Union attack kicked off at dawn, April 7. The Confederates were forced to retreat all the way back to Corinth.

Shiloh was the bloodiest battle of the war at that time. Total casualties were almost 25,000. More importantly, the battle caused everyone on both sides to realize that instead of a glorified duel, the Civil War was going to be a fight to the finish.

Ulysses S. Grant at Shiloh

BATTLE OF ANTIETAM

The deadly battle that lead to the issuing of the Emancipation Proclamation

The dead in front of Dunker church

Confederate strategy in the Civil War was to conduct defensive operations. By forcing the North to invade, it hoped to arouse sympathy for its cause in the North and abroad. That strategy changed when General Robert E. Lee took his Army of Northern Virginia into Maryland in early September 1862. Confederate leaders had many reasons for the change. They believed a victory in the North would cause Great Britain and France to grant them diplomatic recognition, encourage northern voters to elect Democrats in the fall congressional elections who would force President Lincoln to sign a peace treaty, and boost morale in the South.

Shortly after the Army of Northern Virginia invaded Maryland, two Union soldiers discovered in a field a copy of Lee's battle plans wrapped around three cigars, lost by a careless Southern officer. When Army of the Potomac commander General George McClellan saw the documents, he said, "Here is a paper with which, if I cannot whip Bobbie Lee, I will be willing to go home!" However, instead of promptly attacking Lee's troops while they were en route, scattered, and vulnerable, McClellan, whose earlier acts of caution had angered President Lincoln, delayed yet again.

McClellan finally attacked on September 17. Lee's army was still scattered. He had only 26,000 troops in defensive positions between the town of Sharpsburg and Antietam Creek. McClellan had 70,000 men but he made two initial mistakes. The first was thinking Lee had 120,000 troops. The second was not using all his men to smash Lee's army. Instead, McClellan held a large portion back. Those he did use were sent into action piecemeal.

September 17 was the bloodiest day of fighting in the Civil War. At least 6,000 men died and another 17,000 were wounded. Had McClellan continued fighting the next day, he could have destroyed Lee's army. Inexplicably, he did nothing and allowed Lee to retreat back to Virginia unimpeded.

Still, the offensive was stopped. Great Britain and France refused to grant the Confederacy diplomatic recognition. And, though incomplete, Antietam was enough of a victory to prompt Lincoln five days later to issue his preliminary Emancipation Proclamation freeing slaves.

The battle at Antietam

ROBERT E. LEE

Confederate general at the Battle of Antietam (1807–1870)

Robert E. Lee was the son of Revolutionary War hero Henry "Light Horse Harry" Lee. He obtained his military education at West Point (1821) where he graduated second in his class.

Lee served with distinction on the staff of General Winfield Scott during the Mexican-American War. Following the war, he served as superintendent at West Point (1852–1855). In 1859, he led the force that put down the slave rebellion attempt at Harper's Ferry, Virginia, led by abolitionist John Brown.

When his home state of Virginia seceded, Lee resigned his commission in 1861, and was commissioned a brigadier general in the Confederate Army.

When General Joseph E. Johnston was wounded in the Battle of Seven Pines in 1862, Lee was appointed to succeed him. It was as the commanding general of that army, renamed the Army of Northern Virginia, that Lee would become famous. For the next three years, Lee displayed a genius for war that intimidated his enemies. Even after the defeats at Antietam and Gettysburg, they dared not harass his army for fear he would find a way of turning defeat into victory.

What made Lee's victories even more extraordinary was that he accomplished them despite being always outnumbered and short of supplies. His victory at Chancellorsville is regarded by historians as a masterpiece. Despite his tactical successes, Lee was never able to achieve his strategic goal of destroying the Union Army of the Potomac and securing diplomatic recognition of the Confederacy.

Following his defeat at Gettysburg in 1863, Lee returned to Virginia and a defensive strategy that had served him well. Then, in 1864, Lt. General Ulysses Grant, the new Union general in chief, launched a coordinated and unrelenting campaign against Lee and the other Confederate armies. The logistic weaknesses that had dogged Lee proved overwhelming. In the spring of 1865, Lee surrendered to Grant at Appomattox Court House on April 9, 1865.

After the war, he became the president of Washington College in Virginia. He died of heart disease five years later, at age sixty-three. The institution subsequently changed its name to Washington and Lee College.

TELEGRAPH

A communication device used during the Civil War

The telegraph is long-distance communication method that transmits coded messages composed of a series of electronic pulses and pauses over wire. Samuel F. B. Morse invented the device in 1844. The first use of telegraph communications in war was during the Crimean War (1853–1856). The novelty of suddenly being within real-time contact with a distant battlefield proved irresistible to the political leaders in Paris and London, hundreds of miles away. And Napoleon III provided such a steady stream of advice that he precipitated a command crisis. One French commander complained bitterly about being placed "at the paralyzing end of an electric cable."

By the time of the Civil War, telegraph networks in the United States stretched throughout the nation and across the continent. Though often tempted, President Abraham Lincoln exercised self-restraint and avoided meddling in operations the way Napoleon III did. When used properly, as General Ulysses S. Grant did in his campaigns, it proved to be a great boon for coordinating strategy. Telegraph wagons were an integral part of Grant's headquarters and he noted how quickly communications could be set up during a moving campaign, writing, "In a few minutes longer time than it took a mule to walk the length of its coil, telegraphic communications would be effected between all the headquarters of the army."

Because of their greater dexterity, more than half of the 2,000 telegraph operators used in the Civil War were women and many of them served in uniform.

The inventor Thomas Edison, who as a boy was a telegraph operator, invented the "quadriplex method" in 1874 that allowed for messages to be sent simultaneously over one wire.

The British successfully used lighter field telegraphs in their colonial wars of the late nineteenth and early twentieth centuries. One correspondent noted in admiration that telegraph teams became so efficient that field telegraph cables could be laid across country "at a speed limited only by that of the six-horse teams which drew the wagons." Telegraph use began to decline following the development of radio and telephone communication in the twentieth century.

Republican Civil Guards defending telephone & telegraph offices against Nationalist rebels in the Spanish Civil war, one of the last conflicts in which the telegraph was used

BATTLE OF HAMPTON ROADS

Historic first battle of the ironclads: Monitor *vs.* Virginia

Aboard the
Monitor

A key part of the Union strategy for winning the Civil War was a naval blockade system called the Anaconda Plan. Federal warships took position outside the South's main ports and either captured or prevented supply ships, called blockade-runners, from entering or leaving. In the early months of the Civil War, both blockade-runners and federal ships were alike in that they had wooden hulls.

On March 8, 1862, sailors aboard the federal ships off the Virginia coast at Hampton Roads were shocked to see an object resembling a metal outbuilding steaming toward them. It was the CSS *Virginia,* a Confederate warship rebuilt around the hull of the captured USS *Merrimack* and with a superstructure completely clad in iron. Captain Franklin Buchanan's orders were to use the *Virginia* to break the blockade by sinking as many Union ships as he could. In the first battle involving an ironclad, the *Virginia* sank the wooden-hulled USS *Cumberland* and USS *Congress,* forced three other ships to run aground, and wreaked havoc with several other small federal warships before returning back to its home port of Norfolk. Though the *Virginia* had not been seriously damaged, Captain Buchanan had been wounded by Union sharpshooters.

When the *Virginia* steamed out the next day, under the command of executive officer Lieutenant Catesby R. Jones, it found itself facing a new foe: the Union ironclad, the USS *Monitor* captained by Lieutenant John L. Worden. The recently completed *Monitor* had been towed down from the Brooklyn Navy Yard in New York and had arrived just hours earlier. The battle began just before 9 A.M. The *Monitor* was able to travel in circles around the slow, cumbersome *Virginia.* But the advantage was largely wasted. Though both ships repeatedly scored hits on the other, neither side was able to cause serious damage. Both vessels also suffered mechanical problems during the fighting. Almost four hours after it had begun, the two ships turned away. The first battle in history between ironclad ships had ended. And, along with it ended the era of the wooden-hulled ship.

The battle between the *Monitor* and *Virginia*

Ironclad Warship

Metal-hulled ships that first fought at Hampton Roads

The U.S. Civil War was the first conflict that saw the large-scale use of ironclad warships in battle and the first ironclad ship-to-ship engagement. Though both sides used them, there was a wide technological disparity between the Union and Confederate ships because of the more developed industrial base in the North. The Union could construct its ironclads from the keel up. The Confederates had to take existing hulls and basically wrap metal around them.

The French and British were the first to use ironclad vessels, which saw action against land targets in the Crimean War (1853–1856), and by 1861, both had seagoing ironclad ships. Their experience served as a reference for both the Union and Confederacy.

The Union used three ironclad designs, two conventional and one innovative. The innovative design, John Ericsson's *Monitor*, overshadowed all other armored warships with its unprecedented design. The *Monitor*, and the class of ships that bore its name, became the most famous iron-hulled vessels in the war. But its low freeboard, which barely cleared the surface of the water, and pillbox style turret, represented a dead end in naval architecture.

The Confederacy's approach to ironclads can be summarized with Confederate Secretary of the Navy Stephen Mallory's statement, "Inequality of numbers may be compensated by invulnerability." When efforts by the Confederacy to purchase ironclads in Europe proved unsuccessful, Mallory attempted to launch a construction program. However, the South had neither the foundries nor the shipyards to build them. As a result, the Confederacy embarked on a patchwork effort. The *Virginia* was built around the sunken Union steam frigate *Merrimack* and was a typical example. Ultimately, the Confederacy constructed twenty-five ironclads.

The greatest threat posed by the Confederate ironclad navy was that of a "fleet in being." Their mere presence, as the *Virginia* demonstrated in the Battle of Hampton Roads in March 1862, vastly complicated the Union's blockade efforts. Technologically speaking, American (particularly Union) ironclad ship design during the Civil War proved inferior to the designs of other nations, particularly when compared to the Royal Navy's ironclads. The American ships, though, had the virtue of being the first to be truly battle tested—and in so doing, ushered in a new age of seafaring vessels.

A scene from the Hampton Roads battle during the American Civil War

CONTAINMENT

Blockade strategy used during the Civil War

The purpose of containment is to isolate an opponent through the use of military, economic, or ideological force or barriers. Containment strategy essentially falls into two categories: passive sieges and blockade—with the former being exclusively used by the military and the latter including military, economic, and ideological tactics.

The classic military *siege* involved the construction of a barrier, or a line of manned outposts, around a site, usually a fortified city. Once the city is encircled, both sides settle down to wait out the siege until one side or the other gives up. Sometimes there are skirmishes or attempts to breach the defenses or break through the siege line. A city's ability to wait out a siege often depends more on its food and drinking water supplies than on its military strength. Generally military action occurs at the climax of a siege, when the attacking army would break through the city's wall. This was often followed by looting, pillaging, and rape by the invaders.

The most notable example of a *blockade* is the naval blockade of an opponent's forts. The Union's Anaconda Plan of Confederate ports was one such example. The Royal Navy in World War I employed a similar blockade of Imperial German ports in World War I. An example of a reverse blockade—one in which the blockade was not on an enemy's ports but on the ports where it sought to do business—was Napoleon's Continental System against England, which sought to prohibit ports in Europe from receiving British goods. In more recent times, nations have adopted blockade policies called *economic sanctions*. Perhaps the longest-running sanction is the United States's policy against Cuba.

Blockades by their very nature are long-term strategies. Military blockades have the virtue of being straightforward, with clearly defined success or failure results. Economic sanctions, because they have historically been proved to be more porous, have achieved more mixed results.

BATTLE OF CHANCELLORSVILLE

Lee's greatest victory; death of Stonewall Jackson

110th Pennsylvania regiment, which was nearly annihilated at Chancellorsville

On January 26, 1863, the Union Army of the Potomac greeted its third commander in less than four months. McClellan, a great organizer but timid fighter, was relieved in November 1862. Then, Major General Ambrose Burnside was relieved in January 1863 following the humiliating defeat in the Battle of Fredericksburg. Now it was Major General Joseph "Fighting Joe" Hooker's turn. Hooker, like Burnside, promoted from corps command within the Army of the Potomac, talked a good fight. And it appeared he would deliver. First, he reorganized his army and restored its flagging morale. When he marched it into Virginia to battle the Army of Northern Virginia in April 1863, Hooker boasted, "My plans are perfect, and when I start to carry them out, may God have mercy on General Lee, for I will have none."

Hooker's plan was to hold Lee's army entrenched at Fredericksburg with a diversionary attack from part of his army. His main attack would come from Chancellorsville, 9 miles west of Fredericksburg. Caught between the two federal forces, the Rebel army would be destroyed. The plan was brilliant. With 130,000 men, Hooker had enough troops to overwhelm Lee and his 60,000 men.

Skirmishing began on April 30. The strength of the rebel fighting surprised Hooker, causing him to hesitate and lose the initiative. Lee then devised a counterattack, one filled with risk. It involved the rapid shifting of forces back and forth while the battle was raging. The key to success was a 12-mile quick-march by Lieutenant General Thomas "Stonewall" Jackson and his men, who had to get into position for a surprise attack on the unprotected federal right flank.

Lee attacked on May 2. Once again, he outgeneraled his opponent. Lee's rapid troop movements flummoxed Hooker to immobility and he never used the full force of his army. Demoralized, Hooker ordered a retreat on May 4.

Lee had won his greatest victory. But it had come at great cost. His army had suffered 13,000 casualties. His greatest loss was that of his "strong right arm," Stonewall Jackson. Wounded by friendly fire, Jackson died from complications a week later.

The last meeting between the Confederate Army Generals Stonewall Jackson and Robert E Lee

SIEGE OF VICKSBURG

Grant's victory that opened the Mississippi River to Union control

Cutting the levees
at Providence

The Union strategy to control the Mississippi River and divide the Confederacy reached its climax with the siege of the South's last major stronghold on the river, Vicksburg, Mississippi. But capturing Vicksburg would not be easy. The combination of high bluffs on which the city rested, marshlands, and manmade defenses garrisoned by a 40,000-man army led by Lieutenant General John C. Pemberton, gave Vicksburg the well-deserved nickname of "Gibraltar of the Mississippi."

Major General Ulysses S. Grant, commander of the new 72,000-man Army of the Tennessee, made his first attempt to capture Vicksburg in December 1862. After five assault attempts over a four-month period ended in failure, Grant decided to surround the city and starve it into submission.

What followed was a seventeen-day campaign in the first half of May 1863. Grant's army marched 180 miles and fought and won five engagements against separate enemy forces, eliminating any chance of outside help for Vicksburg. Grant then closed the ring around the city with gunboats on the Mississippi River and troops behind fortifications on land. On May 18, 1863, the siege of Vicksburg began.

Grant liberally used his artillery during the siege. Every day, at least 70,000 projectiles of all types, some weighing as much as 300 pounds, fell on the city. The Confederate defenders replied with their artillery until ammunition was exhausted. Because the streets became too dangerous, civilians burrowed in caves in the hillsides to live. Food became scarce and soon pack animals, house pets, snakes, and vermin disappeared into cooking pots. Eventually, even the bark of trees was chewed.

On July 3, 1863, General Pemberton sent a message to General Grant stating that he wished to negotiate a surrender. Once again, "Unconditional Surrender" Grant responded that there were no terms to negotiate, though city and garrison would be treated "with all respect." On July 4, 1863, Pemberton surrendered.

The one-two punch of Union victories at Gettysburg on July 3 and Vicksburg on July 4 caused morale to soar in the North. Grant's reputation as a successful fighting general was sealed. President Lincoln gratefully noted that the Mississippi River "again goes unvexed to the sea."

Champion Hill, the pivotal battle of Vicksburg

Benjamin Henry Grierson

Union cavalry general (1826–1911)

It's ironic that Grierson, a cavalry leader, didn't like horses. When he was eight years old, he was almost killed by one when it kicked him. When war was declared, he volunteered as an aide-de-camp to General Benjamin M. Prentiss. He later joined the 6th Illinois Cavalry and was promoted to major. In April of 1862, he was promoted to colonel. Grierson's service in the Civil War was in the West, first with the Army of the Tennessee and later with the Army of the Mississippi.

Grierson's most notable achievement in the war was an action later called Grierson's Raid. During his Vicksburg campaign, General Grant ordered Grierson to create a diversion to distract Confederate general John Pemberton and his forces so Grant's army could cross the Mississippi River south of Vicksburg.

Grierson departed from La Grange, Tennessee, near Memphis, on April 17, 1863, with 1,700 men and headed south. The raid lasted from April 17 to May 2. During that period he and his men traveled as much as 800 miles (accounts vary), conducted numerous skirmishes with Confederate troops, disabled two railroads, captured a number of prisoners and horses, and destroyed large amounts of military property. The raid concluded at the Union stronghold at Baton Rouge. Grierson's raid was so effective that Grant accomplished his crossing virtually without opposition. Grant later praised Grierson's Raid as "one of the most brilliant cavalry exploits of the war."

In recognition of his service, Grierson received three brevets on February 10, 1865: Major General U.S. Volunteers, Brigadier General U.S. Army (for Grierson's Raid), and Major General U.S. Army (raids conducted in 1864).

Grierson remained in the army after the war, reverting to the permanent rank of colonel. He served at numerous posts in the west before retiring in 1890 with the rank of brigadier general. He died in 1911.

Battle of Gettysburg

Confederate defeat defined the "high water mark of the Confederacy"

Federal dead on the field of battle after the first day

Confederate General Robert E. Lee's second offensive into the North, this time into Pennsylvania, began on June 3, 1863. His objectives were largely the same as before: diplomatic recognition for the Confederacy following military victory, pressure the North, and to relieve war-ravaged Virginia.

One of the hallmarks of Lee's successes was timely intelligence provided by reconnaissance from Lieutenant General Jeb Stuart's cavalry. But this time Lee was denied his "eyes and ears." Union cavalry commander Major General Alfred Pleasonton had successfully stymied Stuart's scouting efforts in the days leading up to the battle at Gettysburg, preventing Stuart from communicating with Lee until after the battle had been joined.

Not only was Lee unaware of the Army of the Potomac's exact location, he was initially also unaware it had a new commander. President Lincoln had become disillusioned with Major General Joseph Hooker and, on June 28, sacked Hooker and replaced him with another corps commander from within the army, Major General George Gordon Meade. Three days later, advance elements from both armies clashed at a strategic road junction in south central Pennsylvania. The Battle of Gettysburg had begun.

Initially, both Lee and Meade were miles away. The first day's fighting was led by subordinate commanders, who struggled to gain the high-ground advantage before the rest of the armies arrived. At the end of the first day, it appeared the advantage lay with the Confederates.

The second day was one of lost opportunity for the Confederates. Significantly, a major attack by Lt. General James Longstreet's corps scheduled for the morning did not occur until the afternoon. It failed, though barely.

On July 3, the most famous attack in the Civil War was launched: Pickett's Charge. Some of Major General George Pickett's men breached the Union lines in what was later called "the high water mark of the Confederacy." But they were quickly overcome. Of the 13,000 Rebels that attacked, fewer than half returned alive.

On July 4, as Lee began retreating back to Virginia, the North celebrated its greatest victory in the Civil War.

The battle at Gettysburg

JAMES EWELL BROWN ("JEB") STUART

Confederate cavalry general during the Battle of Gettysburg (1833–1864)

Stuart was born and raised in Virginia. He attended West Point when Robert E. Lee was the military academy's superintendent and graduated thirteenth out of a class of forty-six in 1854. Stuart's first postings were in the West. During Indian campaigns in Texas, he displayed the first signs of leadership that would make him famous in the Civil War. Stuart was one of the officers, along with Lee, who participated in the suppression of John Brown's raid at Harper's Ferry in 1859. When Virginia seceded from the Union, he resigned his commission and joined the Confederate Army, where he was commissioned a lieutenant colonel of infantry in May 1861. Two weeks later, he was made a captain of cavalry.

Stuart was appointed brigadier general following action at First Bull Run. He achieved worldwide fame during Union General George McClellan's Peninsular Campaign (March–July 1862) in southeastern Virginia by leading his cavalry command in a spectacular reconnaissance and raiding ride completely around the rear of McClellan's army. Promoted to major general, he repeated this end-around feat again at the Battle of Antietam in September of that year. Though the raids had little strategic impact, it was a feat that boosted the morale of the Confederacy and humiliated the Union.

Stuart had a weakness for flashy uniforms. His plumed hat and brightly colored riding cloak and gloves was coupled with his dramatic feats on the battlefield and gracious manners and good humor. He became revered by the public as a dashing, romantic cavalry leader.

As cavalry commander for the Confederate Army of Northern Virginia under General Robert E. Lee, he was, in Lee's words, his "eyes and ears." Stuart's reconnaissance behind Union lines and delivered in timely fashion contributed significantly to Lee's victories. The low point of this relationship was reached during the Battle of Gettysburg. There, a resurgent Union cavalry, previously humiliated by Stuart, successfully prevented him from maintaining contact with Lee and the main body of the Army of Northern Virginia until after the battle at Gettysburg had commenced.

Stuart was mortally wounded at the Battle of Yellow Tavern and died the next day, May 11, 1864.

BATTLE OF MOBILE BAY

The Union's greatest naval victory

Officers positioning a large cannon at Fort Gaines

In the summer of 1864, the only large Gulf port still open for the Confederates was Mobile, Alabama. However, blocking or capturing it would not be easy for Union admiral David Farragut and his forces. A naval axiom states that only a fool uses a ship to fight a fort—and three guarded Mobile Bay. The main harbor channel, protected by Fort Gaines and Fort Morgan, was also strewn with about 180 torpedoes (mines). Rounding out the defenses was a small Confederate fleet that included the ironclad CSS *Tennessee*.

But Farragut had a reputation for audacity. With the help of a corps led by Union general Gordon Granger, Farragut planned to capture the entrance to Mobile Bay and close down the port. His attack began on August 3 with a landing by 1,500 of Granger's men on Dauphin Island, in the middle of the bay's entrance. Farragut hoped the garrison on Fort Gaines would be sufficiently distracted to allow him to take seventeen ships from his fleet through the torpedo-filled gauntlet between Fort Gaines and Fort Morgan.

But Colonel Charles Anderson, Fort Gaines's commander, saw Farragut's ships begin their run at dawn on August 5 and raised the alarm. The Union ships were quickly bracketed by Confederate cannon fire. The first Union victim was the USS *Tecumseh*, which was hit by a torpedo and sank. The Union ships immediately behind the action stalled in confusion, afraid to proceed. Furious, Admiral Farragut shouted the rallying cry that became famous, "Damn the torpedoes! Full speed ahead!" He ordered his flagship, the *Hartford*, to take the lead. The rest fell in behind and successfully ran the channel. Once inside the bay, they encountered the *Tennessee* and three gunboats. Accurate Union cannon fire routed the gunboats and damaged the *Tennessee*, which later ran aground.

Farragut then conducted a series of coordinated pincer attacks to reduce Confederate defenses. Fort Gaines surrendered on August 8. Fort Morgan fell on August 23. Though the city of Mobile remained in Confederate hands until April 1865, with Union forces controlling the bay's entrance, its use as a port was over.

Farragut's fleet set on by the ironclad CSS *Tennessee*

David Glasgow Farragut

U.S. Navy admiral and victor of the Battle of Mobile Bay (1801–1870)

Farragut was born in Tennessee and became a midshipman in the U.S. Navy when he was only nine years old. He was twelve years old when, during the War of 1812, he was given command of a ship captured by the USS *Essex* and successfully brought the prize to port. Following the war, he briefly left the navy to continue his education. He then returned and served on a number of ships and in a number of capacities.

Farragut and his family were living in Virginia when that state seceded from the Union. Though his wife was Virginia-born, they were Union sympathizers and quickly moved to the North. Following the outbreak of the Civil War, he was given command of a squadron and charged with capturing New Orleans. His success in breaching the defenses at the mouth of the Mississippi River and the capture of New Orleans in April 1862 made him a hero in the North. After opening the Mississippi River all the way up to Vicksburg, on July 1862, he was promoted to the rank of rear admiral, the first officer in the U.S. Navy to receive the rank.

In early 1864, Farragut began making plans to capture the last major Confederate port, Mobile Bay. His victory there earned him further glory and honors. In December 1864, he was promoted to vice admiral and, two years later, to full admiral. He was the first American naval officer to hold both ranks.

Farragut was bold, courageous, and headstrong. The last trait occasionally made him an uneasy partner in combined operations, for he sometimes would impetuously foray into action without coordinating with supporting troops. This had tragic results, particularly in the 1863 Battle of Port Hudson on the Mississippi River. There, he prematurely attacked Confederate fortifications and his fleet suffered considerable damage and casualties.

Farragut died in Portsmouth, New Hampshire, in 1870 and was buried in Bronx, New York.

Sherman's March to the Sea

Decisive campaign that shattered the last hope of the Confederacy

Sherman's troops removing ammunition from Fort McAllister in Georgia

On November 15, 1864, Major General William Tecumseh Sherman embarked on the boldest campaign of the Civil War. Starting from his base in Atlanta, Georgia, the Union commander marched his 62,000-man army 285 miles southeast to the Atlantic port of Savannah. Defying convention at the time which demanded he maintain secure lines of communication and logistics, Sherman chose instead to carry all his supplies with him and, when necessary, forage off the land. He accepted the risk that he would be cut off and unable to communicate with his superiors during his campaign. His intent was to cut a 60-mile-wide path of destruction that would destroy Confederate logistics and crush southern morale. In his words, he would "make Georgia howl." By planning the campaign the way he did, he wanted to demonstrate to even the most diehard Confederate that there was nothing the Rebels could do to stop him.

Sherman split his army into two wings as part of a deception to hide his destination. Sherman's men ripped up railroad tracks and burned and looted the Georgia countryside. Though Sherman did not condone wanton acts of violence against Confederate civilians, he tolerated them. Inevitably, some Union troops exceeded their broadly written orders and abuses occurred. Yet, Sherman was unmoved by the civilians' lamentations over the devastation his men wrought on them, their land, and property. He saw his campaign as the surest way to achieve a swift defeat of the Confederacy.

Sherman's army reached Savannah on December 9, having encountered almost no armed resistance worth noting. As his troops prepared to lay siege to the heavily fortified city, the Confederate commander, Lt. General William J. Hardee, evacuated his 10,000-man garrison on the night of December 20. Sherman and his men entered the city on the following day. In a message to President Lincoln, his first communication to the outside world in more than a month, Sherman offered the city as a Christmas present to the president.

Historians have since argued that Sherman's March to the Sea, as it came to be called, was the first example of modern, and total, war.

General Sherman directing troops

WILLIAM TECUMSEH SHERMAN

U.S. general during the March to the Sea Campaign (1820–1891)

Sherman was born and raised in Ohio. He graduated from the U.S. Military Academy at West Point in 1840, near the top of his class. During the Mexican-American War, Sherman was stationed in California and saw little action. He resigned from the army in 1853 and had a successful business career. He was the head of what is now Louisiana State University when that state seceded from the Union. Sherman resigned his position and returned north to volunteer for federal service.

Sherman was commissioned a colonel in the regular army and saw action at Bull Run. He was promoted to brigadier general of volunteers and in October 8, he became the commanding general of the Department of the Cumberland in the west. His outspoken criticism of unrealistic administration policies and his tempestuous relationship with the press during this period almost led to his dismissal. Journalists claimed that he was insane; historians acknowledge that he did show signs of emotional instability.

Sherman was a division commander in the Army of the Tennessee at the time of Shiloh. Sherman was wounded in that battle and was praised in dispatches by his superiors for his role. Sherman became Grant's most important subordinate in the campaign in the West. Promoted to major general of volunteers, he was a corps commander in the Vicksburg campaign and Grant's successor as commanding general of the Department of the Tennessee.

Sherman then succeeded Grant as the commander of the Military Division of the Mississippi when Grant was appointed general in chief of all the federal armies. As such, he was Grant's principal subordinate for military operations in the West. Sherman's campaigns in Georgia and the capture of Atlanta, followed by his March to the Sea, caused historians to rank him as one of the top federal commanders in the Civil War.

After the Civil War, Sherman was promoted to lieutenant general (1866), then full general (1869) and successor to Grant as the commander-in-chief of the army. Sherman retired from the army in 1884. Despite repeated requests, Sherman steadfastly refused to run for president. He died on February 14, 1891.

FIRST BATTLE OF SEDAN

The decisive battle of the Franco-Prussian War

The surrender of
Napoleon III

For years, Emperor Napoleon III of France had nervously observed German Chancellor Otto von Bismarck's successes in unifying the many independent German states under the rule of the Prussian king, Wilhelm. When Prussia attempted to place a member of its royal family on the vacant Spanish throne, Napoleon III saw it as a hostile act and preemptively declared war on July 19, 1870.

France had a large and well-equipped army, though Napoleon III had an exaggerated estimation of its fighting ability. The most glaring weaknesses were with its faction-ridden officer corps and outmoded doctrine. In contrast, the head of the German General Staff, Field Marshal Count Helmuth von Moltke, had completely modernized the Prussian army to take maximum advantage of the latest technological advances in weapon systems, transportation, and communication.

Though the French troops displayed great courage on the battlefield, their generals were repeatedly outmaneuvered. A series of defeats in August saw surviving French troops along the border with Belgium and Germany driven back to the fortress of Sedan on the Meuse River in the border province of Lorraine.

Sedan was ill prepared for the sudden influx of more than 120,000 men and their weapons and equipment. Included in the group was Emperor Napoleon III, who chose to remain at the front. By August 30, German armies had surrounded Sedan. Compounding the French plight was a confusing sequence of command changes that crippled the army's ability to defend itself and organize an effective breakout.

Napoleon III then made the stunning decision to capitulate. On September 1, he personally surrendered to the Prussian king. Following the surrender at Sedan, Napoleon III abdicated and the French Second Empire came to an end. The French government reorganized itself into the Third Republic and continued the war but by this time German victory was inevitable. Fighting ended on May 10. In a ceremony held at Versailles, King Wilhelm of Prussia was crowned Kaiser Wilhelm of Germany. Bismarck's vision of a unified Germany was now complete.

Prince Otto von Bismarck (right) meeting with
Napoleon III after the surrender of the French army at Sedan

ENGINES

Pivotal transport innovation during Franco-Prussian War

Whether the military leader was an Egyptian pharaoh, a Roman general, a conquistador, a George Washington, or a Napoleon, the armies they lead all had one thing in common: They got from one point to another on foot, marching at a pace ranging from 2 to 4 miles an hour and usually no more than 20 miles a day. That typical situation changed with the invention of the internal combustion engine.

Designs for engines, powered by steam, existed as early as the thirteenth century. But it was not until the nineteenth century that technology had progressed sufficiently to create engines large enough to be used in transport. Railroads and their steam locomotives were used by both sides, with varying degrees of efficiency, in the U.S. Civil War (1861–1865). One of the key factors in Germany's success in the Franco-Prussian War (1870–1871) was its use of railroads to move large bodies of troops quickly to the battlefield.

The engine made larger, heavy metal-hulled ships, armored vehicles such as tanks, and airplanes possible. Truck use in logistics and troop movement facilitated the sweeping offensives of World War II. The most famous supply campaign in history was the American Red Ball Express truck convoys in France during World War II. Design variations allow engines to use a wide range of fuels for power, including wind, petroleum, water, and solar energy. Today, all armies and navies rely on mechanical engines as their main power source for movement.

Maintenance crewman working on a helicopter engine in the Persian Gulf

Count Helmuth Karl Bernhard von Moltke (the Elder)

German field marshal and leader during the Battle of Sedan (1800–1891)

Von Moltke, father of the German General Staff system, was one of the great strategists of the second half of the nineteenth century. Called von Moltke the Elder, to distinguish him from his nephew who led the Imperial German army at the outbreak of World War I, he was one of the most unlikely individuals ever to reach the top of the military profession.

He was the son of petty nobility impoverished by the Napoleonic Wars. He entered Prussian military service in 1822. Almost immediately, the junior officer impressed his superiors, eventually including the future Kaiser Wilhelm II, with his intellect. Many of von Moltke's contemporaries in uniform had keen military minds. What set von Moltke apart from his peers was his erudition. He could speak seven languages. He loved music, poetry, art, archaeology, and theater. He was a gifted artist. He was a writer—one of his efforts was the translation into German of Gibbon's *The History of the Decline and Fall of the Roman Empire*. He conducted himself with charm, wit, and diplomacy in royal courts and high society, where he was well received.

Von Moltke served as a military advisor to the Ottoman Empire in the late 1830s. His account of his experiences, which he illustrated, made him famous. In 1857, he was appointed chief of the general staff, a position he would hold for thirty years. As the most powerful military leader next to the Kaiser, von Moltke embarked on a top-to-bottom transformation of the German army and its means of waging war. Two of his most important allies in this effort were the German chancellor, Otto von Bismarck, and the Minister of War, Albrecht von Roon.

Von Moltke's military successes against Denmark (1864) and Austria (1866) were crowned by his greatest achievement, victory over the French Second Empire in the Franco-Prussian War (1870–1871). This victory resulted in the dissolution of the French empire and the creation of the German empire. This war showed his extraordinary skill at using the modern technologies of communication, rail transport, and other advances to rapidly move large armies vast distances.

Von Moltke retired in 1888 and died in Berlin in 1891.

BATTLE OF THE LITTLE BIGHORN

The most famous battle in the Plains Indian wars

Civil War portrait of George Armstrong Custer, then a brigadier general

When the U.S. government tried to buy the Black Hills from the Sioux in 1874, Sioux Chiefs Sitting Bull, Crazy Horse, and Gall refused. The land was sacred to the Sioux. In defiance, they, their followers, and Cheyenne allies went to unceded Indian lands in southeastern Montana. The government decided to take military action to crush these non-treaty Indians.

The campaign called for a three-pronged attack (two from the north, one from the south) in June 1876. The southern prong was turned back by a brilliant attack led by Crazy Horse. The two northern columns planned to meet at the junction of the Yellowstone River and Rosebud Creek to coordinate their two prongs. Brigadier General Alfred Terry ordered Lt. Colonel Custer to take his Seventh Cavalry around the Indian camp and take up a blocking position south of it to prevent the Indians from escaping.

But, Custer, who had presidential ambitions, wanted the glory of defeating the Indians for himself. He commenced a forced march that brought his men near the Indian camp on June 25, well before Terry and Colonel John Gibbons were able to get into position. Ignoring warnings from his scouts of the Indian camp's large size, Custer fatally divided his command of 600 men into three parts. The three groups would simultaneously attack from the southeast.

When they attacked, the 600 troops found themselves confronting a camp of about 7,000, including 2,000 warriors. The forces led by Marcus Reno and Major Captain Frederick Benteen suffered heavy losses. Reno and his survivors barely managed to retreat to Benteen's defensive position where they successfully held out for two days. Meanwhile, Custer and his men were losing the battle to save their lives. Caught in broken terrain east of the Little Bighorn River, Custer and his command of 215 men were massacred.

By June 26, the battle was over. The Indians had left.

But the spectacular Sioux and Cheyenne victory only delayed the inevitable. Within four years Crazy Horse was dead and Sitting Bull, Gall, and the non-treaty Indians were all on reservations.

A romanticized painting of the Battle of the Little Bighorn

SITTING BULL (TATANKA YOTANKA)

Hunkpapa Sioux chief, medicine man, and victor at Little Bighorn (ca. 1831–1890)

In his youth, Sitting Bull distinguished himself as a skilled hunter and capable warrior, and someone who was generous to his own people. These traits caused him to be inducted into a number of important Sioux warrior societies, including the Strong Heart warrior lodge, of which he became a leader at about the age of twenty-five. The American public learned of him in 1866 for his leadership in attacks on the garrison at Fort Buford in western Dakota Territory.

As pressure from the United States government increased on the Sioux Confederation, Sitting Bull emerged as one of the important political and military leaders. He rejected the terms of Treaty of Fort Laramie in 1868, in which the Sioux Confederation made peace with the United States. As one of a number of non-treaty Indians that included Crazy Horse, Sitting Bull took his followers to live in the Sioux ancestral land around the Powder River.

Sitting Bull rejected the government's efforts to revise the treaty and cede the sacred Black Hills to the United States following the discovery of gold there in 1874. This led to the government's campaign in 1876 against Sitting Bull and the other non-treaty Indians to crush their influence. As a medicine man, Sitting Bull did not participate in the battle at the Little Bighorn. Instead he "made the medicine" that was responsible for the victory over Lt. Colonel Custer and his men.

Sitting Bull took his followers into Saskatchewan where they lived in exile for almost four years before returning to Dakota Territory, where he surrendered. He was imprisoned for about three years and then transferred to the Standing Rock Indian Reservation where he struggled against the Bureau of Indian Affairs to maintain Sioux culture. He joined Buffalo Bill Cody's Wild West Show in 1885 and toured with it for two years, to great acclaim. After returning to Standing Rock, he continued his resistance to government policies. He was killed while resisting arrest on December 15, 1890, following the government charge that he was going to use the religious Ghost Dance movement to incite Sioux rebellion.

CRAZY HORSE (TASHUNCA UITCO)

Oglala Sioux war chief and victor at Little Bighorn (ca. 1840–1877)

Crazy Horse's reputation as one of the great military tacticians in history was first demonstrated in the Fetterman Fight (1866) and the Wagon Box Fight (1867) near Fort Phil Kearny in Wyoming Territory. Like Sitting Bull, he rejected the terms of the 1868 Treaty of Fort Laramie and took his followers of the Oglala tribe to live in the ancestral Sioux lands of the Powder River Valley.

Crazy Horse was an implacable foe of any surrender of Sioux land to the United States government. His military success against the U.S. cavalry earned him great respect among his people and, like Sitting Bull, he became a central figure among the non-treaty Indians in their resistance to white encroachment on tribal lands.

In 1868, he was accorded the highest formal honor in his tribe when he was selected as one of the head warriors, or shirt-wearers, of the Oglalas. Crazy Horse lost his position as a shirt-wearer in 1871 as a result of an affair with Black Buffalo Woman, a married woman and the niece of the great Sioux Chief Red Cloud.

Crazy Horse was among the group of non-treaty Sioux to reject the government's demand to cede the sacred Black Hills land to the United States following the discovery of gold in 1874. Like Sitting Bull, and other leaders, he also rejected the demand to leave the unceded land in the Powder River Valley and live in government-allocated reservation territory.

The 1876 campaign was the highlight of his career as a war chief. The U.S. Army created a three-pronged offensive to crush the non-treaty Indians. Leading about 1,500 warriors, Crazy Horse defeated the southern prong led by Brigadier General George Crook at Rosebud Creek in southern Montana on June 17, 1876. Just over a week later, he helped lead the attack that massacred Lt. Colonel George Custer's command at the Little Bighorn.

These victories were followed by a series of defeats that began in the second half of 1876. Crazy Horse and his followers surrendered at Fort Robinson in Nebraska on May 6, 1877. He was arrested in September on the charge of attempting to incite rebellion and was killed while trying to escape on September 5, 1877.

The death of Crazy Horse in 1877 at Fort Robinson, Nebraska

maka 1847 en (ta Sunke Witko) Ktepi (laKota Wanji Ogun Spaka
WiCaSa TanKala eCiyapi

ta Sunke Witko akiCita tu Weya mazowakon
yuHa ope (Washington, D.C. ekta yesipi
tKa WiCaSa Sni Keyapi Heon Ktepi Keyapi

t Robinson neb en)

BATTLE OF RORKE'S DRIFT

A pivotal battle in the Anglo-Zulu War

A Zulu chief

The border Zulu nation had been at peace with the white colonists in South Africa for thirty years. Then its leaders decided to expand its hegemony in the late 1870s. In response, the British Army in South Africa rushed to the defense of its colonists in Natal, which was most threatened.

One British expedition of 3,000 British and African troops were surprised and slaughtered in the Battle of Isandlwana on January 22, 1879. The Zulus quickly began an advance on their next target, the British post at Rorke's Drift. Rorke's Drift was a mission with a small hospital located on a ford of the Buffalo River not far from Isandlwana. On the day of the Zulu attack at Isandlwana, Lieutenant John Chard and his command of 139 men were stationed at the mission. When word of the approach of a large Zulu army reached him, Chard promptly began preparations to defend the mission. The men had barely finished setting up their defenses when the Zulu army, estimated at 4,000–6,000 strong, arrived late in the afternoon of January 22 and surrounded the place.

With odds of more than 20 to 1 against them, and with the well-trained and armed Zulus who possessed both firearms and their deadly iklwas thrusting spears, the British cause looked hopeless. The Zulus launched one assault after another and managed to breach the outer ring of defenses. The British kept up a steady fire as they shortened their perimeter. The Zulus kept constant pressure on the defenders and the battle continued throughout the night.

At dawn of January 23, the exhausted British discovered that the Zulus were gone. Patrols were sent out. They discovered that at least 400 Zulu warriors had been killed in the action. British casualties were an astonishingly low total of seventeen dead and ten wounded.

A total of eleven Victoria Crosses, the country's highest decoration for valor, were awarded to the defenders at Rorke's Drift—the most ever presented for a single battle.

The defense of Rorke's Drift during the Zulu War

GIUSEPPE GARIBALDI

Italian general during the wars of Italian unity (1807–1882)

Giuseppe Garibaldi was acclaimed as the "hero of two worlds" for his successful military campaigns in Italy and in South America. So great were his achievements that at one point President Abraham Lincoln offered him a command in the Union army during the Civil War.

Garibaldi was born into a seafaring family in Nice, France. At that time, the Italian peninsula held a collection of fragmented territories, many under foreign dynastic rule. Garibaldi joined the nascent Italian revolutionary movement in 1834. When the insurrection failed, Garibaldi fled to South America to avoid a death sentence. It was in South America that he learned the art of guerilla warfare. It was also there that he adopted a distinctive red shirt for a uniform, and "Red Shirts" became the identifying name for his troops.

After twelve years of campaigns in Brazil and Uruguay, in 1848 Garibaldi learned of the renewed independence movement, *Risorgimento* (revival), in Italy. He returned to Europe. Early campaigns against the Austrians in the north and the French in the south ended in defeat and he fled to the United States. He returned to Italy in 1854 and five years later was leading a new army of Red Shirts in support of Sicilian independence. Victory there in 1860 was followed by campaigns on the Italian peninsula. This led King Victor Emmanuel II to declare the kingdom of Italy on February 18, 1861.

Garibaldi continued his campaigns to unify all of Italy. Even though he suffered repeated defeats, his efforts added luster to his already enormous reputation. In 1874, after Italy was finally united, he was elected to the Italian Parliament where he served for two years before retiring in 1876. He later became a vocal champion on social issues. He died in 1882 at age seventy-four.

SIEGE OF KHARTOUM

British defeat by Sudanese nationalists seeking independence from Egypt

General Charles
Gordon

In 1883, Egypt, nominally independent but in reality a dominion of Great Britain, confronted an Islamic revolution led by Mohammed Ahmed in its province of Sudan. Ahmed believed he had been called upon by Allah to accomplish a great religious reform. His sermons drew large crowds who proclaimed him a Mahdi—a Messiah sent by Allah. The resultant uprising against the corrupt Egyptian government was called the Mahdist revolution.

In November 1883, the Mahdists slaughtered 11,000 Anglo-Egyptian soldiers under the command of British General William Hicks. The British government under Prime Minister William Gladstone, which had heretofore taken a hands-off role, was forced to intervene. It sent to the Sudan General Charles George "Chinese" Gordon, one of its most distinguished military leaders. In 1876, Gordon had served as Governor-General of Sudan and also had completed noteworthy tours of duty in Africa and Asia.

Gordon entered Khartoum with a small force in February 18, 1884. He realized his force was insufficient and requested reinforcements, which were refused. The Mahdi, meanwhile, organized an army of 200,000 strong and laid siege to Khartoum in March. Gordon had fortified the city well, but time was on the Mahdi's side. The British responded with a relief army commanded by General Sir Garnet Wolseley but it was slow to organize. By the time the army began its journey from Egypt to Khartoum in early January 1885, the plight of the defenders was desperate. A portion of the relief army detached itself and attempted to reach Khartoum but was repulsed. The Mahdi then decided to assault Khartoum before the rest of the British army could arrive.

On February 26, approximately 50,000 Mahdist soldiers attacked. The small garrison and the city's inhabitants were slaughtered. Though the Mahdi had ordered Gordon captured alive, he was killed and his head was cut off and later presented to the Mahdi as a trophy.

Two days later, the relief army arrived. It quickly retreated back to Egypt. Muhammad Ahmad installed himself as the ruler of the new independent state of the Sudan.

Charles Gordon during the assault on Khartoum

WOUNDED KNEE

Massacre of Sioux that was the last military action in the Plains Indians Wars

Bodies of Sioux Indians being unceremoniously piled into a mass grave in the frozen South Dakota soil

By 1890, a religious movement called the Ghost Dance had taken hold over many of the dispirited Plains tribes. It was particularly popular with the Sioux, who were now living on reservation land and totally dependent on the U.S. government for their livelihood. The Ghost Dance blended the Christian belief of a messiah with traditional native beliefs. According to Ghost Dance worshippers, if the Native Americans lived righteous lives and performed the Ghost Dance ritual, the Native Americans would return to life as it was before the arrival of the white man.

Big Foot was a Sioux chief of the Miniconjou Lakota tribe who was not considered a dangerous leader. Even so, after Sitting Bull was killed on December 15, 1890, he was one of a number of influential Sioux chiefs who were kept under close watch by military authorities. When Big Foot took his band of Miniconjous out of the Cheyenne River Agency on December 23, in apparent defiance of orders to remain on the reservation, cavalry forces were ordered to intercept them.

On December 28, Colonel James Forsyth, leading the Seventh Cavalry, found Big Foot and his group—composed mostly of the elderly, women, and children—at Wounded Knee Creek in South Dakota. The next morning, he convened a council and demanded they surrender any and all firearms and that they would be relocated in a new camp.

As nervous soldiers watched, some members of the Miniconjous began singing and conducting Ghost Dance rituals. When a struggle broke out over the refusal of one Miniconjou to surrender his rifle and the weapon accidentally discharged, the troops began firing into the crowd. The outnumbered and outgunned Lakotas began to flee across the snow, followed by the still-shooting soldiers. When the shooting stopped, an estimated 250 to 300 Sioux lay dead in the snow. The Seventh Cavalry lost twenty-five men, believed to be killed by friendly fire. Bodies were found as far away as 3 miles from the camp. Among the dead was Big Foot.

Since then, Wounded Knee has become a tragic symbol of the many failures of the U.S. government's policy toward the Native Americans.

U.S. troops surrounding the Indians at Wounded Knee

TSUSHIMA

The Japanese naval victory over the Russian fleet

Japanese soldiers at Chemulpo

One of the great dreams of the Russian czars was to have a warm water port in both the east and west. Russia's efforts in Asia placed it in conflict with the growing ambitions of Japan. After diplomatic negotiations failed, war was declared on February 10, 1904.

A Japanese fleet blockaded the Russian Far Eastern Fleet at Port Arthur in China. To relieve the blockade and force a decision against Japan, Czar Nicholas II formed the 2nd Pacific Fleet from the Baltic Fleet and ordered it on an 18,000-mile voyage from its port on the Baltic Sea to Japan—a trip that lasted eight months.

The 2nd Pacific Fleet, under Vice Admiral Zinovy Rozhdestvenski, arrived in the Tsushima Straits on May 27, 1905. Confronting him was the Japanese Combined Fleet under Admiral Heihachiro Togo. Though the Russian admiral's fleet was numerically superior in capital ships, Togo's ships were more modern and had better armor and superior gunnery.

The battle commenced in the early afternoon of May 27. Russian fire concentrated on Admiral Togo's flagship, *Mikasa*, which was hit fifteen times in the first half hour. But Japanese return fire scored hits on many of the Russian warships. Admiral Rozhestvenski's flagship, *Suvarov*, was badly damaged and the admiral was wounded so severely that command of the fleet had to be passed to Rear Admiral Nicholas Nebogatov aboard the *Nikolai I.*

The Japanese fleet continued its deadly fire against the Russian fleet and by nightfall the *Suvarov* and three other battleships were sunk. Fighting continued into the night, during which time another battleship was lost. The next day, the Russians lost more ships before Admiral Nebogatov was able to break off action. The Russian fleet scattered in such confusion and disarray that some ships found safety in Manila, others in Vladivostok, some were run aground, others sunk in battle, and still others were captured. The Russian defeat truly ended in debacle.

The blow to Russian prestige was immense and humiliating. For Japan, the victory put her to the forefront as the new world sea power.

Sailors on the deck of the stricken Russian battleship *Borodino*, sunk by the Japanese fleet

HEIHACHIRO TOGO

Japanese admiral and victor of the Battle of Tsushima (1848–1934)

Togo was born in the Satsuma fief (later Kagoshima prefecture), the son of a samurai. He entered local military service at the age of fifteen and saw action during the Anglo-Satsuma War (1863). He joined the newly formed Satsuma navy in 1866. He was a gunnery officer in the Boshin (Restoration) War that overthrew the Tokugawa shogunate. He entered the new Imperial Japanese Navy as a cadet in 1871. Later that year, he was sent to England as a naval student. He served as an ordinary seaman aboard the sailing ship *Hampshire* in an 1875 voyage that circumnavigated the globe. Upon completing his studies in England, he was promoted to lieutenant and returned to Japan.

Togo fought in the Sino-Japanese War (1894–1895), where he achieved notoriety for the sinking of a British transport carrying Chinese troops. By war's end, he had been promoted to rear admiral. Following the war, he held a number of important posts ashore before being appointed to the post of commander in chief of the Imperial Japanese Navy's Combined Fleet in 1903.

When the Russo-Japanese War erupted, Togo fought and then blockaded the Russian Far Eastern Fleet at the Chinese harbor of Port Arthur in 1904. This set the stage for what became the Battle of Tsushima the following year. Togo's decisive victory over the Russian fleet in that battle garnered him enormous prestige at home and abroad. Not only was Russia's attempt for hegemony in the region shattered, Japan was elevated to the third most powerful sea power in the world.

After Tsushima, he was appointed chief of the naval general staff, served as a member of the Supreme War Council, and was made a count. Later, he was promoted to fleet admiral and made responsible for the education of Crown Prince Hirohito. Among his many awards was Japan's highest honor, the Collar of the Supreme Order of the Chrysanthemum (only the third person to receive it). He was elevated to marquis just before his death in 1934. Navies from six countries, including the Great Britain and the United States, sent ships for a naval parade in Togo's honor following his state funeral.

DREADNOUGHT

British battleship that defined the era of the big ship

In the late 1800s and early 1900s, an intense sea power rivalry had broken out among the major world powers of the day. Central to this rivalry was the construction of big warships, most importantly, of battleships. In America, President Theodore Roosevelt had the Great White Fleet, so named because of the color of the ships' hulls. The Great White Fleet contained sixteen battleships.

The Japanese and the Germans also had modern fleets but the apogee of big ship doctrine was reached by the British with the battleship HMS *Dreadnought*, commissioned in 1906. The *Dreadnought* was such a revolution in design, size, and armament that her name became a generic term for modern battleships. Battleships in service before her launch became known as "pre-dreadnoughts."

The *Dreadnought* was the first capital ship to use steam turbine propulsion. With a top speed of 21 knots, she was the fastest battleship in the world. Unlike other battleships that had a variety of cannon sizes for their main batteries, the *Dreadnought* was what came to be called an "all big-gun" battleship. Her main battery was uniform: ten 12-inch guns (so-named for the diameter of the shell). The *Dreadnought* incorporated the latest in electronics technology, communications, fire control, and range finding. Compartments were redesigned to increase structural integrity.

The *Dreadnought* would serve as the flagship of the Royal Navy's Home Fleet for five years. The *Dreadnought* was followed by a new class of battleship, the "super-dreadnoughts." It caused Germany's Kaiser Wilhelm II, an apostle of Admiral Mahan's doctrine of sea power, to begin a fast-paced building program for the German High Seas Fleet to outmatch the Royal Navy.

In 1910, the *Dreadnought* became the victim of a practical joke perpetrated by the infamous prankster Horace de Vere Cole. He managed to trick the Royal Navy into giving a guided tour of the battleship to a visiting group of Abyssinian royals. The "royals" were members of the Bloomsbury Group that included author Virginia Woolf. The *Dreadnought*'s years of supremacy were brief. By the time World War I began, she had already been out-classed by newer battleships.

The most powerful battleship in the world, the HMS *Dreadnought* at its launch by the King at Portsmouth in 1906

ALFRED THAYER MAHAN

American admiral, educator, and sea-power theorist (1840–1914)

Mahan was born at West Point, New York, in 1840, the son of Dennis Hart Mahan, a professor at the Military Academy. Instead of an army career and against his parents' wishes, Mahan transferred from Columbia University to the U.S. Naval Academy at Annapolis and graduated second in his class in 1859. He was commissioned a lieutenant and served in the Union Navy during the Civil War as a junior officer on a number of ships, participating primarily in blockade duty. Mahan was a lieutenant commander at the end of the war and received a number of routine assignments. In 1872, he was promoted to commander and, in 1885, to captain.

Ironically, Mahan was at best an indifferent shipboard naval officer (he hated the coal-fired ships of the period). Instead, he was an intellectual in a service that at the time largely viewed such individuals with deep suspicion. Mahan was a prolific writer who held strong views about the role of sea power and empire. He resented his tours of duty on ships, much preferring to be behind a desk, in front of a typewriter. In 1885, he was appointed lecturer in naval history and tactics at the Naval War College. He then was appointed its president and served two terms, 1886–1889 and 1892–1893.

Mahan wrote his two most influential books, *The Influence of Sea Power upon History, 1660–1783* (1890) and *The Influence of Sea Power upon the French Revolution and Empire, 1793–1812* (1892) at an important junction in American history. The United States had gained an empire as a result of its victory in the Spanish-American War and President Theodore Roosevelt was looking to expand America's influence around the world. In addition, the great imperial nations in Europe and elsewhere were looking to expand their own world influence. Mahan's central thesis was that whoever was master of the seas during war, would eventually win that war. It was a self-evident truth, never before expressed in print, whose simplicity and accuracy hit the world's political and military leaders like a thunderbolt. Mahan's books were instant worldwide bestsellers and made their author famous. Military and naval colleges throughout the world translated and studied his books. Mahan received numerous honors and was feted in royal courts. Kaiser Wilhelm II was enormously influenced by Mahan's work. He was promoted to rear admiral in 1906 and died in Washington, D.C. in 1914.

First Battle of the Marne

French army defense that ended the German Schlieffen Plan offensive

A soldier at
St. Mihiel

In 1900, Count Alfred von Schlieffen was chief of the German General Staff. He presented to Kaiser Wilhem II a plan for an offensive campaign to defeat the Allies in the west. As originally drafted, the Schlieffen Plan, as it came to be known, called for a strong German right wing attack through the Netherlands and Belgium that would smash into western France. Then, once the German armies were south of Paris, they would wheel east, encircle the French capital and crush any lingering resistance. Von Schlieffen estimated the campaign would last no more than six weeks. After his death in 1913, his successor, Field Marshal Helmuth von Moltke, revised the plan, fatally weakening it.

In World War I, the German offensive in the west was launched on August 14, 1914. The German First, Second, and Third Armies drove through Belgium and into northern France. The German First Army, northwest of Paris, was well ahead of the other two German armies when, on August 30, its commander, General von Klück, decided to change the axis of attack. Instead of continuing south until it was past Paris before turning east to envelope the city, he decided to make his turn north of the city along the Marne River. His intent was to trap the French Fifth Army between his troops and those of the German Second Army. Once the French army was destroyed, the advance on Paris would resume.

But Paris military governor General Joseph Gallieni saw that von Klück's maneuver had given the French an opportunity. He requisitioned 600 Parisian taxicabs to rush a fresh division to the front.

What happened next came to be called the "miracle of the Marne." French and British armies rallied on September 6 and surged through the gap in the German lines. At the same time, further east, French troops threw up a strong defense. The German offense was stopped cold. Von Moltke lost his nerve and on September 10, ordered his armies to fall back and regroup along the Somme River.

Though France had been saved from imminent defeat, no one knew when victory against the Germans would come. British Foreign Minister Sir Edward Grey spoke for a generation when he said, "The lights are going out all over Europe. We shall never see them again in our lifetime."

French soldiers during the Battle of the Marne, likely a recreated scene

BATTLE OF TANNENBERG

German victory against Russia in the opening days of World War I

Poster encourages war fund donations on anniversary of Tannenberg

Germany faced a two-front war in August 1914, against the allied French and British armies in the west and Russia in the east. The chief of the German General Staff, Field Marshal Helmuth von Moltke, decided to launch his first offensive in the west—the Schlieffen Plan. He chose to leave a relatively weak army guarding the eastern front, gambling that the Russian armies would not be able to attack until after Germany had triumphed in the west.

Thus, he was surprised when not one, but two massive Russian armies, the First and the Second, attacked East Prussia at the same time the bulk of the German army was marching through northern France. Von Moltke immediately began stripping divisions from the western armies. But in the time it would take to send them east, it appeared that the "Russian steamroller" would win. The German commander of the German Eighth Army in the east, General von Prittwitz, lost his nerve and recommended a retreat that would abandon the whole of East Prussia. He was relieved on August 20 and was replaced with generals von Hindenburg and Ludendorff.

The two Russian armies, meanwhile, failed to coordinate their advance. This allowed the new German commanders to implement a counterattack that had been drawn up by the Eighth Army staff. It called for the main blow to fall on the Russian Second Army. The Russian First Army would be prevented from helping by a German screening force. Success of the Russian offensive made General Samsonov, commander of the Russian Second Army, overconfident. When he saw that the Germans had taken position near the city of Tannenberg, on August 24, he ordered his troops to attack. They rushed into a trap. Fighting continued through August 29, when Samsonov, humiliated by Russian losses that exceeded 125,000 men, committed suicide. By August 31, the Russian Second Army ceased to exist.

Von Hindenburg and Ludendorff promptly followed up the victory at Tannenberg with a strong counterattack on the Russian First Army that inflicted an additional 125,000 casualties. German casualties from both actions totaled approximately 20,000 men. Though the Russians suffered a great strategic defeat, their sacrifice contributed to a strategic victory in the west. By forcing von Moltke to reroute troops to the east, he fatally weakened the drive to Paris. The German advance was stopped at the Marne River. France was saved.

German general Paul von Hindenburg (center) and his chief of staff Erich Ludendorff on their way to a meeting with King Ferdinand of Bulgaria

Paul von Hindenburg

German field marshal and president (1847–1934)

Von Hindenburg was the son of a Prussian army officer who entered the service in 1860. He had a respectable career in the army prior to his retirement in 1911. He fought in the Austro-Prussian War (also known as the Seven Weeks War) (1866) and the Franco-Prussian War (1870–1871). He attended the Kriegsakademie (War College) and later was an instructor. In 1877, he became a member of the German General Staff and, in 1883, he was head of the War Department's Infantry Bureau. He was called out of retirement in 1914 at the onset of World War I. He succeeded the commander of the Eighth Army in Prussia in August, who had lost his nerve shortly after the Russian offensive in the east was launched. Despite the fact that he had been out of uniform for three years, he displayed an imperturbable calmness when he arrived at his new headquarters with his chief of staff, Erich Ludendorff. He oversaw the German counterattack that became the Battle of Tannenberg. Von Hindenburg followed this up with the campaign in Poland. In November 1914, he was promoted to field marshal and made commander in chief of Austro-German forces on the Eastern Front.

In August 1916, von Hindenburg succeeded von Falkenhayn as chief of the German General Staff. He brought with him Ludendorff, whose mercurial personality and genius for planning complimented the staid von Hindenburg. When Kaiser Wilhelm II and the Reichstag abdicated responsibility governing the nation, von Hindenburg and Ludendorff became de facto military dictators of Germany.

Von Hindenburg oversaw the proclamation of unrestricted submarine war that led to the United States's entry on the side of the Allies, as well as the Peace of Brest-Litovsk (March 1918) that ended Germany's war with Russia. When Germany's defeat was imminent that fall, he was instrumental in convincing the Kaiser to abdicate to avoid social chaos. Following the war, von Hindenburg retired for a second time.

Von Hindenburg returned to public life as president of the German republic in 1925. Adolf Hitler, whom he didn't like, became his chancellor during his second term. He died in office in 1934.

ERICH WILHELM LUDENDORFF

German general (1865–1937)

Ludendorff, the son of a Pomeranian merchant and landowner, entered the Cadet Corps in 1877 and, upon graduation, the German army. His intelligence, flair for mathematics, and excellent work ethic impressed his superiors and in 1894 he was appointed to the German General Staff.

He was a brigadier general on the Western Front at the start of World War I and participated in the capture of Liége in early August 1914. Later that month, he was sent east to be von Hindenburg's chief of staff and help turn around the disaster looming on the Eastern Front as a result of the Russian offensive. Though both von Hindenburg and Ludendorff arrived too late to do little more than approve the counterattack plans that had been drawn up, they became famous as the victors of the Battle of Tannenberg. The two remained a team from that point on to the end of the war.

Ludendorff became known as the brains of the team, for it was he who originated most of the plans of their operations. When von Hindenburg became chief of the German General Staff, he brought in Ludendorff as his deputy. The structure of the German government at that time was such that the military had great influence over civil and economic affairs of the nation; Ludendorff and von Hindenburg soon effectively became military dictators. It was Ludendorff who pushed for unrestricted submarine warfare, a miscalculation that ultimately led to Germany's defeat because it contributed to the United States declaring war against Germany.

Following the victory over Russia that led to the signing of the Treaty of Brest-Litovsk, Ludendorff laid plans for an all-out offensive in the west in the spring of 1918. That offensive's failure, and the powerful Allied offensive that followed, caused the first breach in his relationship with von Hindenburg. Ludendorff's behavior in the final weeks of the war was a messy series of demands, accusations, on-and-off resignations, and political meddling. He fled to Sweden following the armistice.

Ludendorff briefly became associated with the Nazi party and participated in the abortive 1923 Beer Hall Putsch. Following that incident, Ludendorff retired from public life and died in 1937.

Paul von Hindenburg, Kaiser Wilhelm II, Erich Ludendorff

Battle of Gallipoli

British-led amphibious assault on the Dardanelles Strait

Gallipoli battle map

When World War I began to degenerate into trench war stalemate, two schools of thought arose among senior leaders in the British government and military about how to further prosecute the war. The "Westerners" believed that the decisive theater was in France and all effort should be applied there. "Easterners" believed no good would come from the war of attrition in France. Their proposal was to attack Germany's weakest ally, the Ottoman Empire. Knocking out the Ottoman Empire would not only eliminate one of the three Central Powers but it would also open a supply route to Russia.

First Lord of the Admiralty Winston Churchill was the main supporter of an attack against the Ottoman Empire. What eventually emerged was a plan for a British, Commonwealth, and French amphibious assault of Turkey's Gallipoli Peninsula at the mouth of the Dardanelles Strait. Once Gallipoli had been secured, the army and navy would then advance on Turkey's capital, Constantinople (Istanbul). Its fall would trigger the Ottoman Empire's surrender.

Unfortunately for the Allies, things began to go wrong almost from the beginning. A premature British naval bombardment of the Gallipoli defenses in 1914 alerted the Turks. Prior to the amphibious assault, an opportunity to seize the straits by the British fleet providing the preparatory bombardment vanished when the admiral lost his nerve. Logistical problems delayed the amphibious assault. Finally, on April 25, 1915, the Australian, New Zealand, British, and French troops landed on the beaches. But two factors set the stage for the disaster to come. The landings occurred at sites too widely separated to be mutually supporting. And instead of rapidly moving inland and seizing the heights that dominated the landing sites, the British commanders fatally delayed.

The Turks responded with alacrity and invested the heights. The British command's incompetence coupled with the Turkish command's brilliance (one of the Turkish officers was Mustafa Kemel, the future ruler of Turkey) made the beaches a nightmare for the Allied troops. The Gallipoli campaign became a stalemate that lasted almost a year before the Allies evacuated. In the acrimonious political fallout, Churchill received much of the blame and was forced out of office.

A 60-pound heavy field gun in action on a cliff top at Helles Bay at Gallipoli

BATTLE OF THE SOMME

Britain's controversial first major offensive in World War I

Removing the dead from the trenches

The Battle of the Somme in northern France was the outgrowth of two circumstances: the Allied strategy meeting at Chantilly in December 1915 and the siege of Verdun. Initially, the Somme campaign was to be an equal Anglo-French battle but, when the German army attacked Verdun, Britain contributed most of the troops. Its original intent was to be a breakthrough of the German lines—the "big push" that would lead to victory in 1916. But the ongoing siege of Verdun added the goal of relieving pressure on the French defenders by drawing German troops away to the north.

Since the small British army had been decimated by the battles of 1914 and 1915, most of the British Expeditionary Force (BEF) troops were all-volunteer "New Army" and many regular army officers who led them were recently promoted survivors of the earlier battles. Many generals, including BEF commander General Sir Douglas Haig, were new to their roles.

Following a one-week preliminary bombardment in which British artillery fired more than 1.5 million shells, the attack commenced on July 1. British troops confidently expected to find the Germans obliterated by the artillery. Instead, the cannon fire had proved ineffective. Rows of barbed wire that should have been destroyed remained intact. It was the British who were slaughtered. By the end of the day, more than 57,000 troops were casualties, including at least 19,000 dead. Haig launched smaller attacks for the next three months, gaining ground—but at frightful cost. On September 15, Haig ordered another major attack, one where tanks were used for the first time. Unfortunately, the tanks were too few and unreliable to affect the course of battle. By November, the autumn rains had turned the battlefield into a quagmire. The campaign finally concluded on November 19.

To liberate land in northern France about 20 miles long, 6 miles deep, and of no strategic importance, the British suffered more than 420,000 casualties and the French lost about 200,000 men. German losses were equally horrendous, an estimated 400,000 to 600,000 casualties. The campaign deeply shocked the British and foreshadowed the war of attrition to come.

Canadian troops with fixed bayonets leaving their trenches for a raid on the Somme

Barbed Wire

Metal fencing material

Barbed wire arose out of the need for inexpensive fencing material. Barbed wire technology was developed simultaneously by a number of people. Joseph F. Glidden of DeKalb, Illinois, is credited with receiving in 1874 the first patent for his wire, which he named "the Winner." It was a double strand of twisted wire interspersed with shorter lengths wrapped around it to form barbs. More than 570 patented wires are registered and more than 2,000 variations exist, some having rather fancy, even decorative, barbs. One type, called razor wire, was created in Germany during World War I but widespread use did not occur until the 1960s.

Barbed wire became instantly popular in the Great Plains because of its resilience in extreme weather, its ease of installation, and its low cost in a region where wood for fencing was expensive or not available. It was initially used to confine cattle and to indicate farm and ranch property lines. Railroad companies were the first major businesses to use barbed wire. They constructed the fence along their tracks to protect them from roving herds of cattle.

Warwire—barbed wire for military use—was first used in the Civil War in 1864 at Vicksburg. Regular barbed wire designed for cattle confinement was used by the military up until 1898, when designs created specifically for the military, with sturdier coils with heavier barbs, began to be manufactured.

The British used barbed wire in the Boer War (1899–1902) and it appeared in defensive positions in the Russo-Japanese War. World War I was the first major conflict in which barbed wire was widely used. Long coils of concertina wire, so named because they can be expanded like the bellows of the concertina, were erected as barriers to protect the trenches. Since then, barbed wire or razor wire have become an ubiquitous presence around military installations—whether temporary or permanent—and other facilities where security is important, such as prisons.

While the machine gun was a factor of the decline of horse cavalry, barbed wire, in fact, was a major contributor to this decline because horses would refuse to charge a barbed wire barricade.

An American soldier advances across barbed wire obstacles in
No Man's Land during a battle on the Western Front in World War I

BATTLE OF VERDUN

Von Falkenhayn's campaign designed to knock France out of the war

Soldiers marching into a shelled Verdun

General Erich von Falkenhayn succeeded the younger von Moltke in September 1914 as chief of the German General Staff. In his Christmas memo of 1915 to Kaiser Wilhelm II, von Falkenhayn proposed a campaign where the seizure of territory was secondary to the real goal: the taking of lives. This battle would, in his words, "bleed to death" the French army. Von Falkenhayn chose Verdun as his target, a lightly garrisoned city in the northeast province of Lorraine. Though it had little strategic significance, von Falkenhayn astutely saw that French pride would cause them to defend the place to the last man.

The battle opened with a bombardment by about 1,400 cannon on February 21, in the greatest artillery barrage at the time. The next day, with artillery support also firing poison gas shells, the advancing German troops discovered that parts of the French defensive line had disintegrated. During the next few days, one key objective after another fell to the Germans, including the centerpiece of the area's fortress complex, Fort Douaumont.

As von Falkenhayn predicted, reinforcements were rushed in. General Philippe Pétain was made overall commander of the city's defenses. Verdun's only means of supply was a narrow, 40-mile long road to the vital railhead at Bar-le-Duc. Pétain used the road, later christened the *voie sacrée* (sacred way), around the clock to send in troops and supplies.

Von Falkanhayn had not anticipated the battle becoming a virtual meat grinder of German troops as well. By July, the campaign had failed. Verdun had turned into a slaughterhouse of both French and German troops but France refused to capitulate. Von Falkenhayn was replaced by Field Marshal von Hindenburg.

The French launched their counteroffensive in October. By December 15, the Germans were back in their original trenches. Total casualties for both sides were an estimated 1.2 million men. One long-term impact of the battle was the effectiveness of Verdun's fortress complex. Its success in stopping entire divisions led to the French government's construction of the Maginot Line after the war.

French soldiers on the battlefield, during an offensive action on the French fortress town of Verdun

ATTRITION

Strategy of wearing down an enemy through sustained attack used at Verdun

Attrition is the most brutal type of strategy employed in war. It requires such an extraordinary political will to sustain, that democracies rarely employ it. Only dictators or totalitarian societies possess the unquestioned authority necessary to continue it over the long term.

At the operational (battlefield) level, attrition is the annihilation of an enemy's army—"bleeding it white." Examples include General Ulysses Grant's Overland (or Richmond) Campaign in May–June 1864 and the siege of Verdun in World War I. In World War II, the Japanese employed a de facto attrition strategy following the Battle of Tarawa. Had the strategy been employed less haphazardly, the Japanese could have arguably extended the war into 1946.

On the grand strategy, or national security policy, level, the greatest example of the strategy of attrition and its cost to both sides is World War I on the Western Front. As the war continued, both the Allies and Germany found themselves locked in a vicious cycle of escalating bloodletting that neither could end, even though their economies and governments faced ruin and revolt.

The Eastern Front in World War II is another example of the high cost of a policy of attrition. The Soviet Union paid a fearful price for its victory and in so doing was one of the very few nations to successfully employ a strategy of attrition. The reasons it could do so included having a large population, a totalitarian society, facing an enemy more brutal than the Soviet government, and a callous disregard for casualties.

The Allies' air campaigns in World War II are examples where the price of attrition was paid by the enemy through the destruction of its cities and industries. This form of strategy arguably reached its signature moment with the dropping of the atomic bombs on Hiroshima and Nagasaki.

The St. Mihiel American Cemetery in France

Battle of Jutland

The largest naval battle of World War I

Admiral Jellicoe

Kaiser Wilhelm II had long been jealous of British sea power and wished to supplant the Royal Navy with Germany's High Seas Fleet. Though the Royal Navy had more ships, Germany's were more modern, with better armor, cannon, and shells. A plan was developed to destroy the Royal Navy in stages, beginning with a fleet action in spring 1916. That fleet action became the Battle of Jutland, involving 250 ships, including 44 battleships (28 British, 16 German) and about 100,000 men.

The British had cracked the German naval codes, so they knew Vice Admiral Reinhard Scheer's plan when the High Seas Fleet weighed anchor for the North Sea on May 31. Preceding the High Seas Fleet was a battle cruiser squadron commanded by Vice Admiral Franz Hipper. What the Germans didn't know was that Admiral Sir John Jellicoe, leading the British Grand Fleet, and a fast battle cruiser squadron, led by Vice Admiral Sir David Beatty, had left their ports a day earlier and were on a path to intercept the German fleets.

The two battle cruiser squadrons clashed first, sighting each other at 3:31 P.M. on May 31. The effectiveness of the German gunnery was an unpleasant shock. Two ships were soon sunk and several others, including Beatty's flagship, were damaged. In a comment that later became famous, Beatty said, "There seems to be something wrong with our bloody ships today." Hipper's squadron was soon joined by Scheer's fleet and Beatty turned around to lure the German ships within range of Jellico's fleet.

The fleets met at 7:15 P.M. Jellico succeeded in positioning his ships in a maneuver called "crossing the 'T'" where his ships were able to fire full-power broadsides at an enemy that could only use its forward turrets. As darkness settled, the battle became a confused night action. By the following morning, both sides had retired.

Each claimed victory. The British lost 6,784 men and ships totaling 111,000 tons; the Germans 3,058 men and ships totaling 62,000 tons. In strategic terms, the British won. The German High Seas Fleet never again challenged the Royal Navy.

The battleships HMS *Colossus* and the HMS *Vanguard* during the Battle of Jutland

COLOSSUS

VANGUARD

Battle of Passchendaele (Third Battle of Ypres)

Failed Allied campaign to the North Sea

Adolf Hitler, who served as a messenger during the Battle of Passchendaele, is sitting on the far left in this group of German soldiers.

In early 1917, BEF commander in chief General Sir Douglas Haig made plans for the largest British and Commonwealth campaign on the Western Front. It would be launched from the Belgian town of Ypres, the setting of two previous major campaigns, and its objective was the city of Ostend on the North Sea. Months of meticulous planning went into the offensive that kicked off with a successful preliminary attack to seize important high ground by the British Second Army on July 13. The British Fifth Army followed this up with the main attack, launched on July 31, following an intense three-day artillery barrage.

Things started going wrong for the British and Commonwealth troops shortly after they began to advance. The land for the attack had a high water table. The explosions of the artillery shells so churned up the terrain that it had become a gigantic sea of mud. The Fifth Army's advance literally bogged down, with some men drowning in the mud. The troops' misery was compounded by the onset of heavy unseasonable rains. By the end of August, the Fifth Army's advance, which had halted, could be measured in yards.

Yet, Haig chose to continue with his plan. He turned to the Second Army, which initially had some incremental success despite the inclement weather. But by October, with the rains continuing to soak the ground, attacks through the mud against the strong German fortifications had thoroughly exhausted the Second Army. And the town of Passchendaele, an important high-ground objective in the October push, had been pulverized to nonexistence by artillery from both sides.

Not until November 10, when Passchendaele—or what was left of it—had been captured, did the campaign conclude. Once again, much blood was shed for little gain: At least 300,000 British and Commonwealth casualties and only 5 miles of Belgium were liberated. The battle so disgusted British Prime Minister David Lloyd George that he never again trusted Haig.

British casualties litter the battlefield outside the town of Passchendaele

POISON GAS

Chemical aerosols used in the Battle of Passchendaele

Poison gas is one weapon in the chemical warfare arsenal. It is also one of a number of weapons of mass destruction, or WMD, so-named because of their widespread and lingering capability once employed.

World War I was the first conflict that had the widespread use of gas weapons, ranging from the disabling (tear, mustard) to the lethal (chlorine, phosgene). Poison gas was first used on April 22, 1915, in the Second Battle of Ypres during World War I. The Germans released chlorine gas over the French lines on the Flanders front. Within ten minutes, approximately 6,000 French and colonial troops were killed, most through asphyxiation caused by fatal damage to the lungs. Thousands more were blinded. Gas then became an important weapon in the arsenal of both sides.

The most famous gas used in World War I was mustard gas. As a vesicant, or blister agent, mustard gas causes severe irritation of the skin and mucus membranes upon contact. Germany introduced it in the Battle of Passchendaele. Depending on weather conditions, it could linger in the soil and remain active for weeks, sometimes months. It was also heavier than the atmosphere. In extreme cases, it completely replaced the air in the trenches.

Because gas is dispersed by the atmosphere, it is a fickle weapon that could, with a wind shift, turn on the combatant that used it. This happened to the British in the Battle of Loos in 1915.

Revulsion over the use of poison gas led to the Geneva Protocol of 1925 prohibiting the use of chemical and biological weapons. Even so, poison gas remained in the arsenals of all the major powers. Stockpiles accompanied the armies of both sides during World War II, though were never used on the battlefield. Poison gas was one of the weapons used by Hitler in his Final Solution.

Though there have been other international agreements ending the stockpiling and use of such weapons, they remain in the arsenals of almost all military powers. Some leaders, such as the late Saddam Hussein of Iraq, had no inhibitions regarding their use.

German soldiers taking advantage of a suitable wind to emit poison gas from cylinders

MACHINE GUN

Repeating firearm used in World War I battles

Few weapons in military history had as revolutionary an impact on the prosecution of warfare as the machine gun. Machine guns in the early twentieth century were capable of firing 600 rounds per minute. By century's end, that number had increased tenfold. It would take the spilling of the blood of a generation on the battlefields of World War I before generals would succeed in developing tactics to counter the machine gun's firepower.

The first known functioning repeating firearm was James Puckle's "Puckle Gun." Built in 1718, it was a tripod-mounted, single-barreled flintlock gun fitted with a multishot revolving cylinder.

Three Americans—Hiram Maxim, John Browning, and Isaac Newton Lewis— were the most important machine gun inventors in the years between the Civil War and World War I. Armies around the world soon purchased the automatic weapons that bore their names. The original Gatling gun, adopted by the U.S. Army in 1866, was a hand-cranked, multibarrel machine gun. Versions in use today are automatic and fire 6,000 rounds per minute.

Maxim was the first to produce, in 1883, a practical, single-barreled machine gun. It came about as the result of a conversation at the 1881 Paris Electrical Exhibition where he was evidently told, "If you want to make a lot of money, invent something that will enable these Europeans to cut each other's throats with greater efficiency."

Lewis demonstrated the first practical lightweight machine gun installed in aircraft.

Browning, regarded by many weapons inventors as the greatest firearms designer ever, created machine gun designs so efficient that the models in use today are little changed from the versions developed during World War I. Reichsmarshal Hermann Göering reportedly said that if his Luftwaffe had had the Browning .50-caliber machine gun in its fighters, the Battle of Britain would have been a German victory.

Inventor John T. Thompson's experience in World War I inspired him to design a one-man, handheld version. The Thompson submachine gun became the weapon of choice among Prohibition gangsters and was widely used by the Allies in World War II.

Two soldiers readying their .50 caliber machine gun prior to participating in a training exercise

BATTLE OF BEERSHEBA

Opening victory that led to British conquest of Palestine

War cemetery at
Beersheba

An important defensive fortification protecting the Ottoman Empire's southern border with British-controlled Egypt was the Gaza–Beersheba Line. It was about 30 miles long, running from the port of Gaza on the Mediterranean coast inland to the town of Beersheba.

General Edmund Allenby assumed command of Britain's Egyptian Expeditionary Force (EEF) in June 1917. Morale in the EEF was low. Two earlier campaigns against the Gaza–Beersheba Line had failed, prompting the previous commander's replacement by Allenby. Though Turkish fortifications at Gaza were strong, they noticeably weakened for a stretch further inland, becoming strong again at Beersheba. The reason for this was water: The only reliable sources were at Gaza and Beersheba. The Turks were confident that lack of water would continue to limit British inland attacks to small raids.

Allenby's plan to crack the Gaza–Beersheba Line focused on the quick capture of Beersheba before his water supplies ran out. He set up a forward base near the town under strict secrecy and cleverly disseminated into enemy hands false battle plans to deceive them.

His attack commenced with an artillery barrage just before dawn on October 31. Allenby's plan called for an infantry assault followed by the capture of Beersheba with dismounted troops. But it had taken more time than anticipated for the infantry to seize its objectives. The second wave would have to be a full-fledged cavalry charge.

Two mounted regiments charged the Turkish trench lines in the late afternoon. The Turks were taken by surprise and even though they were equipped with machine guns, they proved inexperienced in their use and were unable to stop the mounted attack. The Turkish troops began to lose their nerve once the horses began leaping over the trenches and only put up sporadic resistance. While some troops retreated in good order to Beersheba, most began surrendering.

Allenby's men continued into the town and by nightfall Beersheba and its precious water were in British hands at a cost of only thirty-one killed and thirty-six wounded. The battle proved a successful harbinger of the campaign to capture Palestine.

Australian Infantry commemorate Battle of Beersheba in Israel

EDMUND HENRY HYNMAN ALLENBY

British field marshal (1861–1936)

"Bull" Allenby (so named for his large size and fiery temper) graduated from the Royal Military College at Sandhurst in 1881. His first posting was in South Africa and he fought in the Boer War (1899–1902). By war's end, he was a colonel. When World War I began, Allenby was a division commander of horse cavalry. On a trench warfare battlefield where the machine gun dominated, horse cavalry operations were obsolete. Allenby adapted and distinguished himself as a corps commander and later as an army commander. An ongoing feud with General Douglas Haig over tactics caused him to be transferred to Palestine. He arrived as the new commander of the Egyptian Expeditionary Force (EEF) in June 1917.

Even though horse cavalry warfare was in eclipse, Allenby was now in an environment where it could have a last hurrah. He restored the dispirited morale of his troops and reorganized his army. He formed his camel and horse detachments into the highly mobile Desert Mounted Corps, which would become famous in the upcoming campaigns. Allenby began his campaign against the Turks in October 1917 with the capture of Beersheba in southern Palestine. As the Turks began to retreat north, Allenby used his cavalry to constantly pressure the enemy, not allowing it time to form defenses. In December, three weeks ahead of schedule, Allenby capped the success of his first campaign with the capture of Jerusalem.

The German Spring Offensive in 1918 forced Allenby to transfer to France many of his troops. He had to halt offensive operations for nine months until sufficient replacements arrived. In September 1918, Allenby was ready. Using massed cavalry once again, he routed the Turks at Megiddo. His army's advance north was a remarkable achievement. By the end of October, he had captured most of Syria and had forced the Turks to sue for peace. An armistice was signed on October 30.

The combination of battlefield success and low casualties make Allenby perhaps the most successful British commander in World War I. He was promoted to field marshal and made a viscount. He later served as high commissioner of Egypt. He died in London in 1936.

Battle of Cambrai

First great tank battle in history

Cambrai, France

The Allies in 1917 had almost reached the limit of their endurance. For years, the only progress on the Western Front had been the lengthening list of dead troops. Russia had been knocked out of the war and replaced by an unprepared United States. Months would pass before America's involvement would be felt. To boost flagging morale before winter set in, Field Marshal Douglas Haig, the overall commander of British and Commonwealth troops in France, approved a surprise attack by his Third Army at Cambrai, a key supply town behind the German trenches in northern France.

Colonel J. F. C. Fuller and Brigadier General Hugh J. Ellis had begun planning for the attack in the summer. Its purpose was to break the German Hindenburg Line along a 5-mile front in front of Cambrai and sever the important rail and communications networks there. Haig allocated nine infantry divisions, five cavalry divisions, and three brigades of tanks. The tanks—almost 500—were the most important element. The terrain was flat and firm, and had not been heavily cratered by shellfire, making it ideal for tank travel. New tactics were developed to maximize the tanks' shock force.

The attack, organized in secrecy, began at 6:20 A.M. on November 20 with a short, rolling artillery barrage. The sudden appearance of hundreds of tanks astonished the Germans and many fled in panic. By midday, almost all the objectives of the attack had been seized. The one, crucial, exception was in the center at Flesquières, where a division commander had disregarded the new tank battle tactics and substituted his own. The division suffered heavy losses and was unable to keep pace. The Germans recovered and plugged the hole in their lines. The attack began to bog down. On November 29, the Germans counterattacked. The British fell back. By December 7, the British had abandoned almost all of their gains.

The battle's inconclusive end could not mask its importance as a harbinger of the future. Tanks, employed en masse, had demonstrated that the stalemate of trench warfare could be broken. The age of armored warfare on land had begun.

A British tank of the kind that managed to break down the German barbed wire defenses at Cambrai.

SECOND BATTLE OF THE MARNE

The battle that proved American troop ability and resolution

In 1918, German Field Marshal Paul von Hindenburg and General Erich Ludendorff were determined to follow up on their Spring Offensive and achieve victory before the full weight of the growing American Expeditionary Force (AEF), still training in France, could be felt. The knockout blow, later known as the Second Battle of the Marne, was launched on July 15. Specially trained "shock units" advanced in a three-pronged attack that smashed into the British and French lines. In less than two days, the German Army was at the Marne River. Once again, the Germans had victory within their grasp, and once again, the road to Paris, about 50 miles away, was wide open. In 1914, France had its "Miracle of the Marne." This time, France, with its troop strength exhausted, had no miracles of her own remaining. The Allies' supreme commander, General Ferdinand Foch, turned to the AEF's commander, General John Pershing, and asked for help.

Previously, Pershing had refused to release American units piecemeal to reinforce depleted British and French divisions, believing they would become just cannon fodder. He stated that when the Americans fought, they would do so only as a unified army. But Pershing recognized that the present crisis overrode national considerations and temporarily released five divisions to Foch's command. The untested American troops were flung into battle in the most desperate of situations. As a unit of Marines arrived at its jumping off point near Belleau Wood, they were confronted by demoralized, retreating French troops. One French officer called for them to join in the retreat. A Marine captain responded, "Retreat, hell! We just got here!"

The American Marine and Army units counterattacked. The U.S. Army 3rd Division blunted the point of the German attack. Troops were locked in bloody hand-to-hand fighting but the 3rd Division refused to give ground. German assault troops soon spread the rumor that "The Americans are killing everyone."

By July 20, the Germans had begun to retreat, the offensive had failed. American forces had been "blooded" and, despite their inexperience, had proved themselves and earned the respect of both their enemy and Allies. The 3rd Division, because of its steadfast defense, received particular acclaim with the title "The Rock of the Marne." Pershing's belief in the American troops had been vindicated.

An American gun position on the front line in France

JOHN JOSEPH PERSHING

American general during the Second Battle of the Marne (1860–1948)

Pershing, one of only two Americans (Washington being the other) to hold the rank of General of the Armies, was born to a Union sympathizer family in Missouri just before the outbreak of the Civil War. He graduated from West Point in 1886 and initially served in the cavalry, campaigning against the Apache Indians and later in the northern plains. He got his nickname "Black Jack" during the Spanish-American War, when he commanded a unit of all-black troopers. It was during this conflict that he came to the attention of Theodore Roosevelt.

Captain Pershing then served in the Philippines. His work pacifying the rebellious Moros in the southern Philippines so earned their respect that the Moros made him a chief. In 1906, Theodore Roosevelt, now president, promoted Pershing directly from captain to brigadier general, causing great resentment among many older officers.

In 1916, President Woodrow Wilson ordered Pershing to lead a punitive expedition into Mexico to capture the bandit Pancho Villa and his men. Although the military action proved fruitless, Pershing handled his duty with great diplomacy, doing as much as he could not to offend the Mexican populace.

Upon America's entry into World War I, Wilson appointed Pershing as the commanding general of the American Expeditionary Force. He arrived in France in June 1917 at the head of an army that would grow to more two million men. From the beginning, Pershing found himself fighting two wars—one against the Germans and the second against his Allies. Because England and France were war weary and their ranks had been decimated by years of trench warfare, they repeatedly attempted to siphon off American units to increase their ranks. Pershing steadfastly refused. He believed that doing so would undercut the morale and contribution of the American troops. Also, he was philosophically opposed to the trench warfare tactics favored by the Allies, favoring "open warfare" tactics of speed and maneuver.

American participation in the Aisne–Marne, Saint Mihiel, and Meuse–Argonne offensives in 1918 seemed to vindicate Pershing's belief. Upon war's end, Pershing was promoted to the rank of General of the Armies. He served as Army Chief of Staff and retired in 1924. His memoirs were published in 1931. He died at Walter Reed Hospital in 1948.

BATTLE OF MEGIDDO

British campaign in Palestine that featured the last successful cavalry charge in history

Landing party from British ship against Arabs on Persian Gulf

If there was one bright spot on the battlefield for the Allies in the end of 1917, it was General Edmund Allenby's capture of Jerusalem, the crowning achievement of his campaign that year. Unfortunately, the German 1918 Spring Offensive forced Britain to transfer many troops from his command to France. While awaiting reinforcements, he began to make plans for a campaign to knock the Ottoman Empire out of the war. The Turks, meanwhile, used the respite to build a new line of defenses between the Mediterranean port of Jaffa and the Jordan River Valley. One of the important parts of the defensive line was Megiddo, a town whose strategic location had made it a focus of battles throughout history.

Allenby was finally ready to launch his campaign in September. As in the Battle of Beersheba, Allenby employed a variety of deception tactics. These included having Major T. E. Lawrence—Lawrence of Arabia—ordering his agents to openly forage along "planned" paths of attack.

Allenby's assault began on September 17, with Lawrence leading his Arab irregulars on a diversionary attack of the Turkish rail junction at Deraa, east of the Sea of Galilee. Allenby's main attack commenced on September 19. Cavalry troops, supported by aircraft and infantry, led the attack on Megiddo. The Turks were efficiently led by German general Otto Liman von Sanders. But an air strike on Liman von Sanders' headquarters destroyed his communications center, leaving him out of touch at a key moment in the beginning of the fast-moving battle.

By September 22, Allenby's advancing troops had captured Amman in the east. Damascus, in the north, fell on October 1. In a little less than a month, Allenby's campaign begun at Megiddo had covered 360 miles, destroyed three Turkish armies, and captured about 76,000 men at a cost of less than 6,000 casualties. Allenby's men were ready for a final push into Turkey itself when they received news of the Ottoman Empire's capitulation on October 30. World War I in the Middle East ended with a spectacular triumph for the British.

General Edmund Allenby's capture of Jerusalem

BATTLE OF KHALKIN GOL

Soviet victory over Japan prior to the outbreak of World War II

Russian soldiers look down on a trench filled with corpses of Japanese soldiers

Few battles are so important, yet so unknown, as the Battle of Khalkin Gol along the disputed Mongolian–Manchurian border in the summer of 1939. Clashes between Japanese and Mongolian and Soviet troops began occurring after Japan invaded Manchuria and made it the puppet state Manchukuo. Japan, in a step toward extending its hegemony in the region, insisted that the border ran along the Khalkin Gol (Khalkin River). The Mongolians and their Soviet allies insisted it was east of the river. A series of border incidents escalated to the point of undeclared war.

General Georgi Zhukov, commander of Soviet troops in the remote region, faced a daunting tactical situation. His logistic lines were extraordinarily long, making resupply and reinforcement enormously complicated. Also, his troops faced the Japanese Kwantung Army, which had never been defeated in battle.

The Japanese had already conducted two offensive operations and were in the process of launching a third in August 1939 when Zhukov struck back. Zhukov had been building up his forces for an overwhelming counteroffensive, which he launched on August 20, just before the Japanese were going to begin theirs. With infantry in the center holding the Japanese troops, Soviet heavy armored forces spearheaded powerful attacks on the right and left wings. The Soviet mechanized units smashed through the Japanese lines and thrust deep behind them. They then turned inward in a classic double envelopment maneuver and surrounded the trapped Japanese army.

Attempts to relieve the Japanese troops caught in the envelopment failed. When they refused to surrender, Zhukov annihilated them with artillery and air attacks. On August 31, the battle was over. But Zhukov's victory was overwhelmed by circumstances beyond his control. The next day, Hitler attacked Poland and World War II in Europe commenced.

Zhukov's victory was so complete, it ended Japan's attempts to expand its empire at the expense of Mongolia and the Soviet Union. The two countries signed a peace treaty in the middle of September that remained in effect until the Soviet Union declared war against Japan in 1945.

Two Russian soldiers congratulating themselves on their victory

SIR BASIL HENRY LIDDELL HART

British military theorist and historian (1895–1970)

American military historian Martin Bluemenson observed, "The essential tragedy of Basil Henry Liddell Hart was that he was understood, appreciated, and followed, but only by the enemies of his nation."

Liddell Hart served as a junior officer in World War I, was gassed in the Battle of the Somme in 1916, and retired a captain in 1927. The writing career that made him famous began in 1916 as he was recovering from his wounds. He jotted down his observations of the battle and the generals who led it. Assigned light duty following his recovery, he had time to further his studies and to write. His work in revising training manuals led him into a deeper study of how to wage war.

In 1920, he met tank advocate Colonel J. F. C. Fuller and from him developed an appreciation of tank operations and their application in mobile warfare. He began publishing his thoughts on combined tank-and-infantry mobile warfare operations in 1922. His ideas, which included the advocacy of the *indirect approach* and the *expanding torrent* were visionary, widely translated, and generally ignored by the British military hierarchy. In 1939 and 1940, his theories would become reality with the German blitzkrieg. Liddell Hart would later remark of the "tragic irony" in seeing his ideas "put in extreme jeopardy" his country. General Heinz Guderian acknowledged, "I owe many suggestions of [panzer warfare] development to Captain Liddell Hart." And General Fritz Bayerlein, a chief of staff to Field Marshal Erwin Rommel, said, "[Rommel], like Guderian, could in many respects be termed Liddell Hart's pupil." On the Allied side, General George S. Patton Jr. was the best practitioner of his theories.

With his reputation secured, Liddell Hart's fame reached its pinnacle in the years following World War II. He received numerous honors, including knighthood, and he continued to write and lecture. Among his many admirers were officers in the Israel Defense Force who praised him as "the captain who teaches generals."

Liddell Hart died of a stroke in 1970.

John Frederick Charles Fuller

British general, military historian, and theorist (1878–1966)

Fuller was one of the visionary proponents of armored warfare in the interwar years. His writings on the tactical problems, political and social aspects of war, and military history greatly influenced many World War II and postwar leaders.

Fuller was the son of a clergyman. He entered the Royal Military Academy at Sandhurst in 1897. Upon receiving his commission, he served in South Africa and fought in the Second Boer War (1899–1902).

In the early days of World War I, Fuller, as a staff officer, made numerous observations about trench warfare tactical conditions. He began to formulate theories to overcome the obstacles of barbed wire, machine guns, and heavy artillery. When he was introduced to tanks in 1916, he saw that it was the weapon to make his ideas a reality. When the British Tank Corps was formed in December, Fuller became its chief general staff officer.

Fuller created the plan for the Battle of Cambrai, the first massed tank attack in history, launched on November 20, 1917. Later, Fuller continued his role as the primary planner of British tank operations. His Plan 1919 called for a combined force operation utilizing aircraft, 5,000 tanks, and infantry in an offensive that presaged the German blitzkrieg of World War II. World War I ended before it could be used.

After the war, Fuller successfully lobbied for a permanent Royal Tank Corps. He also wrote articles and books that expanded on his theories. His books included *Tanks in the Great War* (1920), *The Reformation of War* (1923), and *The Foundations of the Science of War* (1926), a collection of his lectures, and *Field Regulations III* (1932). Translated into other languages, they were among the books studied by German officers. During this time, he also met and befriended fellow military theorist Basil Liddell Hart.

Fuller became a member of the Imperial General Staff in 1926. He retired in 1933 with the rank of major general. He continued his writing and by the time of his death in 1966, had published more than forty books and hundreds of newspaper and magazine articles.

POLISH CAMPAIGN

Start of World War II in Europe; first use of blitzkrieg

German troops parade through Warsaw

World War II in Europe officially began with Nazi Germany's invasion of Poland on September 1, 1939. The invasion was the culmination of German leader Adolf Hitler's effort to abrogate the Versailles Treaty, destroy Poland, and return to Germany the territory it had been forced to cede to Poland.

After Hitler had absorbed Czechoslovakia in the spring of 1939, Poland obtained a defense alliance with Britain and France. But, when Germany countered with the Nazi-Soviet Pact with the Soviet Union, Poland's fate was sealed.

Germany's plan, Fall Weiss (Operation White), was launched with sixty divisions. The key element of the German offensive was the *blitzkrieg*, or lightning war. Blitzkrieg was an attack conducted by mechanized forces led by tanks and supported by aircraft that would smash through enemy defenses and swiftly thrust deep into enemy territory before opposing armies could recover and regroup.

The Polish army fought bravely. But its weapons and tactics were obsolete. Photographs showing Polish horse cavalry units charging German tanks epitomized the hopelessness of Poland's situation.

The collapse of Polish resistance accelerated when the Soviet Union, as part of the secret terms of the Nazi-Soviet Pact, attacked from the east on September 17. The Polish troops that could escape moved south, with many eventually arriving in England. Organized resistance in Poland ended on October 5. Once again, the nation was partitioned between its more powerful neighbors. Only a small portion remained, but under Nazi control.

With its blitzkrieg in Poland, Germany showcased a new method of waging war that stunned the world—and the lessons of what a lightning war could achieve would be demonstrated the following spring with the German invasion of France.

German air patrol flying over Poland in wake of invasion

TANK

Self-propelled, armored offensive vehicle used in the Polish campaign

---

The tank was another of the long list of revolutionary weapons systems to emerge in World War I. The tank was created out of military necessity—generals were desperate to find something that could overcome the barriers of barbed wire, machine gun, and trench lines that had stopped offensive actions cold. The British were the first to develop tanks, and Winston Churchill, then First Sea Lord, was one of the weapon's sponsors. The word *tank* was actually a code word (referring to boiler or storage tank) used as part of a deception to shroud its true nature from the Germans. Originally referred to as "land ships," the parts of tanks (hull, hatch, turret, deck, and so on) take their names from naval ships.

Tanks first saw action in September 1916 when a handful of Mark I tanks fought in the Battle of the Somme. The largest use of tanks in a combined force operation was the Battle of Cambrai in late 1917. These first tanks were slow and mechanically unreliable.

During the interwar years, American automotive engineer J. Walter Christie developed a suspension system that allowed tanks to achieve high speeds and better overland performance. But budget cutbacks and bureaucratic resistance caused the U.S. Army to reject Christie's design. Ultimately, the tank branch itself was eliminated. Christie would later sell his design to the Soviet Union, which would use it as the basis for their T-34, regarded as the best tank used in World War II.

Improved tank design and tactics, particularly the blitzkrieg (lightning war), resulted in some of the greatest campaigns and battles of World War II, such as Germany's conquest of Poland and France and the Allies' later campaign in France.

Tank design followed a number of paths during the Cold War. Some notable examples include the British Centurion, regarded as the best all-around tank in the West in the 1950s and 1960s, the Soviet Union's JS-S Stalin heavy tank and T-64 and T-80 medium tanks, and the United States's Abrams M-I and M-IA main battle tank.

Innovations in armor design include explosive reactive armor (ERA) and composite armor, also known as Chobham armor, that have the twin virtues of increased protection and reduced weight.

A German panzer tank in winter combat on the Eastern Front, 1943

Heinz Wilhelm Guderian

German general during the Polish campaign (1888–1954)

The creator of the panzer forces and developer of blitzkrieg warfare doctrine was born in East Prussia, now a part of Poland. He became a signals specialist in the Imperial German Army and served with distinction in a variety of positions including staff officer in World War I.

Guderian was chosen as one of the few officers retained in the army following the manpower restrictions mandated by the Versailles peace treaty that limited Germany to a 100,000-man army. During the interwar years, Guderian immersed himself in the theory and application of motorized weapons and transport in war. The result of his studies was the book *Achtung! Panzer!*, which was published in 1937 and presented his theories of tank warfare. It was an immediate success. Translated into many languages, it was studied by forward-thinking officers like George S. Patton Jr. and is still an important reference in military academies.

Guderian was a corps commander of panzers at the outbreak of the war and his campaigns in Poland and France demonstrated to the world the effectiveness of the theories he expounded in his book. Following the French campaign, he was promoted to Generaloberst (four-star general) in July 1940.

In Operation Barbarossa, he commanded the 2nd Panzer Group and participated in the gigantic envelopments of Soviet armies at Minsk, Smolensk, and Kiev. In September 1941, his command was reorganized as the 2nd Panzer Army and he participated in the failed drive to Moscow.

The strong-willed and opinionated Guderian repeatedly clashed with Hitler and his superiors over strategy in the Eastern Front. At the end of December 1941, he was sacked for being a "difficult subordinate."

He was recalled to duty as Inspector General in March 1943. Guderian was a member of the Army Court of Honor that reviewed the cases of all accused army officers following the July 20, 1944, plot to assassinate Hitler.

Guderian was appointed chief of the Army General Staff in July 1944. After more clashes with Hitler over strategy, he was relieved on March 28, 1945. Following Germany's defeat, he retired and wrote his memoirs. He died in 1954.

INDIRECT

Strategy used in Polish campaign that struck weak spots

Indirect attacks—flanking maneuvers—have existed since the dawn of war. But Sir Basil Liddell Hart was the first to codify the tactical method into a full-fledged strategy. His book, *Strategy*, was the result of bitter experience learned in the killing fields of the Western Front during World War I.

Indirect strategy often involves less violence and typically includes a series of military, economic, diplomatic, or psychological actions completed in no particular order but all targeting enemy weaknesses. Often these weaknesses are in territories beyond the enemy's home boundaries: insecure allies, vulnerable overseas territories, recently conquered land, and so on.

The military historian James L. Abrahamson wrote, "Maritime and airpower strategies have an indirect character in that they aim to undermine the enemy's will to resist or deny his armed forces the means to make war."

Bluff is an important aspect of the indirect strategy. In the early years of the U.S. Civil War, the Union Army of the Potomac was rendered virtually immobile because its general, George McClellan, succumbed to "show of superior force" bluffs by Confederate generals, even though the Army of the Potomac substantially out-numbered the enemy.

Many examples of the use of indirect strategy exist in World War II. The first was the German blitzkrieg in Poland and France. The British, together with a not-altogether-willing America, used it in the Mediterranean campaigns in North Africa, Sicily, and Italy. The "island-hopping" campaign by American forces in the Pacific Ocean is a classic case of the indirect approach. Islands that had large Japanese forces were bypassed and less well-defended islands were seized during the advance toward Japan.

American troops landing on the beach of Rendova Island in the Solomons during World War II

GEORGE CATLETT MARSHALL

U.S. general, secretary of state, and secretary of defense (1880–1959)

America's greatest general of the twentieth century never attended West Point nor did he hold a combat command during his military career. Marshall entered the army as a second lieutenant following graduation from the Virginia Military Institute. His first tour of duty was in the Philippines. During World War I, Marshall served in a variety of staff positions where he established his reputation as a brilliant staff officer.

Marshall remained in the army after World War I ended and led a seemingly fruitless, nomadic military life, typical of service in the 1920s and 1930s. Marshall was rescued from obscurity in 1938 when he was appointed deputy chief of staff of the army and transferred to Washington, D.C. The following year, he was sworn in as the new army chief of staff on September 1, 1939, the same day Germany attacked Poland to start World War II in Europe.

Upon the United States's entry into World War II, Marshall was responsible for the strategic planning of a two-ocean war. Under Marshall, the army went from 200,000 to 8 million soldiers. He selected top leaders such as Eisenhower, Patton, Bradley, Stilwell, and others who would achieve battlefield success.

His reputation for honesty earned him the respect of Congress. In fact, it was his success with Congress that caused President Roosevelt to decide to keep Marshall in Washington instead of making him the commander of Operation Overlord, a post which was filled by General Dwight Eisenhower. Marshall retired at the end of World War II with the rank of general of the army. Within ten days, President Harry Truman sent him on a mission to China in a futile attempt to resolve differences between the Nationalist and Communist forces.

Truman named Marshall the secretary of state in 1947. Under Marshall, the European Recovery Plan, popularly called the Marshall Plan, was enacted which restored the devastated European economy. Marshall resigned for health reasons in 1949 but returned to the Truman administration in 1950 and served as Secretary of Defense during the first year of the Korean War. Marshall retired in 1951, this time for good. Two years later, in 1953, he was awarded the Nobel Peace Prize for his Marshall Plan. He lived quietly in Leesburg, Virginia, until his death following a stroke in 1959.

Marshall (seated) and some members of the Joint Chiefs of Staff during World War II

FALL OF FRANCE

Decisive defeat of France by German blitzkrieg

Adolf Hitler in Paris

Following Poland's defeat by Germany, there was a pause in land operations in Europe known as the Phony War. During this period, the French Army warily observed its German counterpart from behind its Maginot Line of fortifications. The German High Command, meanwhile, was laying plans for a decisive campaign in the West.

The offensive kicked off with a diversionary invasion of the Netherlands, Belgium, and Luxembourg, designed to draw the British Army in northern France into northeast Belgium. This opened a gap between the British and French lines.

The main German attack was a surprise assault through Belgium's Ardennes Forest just north of the Maginot Line. Because Allied leaders believed the terrain was impassable for tanks and armored vehicles, it was lightly defended. As a result, German armored units were able to quickly break through and reach the flat plains of northern France that were ideal tank country. The devastating power of the German thrust was aided by the Allies' tangled chain of command, ineffective and obsolete communications, and the rapid collapse of the morale of French senior commanders and troops.

As the Germans expected, the British Expeditionary Force was lured out of its defensive positions in the opening days of the offensive. Exposed and in danger of being cut off and destroyed, the British troops managed one of the most successful rearguard actions in history, the fighting retreat and evacuation at Dunkirk, France. Though all vehicles, heavy weapons, and most small arms had to be abandoned, approximately 340,000 British and French troops were successfully evacuated to England.

Meanwhile, the German offensive continued through France. On June 14, German troops captured Paris. On June 22, 1940, at the site and in the same railroad car used to sign the German surrender in 1918, France capitulated.

The fall of France was a spectacular triumph for Germany. Now it was master of Europe from the Pyrenees to the Arctic Circle.

Refugees from a French town escaping the Nazi onslaught

BATTLE OF BRITAIN

British aerial defense that stopped the invasion of England

Aircraft spotter on the roof of a building in London

In the wake of France's surrender, Hitler attempted to reach a diplomatic settlement with Great Britain. When that effort failed, he issued a directive on July 16, 1940, for the invasion of England. Codenamed Operation Sealion, it called for German amphibious landings along England's southern shore once Luftwaffe aircraft had defeated the British Royal Air Force (RAF).

Initially, it appeared that German success was only a matter of time. The British army had almost no weapons. It had been forced to abandon everything at Dunkirk. The RAF had suffered severe losses during the Fall of France and sufficient replacement pilots and aircraft were still weeks away.

Yet the disparity in aircraft numbers that seemed to favor the Germans was deceptive. With the Battle of Britain, the Luftwaffe was handed a strategic role for which it had not been designed. Hitler had planned for a quick war. The Luftwaffe was created as a tactical air force to be used in support of blitzkrieg operations. It had no heavy bombers, its dive-bombers were too slow, and it had no long-range fighters needed to provide maximum protection for the bombers. These weaknesses only became apparent well after the Battle of Britain commenced.

Initially the Luftwaffe was able to use its superior numbers to hit an array of coastal targets. Despite assistance from radar stations that tracked enemy flight paths and guided them to efficient intercept courses, the RAF squadrons were stretched to the breaking point. The Luftwaffe began targeting RAF airfields in August; had these attacks continued, the RAF might have been defeated. The Luftwaffe made another strategic mistake in not attacking the radar stations that were the invaluable long-range "eyes" of the RAF. Instead, by the end of August, the Luftwaffe was attacking cities, beginning with London.

Unable to defeat the RAF, Hitler indefinitely postponed Operation Sealion on September 9, 1940. Great Britain was saved. As Prime Minister Winston Churchill said of the RAF in a speech before Parliament, "Never in the course of human endeavor has so much by so many been owed to so few."

An English Sunderland flying boat attacks a German plane during a dogfight

Operation Barbarossa

The German invasion of the Soviet Union

German soldier in Russia

Planning for the German invasion of the Soviet Union began in the summer of 1940 following the fall of France. From the beginning, Operation Barbarossa suffered from an unfocused strategic objective. Hitler advocated thrusts north to Leningrad (St. Petersburg) and south to the agriculture and mineral rich Ukraine. The Army High Command proposed that the main thrust be in the center, with the goal being the capture of Moscow. This strategic shifting would continue after the campaign began and last up until Germany went on the defensive following its defeat at Stalingrad (Volgograd) in January 1943.

Soviet dictator Josef Stalin received numerous warnings of German troop buildup and invasion plans in the months leading up to the offensive. He refused to believe them, insisting that Hitler would not break the Nazi-Soviet Pact. He was shocked when, on June 22, 1941, 153 German divisions—containing approximately 3.6 million men, 3,600 tanks, and 2,700 aircraft—crossed the border and invaded.

Arrayed against the Germans was a Red Army containing about 2.9 million men, 15,000 tanks, and 8,000 aircraft. Though the attack was launched along a front that stretched from the Baltic to the Black Seas, initially the main thrust was in the center toward Moscow.

The opening weeks of Operation Barbarossa were chronicled with one disaster after another for the Soviet Union. But the deeper the German troops thrust into the Soviet Union, the greater their challenges grew. Autumn rains turned the unpaved Russian roads into quagmires. Then, in November, winter set in. Still, by early December, the Germans managed to reach the suburbs of Moscow. However, they were at the end of their tether, both in terms of logistics and endurance.

On December 5, the Soviet Army, led by General Georgi Zhukov, launched a surprise counterattack and tore huge holes in the ragged German lines. The Eastern Front was on the verge of collapse when Hitler took direct command and through force of will stabilized the front.

Operation Barbarossa was designed to be a quick campaign to defeat the Soviet Union in 1941. That goal had failed. Germany was now locked into a war of attrition and annihilation.

Exhausted Nazi soldiers rest by the road

GEORGI ZHUKOV

Victor of Battle of Moscow, Soviet Field Marshal, Minister of Defense (1896–1974)

The Soviet Union's greatest general was born a peasant and his early life was one of crushing poverty. During World War I, he was a junior officer in the czarist army where he was wounded and decorated for valor. Following the rise of the Bolsheviks, Zhukov joined the Red Army in 1918 and fought for the Communists in the Russian Civil War.

Zhukov narrowly survived Josef Stalin's brutal purges of the Red Army's senior commanders in the 1930s. In 1939, he was a corps commander and responsible for defenses in Outer Mongolia. For his victory over the Japanese at Khalkin Gol, Zhukov received the first of four Hero of the Soviet Union medals (Medal of Honor equivalent). He was promoted to General of the Army and made commander of the Kiev Military District, a prestigious post.

When the Germans launched Operation Barbarossa in June 1941, Zhukov became Stalin's "fireman," moving from Moscow to Leningrad and back, commanding defenses in those cities. As the principal commander in the Battle of Moscow in December 1941, he led the counteroffensive that drove the Germans back.

In August 1942, he became the deputy supreme commander of the Red Army. In this capacity he oversaw the successful lifting of the siege of Leningrad and the destruction of the German Sixth Army at Stalingrad. He was promoted to Marshal of the Soviet Union in February 1943. He was the main planner of the Battle of Kursk, the largest tank battle in history. His campaign in the east culminated in the capture of Berlin in May 1945.

Zhukov was the most famous and popular military leader in the Soviet Union. That popularity aroused Stalin's jealousy. Zhukov narrowly avoided imprisonment but found himself stripped of his Communist party responsibilities and posted to remote and inconsequential commands.

Following Stalin's death, Zhukov returned to power as first deputy defense minister and later minister of defense under Nikita Khrushchev. But he also feared Zhukov's popularity, so Khrushchev sacked him in 1957 and forced him into retirement. Zhukov died in 1974.

Georgi K. Zhukov (center) inspects the Guard of Honour with British Field Marshal Montgomery

BATTLE OF MOSCOW

The German campaign to seize the Soviet capital

When Operation Barbarossa commenced, the German Army High Command insisted that Moscow be the primary objective. Not only was it the Soviet Union's political center, it was its most highly developed industrial and rail network region. The General Staff reasoned that Stalin would fight to the death to defend it, giving the superior German armies the opportunity to achieve a decisive victory and conquer the Soviet Union.

But, in August 1941, Adolf Hitler gave higher priority to the thrusts in the north and south. Army Group Center, commanded by Field Marshal Fedor von Bock, had to halt. Von Bock did not receive authorization to launch Operation Typhoon, the campaign to capture Moscow, until October 2. But, October rains turned the unpaved Russian roads into seas of mud that made progress all but impossible.

Meanwhile, Soviet dictator Josef Stalin had appointed General Georgi Zhukov as commander of the West Front (Army Group) and charged him with the defense of Moscow. Zhukov used the reprieve granted by his ally, "General Mud," to train the raw recruits in the hastily organized army. He also organized a strategic reserve of veteran divisions newly arrived from Siberia. His was a desperate gamble. He planned to initially sacrifice superficially trained soldiers before the veteran German troops. Only after the other great Russian ally, "General Winter," arrived would he unleash his strategic reserve.

When the weather began to freeze the ground sufficiently, in early November, von Bock resumed his attack. On November 27, units entered the Moscow suburbs, with some just 12.5 miles away from the capital and within sight of the city's minarets. But then the fury of the Russian winter began to take its toll: Temperatures dropped to −40°F at night. German motorized vehicles were immobilized and ill-clad German troops began to suffer from exposure.

Zhukov counterattacked using his strategic reserve on December 6. Huge rents were torn in the German lines. The counterattack escalated into a counteroffensive.

Zhukov had delivered the Germans their first crushing reverse. But they were far from defeated, as events the following year would demonstrate.

Soviet troops push a piece of anti-tank artillery through a snowy field during the Battle of Moscow

PEARL HARBOR

The Japanese surprise attack that prompted the United States to enter World War II

Cheering Japanese soldiers on a carrier before the attack on Pearl Harbor

Only the most die-hard isolationist refused to believe that the United States could stay out of the war raging in Europe and Asia. For many, it was more a question of "when" than of "if." For President Franklin D. Roosevelt and his top military advisors, it was also a question of "where?" By November 1941, diplomatic efforts to avert war between Japan and the United States had reached an impass. War was imminent.

In anticipation of this scenario, the U.S. Pacific Fleet had been ordered earlier that year from its home port in San Diego to Pearl Harbor on the Hawaiian island of Oahu. War warnings had been issued to American commanders in the Pacific but the warnings did not contain a firm timetable. Plus, the Japanese navy had a wealth of strategic targets it could attack, including the Philippines with its American military ports and bases, the rubber- and oil-rich Dutch East Indies, the British bases and colonies of Hong Kong and Singapore, and the American bases on Oahu.

On Sunday morning, December 7, 1941, Japanese navy warplanes made a surprise attack on the American military airfields of Schofield, Wheeler, Ewa, and Hickam and the naval base at Pearl Harbor. Within two hours, American air and naval forces had been gutted. Nineteen warships, including seven battleships, were sunk or badly damaged and 188 aircraft were destroyed. More than 2,400 American servicemen were killed. Japanese losses were 29 aircraft, approximately 100 men, and 5 midget submarines.

News of the sneak attack sent a shock wave throughout the United States. Because of the delay in decoding the declaration of war, the Japanese ambassador delivered the declaration after the attack had started, instead of before.

In a speech that expressed the nation's outrage, President Franklin Roosevelt asked Congress to declare war against Japan, referring to the attack on December 7 as "a day of infamy." Before the week concluded, declarations of war were also exchanged with Germany and Italy.

Historians have since stated that, although the sneak attack was a tactical victory for Japan, it was a strategic mistake because the manner of the attack united the American people as few other actions could have done.

Black clouds of smoke pour from aircraft ablaze on the naval seaplane base on Ford Island

Isoroku Yamamoto

Japanese admiral and planner of the Pearl Harbor attack (1884–1943)

Isoroku Takano was born into an impoverished samurai family in an isolated region along the west coast of the Japanese main island of Honshu. He was later adopted by the prominent Yamamoto family and took their name. He entered the Japanese Naval Academy and graduated in 1904, seventh in his class. He then participated in the decisive Battle of Tsushima in the Russo-Japanese War, where he was wounded, losing two fingers from his left hand.

Yamamoto held a number of shipboard and diplomatic assignments. He studied at Harvard University (1919–1921). It was during this period that he gained respect for American industrial potential. In Japan, Yamamoto rose rapidly through the ranks. In August 1939, he was promoted to admiral and appointed commander in chief of the Combined Fleet of the Imperial Japanese Navy. As Japan prepared for war against the United States, Yamamoto said that he would "run wild" for six months to a year but that he had "utterly no confidence" after that.

Yamamoto planned the attack on Pearl Harbor. That Japanese victory made possible the stunning string of Japanese conquests over the next four months, which put almost one-third of the globe under Japanese control.

If Pearl Harbor was Yamamoto's pinnacle, then the Battle of Midway six months later is when he suffered his nadir. Midway was the first major defeat of the Japanese navy since the sixteenth century. Yamamoto recovered and devoted all his energies into the Guadalcanal campaign.

Yamamoto was killed on April 18, 1943, when American fighter planes shot down the transport carrying him on an inspection tour of Japanese troops on Bouganville. He was posthumously promoted to fleet admiral and given a state funeral.

CHESTER WILLIAM NIMITZ

U.S. admiral during World War II (1885–1965)

Quiet and self-effacing, this son of the Texas hill country north of San Antonio originally wanted to go to West Point. Instead, he wound up applying to the U.S. Naval Academy at Annapolis. Eventually, he would become America's greatest naval commander in World War II.

Nimitz graduated from Annapolis near the top of his class in 1905. But it appeared his career would be over before it had a chance to begin when, three years later as captain of the destroyer *Decatur*, Ensign Nimitz ran his ship aground at night in poorly charted waters. Fortunately, he only received a reprimand.

In 1909, he was assigned to the new submarine service and over the years became the navy's foremost expert, instituting a number of important design changes. Nimitz gradually rose through the ranks and, in December 1941, following the disaster at Pearl Harbor, Vice Admiral Nimitz was appointed commander in chief of the Pacific Fleet.

Nimitz successfully transformed a command shattered by defeat into the most powerful naval force in American history. In coordination with General Douglas MacArthur, Nimitz successfully conducted an island-hopping offensive campaign against Japan. The victories under his command are among the most famous in military history: the Doolittle Raid, Coral Sea, Midway, Guadalcanal, Tarawa, the Battle of the Philippine Sea, the Battle of Leyte Gulf, Iwo Jima, and Okinawa.

At the Japanese surrender ceremony held on the battleship USS *Missouri*, Admiral of the Fleet Nimitz signed the peace treaty as the official representative of the United States. Following the war, Nimitz served as chief of naval operations and oversaw the demobilization of the fleets he helped create. Nimitz became a regent at the University of California at Berkley and died in San Francisco in 1966.

BATTLE OF THE ATLANTIC

The Allied campaign to secure the Atlantic sea routes during World War II

Officer at periscope in control room of submarine

The German Navy was caught in the beginning of a long-term construction program when war broke out in 1939. Not strong enough to take on Britain's Royal Navy, German ships focused on intercepting the merchant fleets that supplied England. But its surface ship campaign against the British suffered early blows when the pocket battleships *Admiral Graf Von Spee* and *Bismarck* were sunk. After May 1941, the remaining surface ships were concentrated in Norwegian waters. There they threatened Arctic convoys to the Soviet Union through occasional direct action, but mostly by their presence, since they rarely left harbor.

Far and away the German Navy's greatest success was with its U-boat submarines, particularly once they were able to operate out of Norwegian and French ports along the Atlantic coast. In a spectacular mission, Günther Prien, commander of *U-47*, successfully entered the Royal Navy base at Scapa Flow in the Orkney Islands north of Scotland, torpedoed the battleship *Royal Oak*, and escaped. U-boat sinking of merchant ships was deadly. Hunting in groups called wolf packs, U-boats sank millions of tons of ships and cargo.

Allied countermeasures included the doctrine of escorted convoys, the use of ASDIC (an early form of sonar), the construction of small escort aircraft carriers, the cracking of German naval codes, and maintaining shipping construction that outpaced losses. These measures slowly tipped the scales in the Allies' favor.

The German Navy countered with new U-boat designs and tactics but construction could not keep pace with its losses. After 1942, the number of ships sunk by U-boats began to drop. By the summer of 1944, following the losses of its bases in France, the U-boat threat had been reduced to the level of harassment. By the end of that year, the German U-boat threat had all but ceased to exist.

Prime Minister Winston Churchill confessed that the war against the U-boats was the only one he feared.

Sailors aboard a British destroyer prepare to fire their gun

SUBMARINE

The war boat that was the pivotal weapon in the Battle of the Atlantic

Submarines are boats (not ships) designed to travel primarily underwater. Strictly speaking, true submarines did not become operational until the launching of the nuclear-powered USS *Nautilus* in 1954. Prior to that, U-boats and other so-called submarines were actually submersibles—sea craft that primarily traveled on the surface of the water and only went below its surface for short periods of time.

Initially, submarine design reflected the idiosyncrasies of designers' dreams and the limits of primitive technologies. Eventually, submarines became an integral part of the navies of the world due to developing technologies beginning with glass, wood, and hide, and later with iron and steel alloys, and the utilization of energy sources including human muscles, gasoline and diesel fuel, chemicals, electricity, steam, and eventually atomic power.

According to legend, Alexander the Great was the first to use an underwater craft. In 332 B.C. near Tyre, he entered a primitive diving bell and was lowered below the surface of the Mediterranean Sea. Over the centuries, a number of inventors, including Leonardo da Vinci, created submarine designs. American David Bushnell, in 1775, achieved the dual distinction of inventing the first submarine and embarking it on a combat mission. In September 6, 1776, his *Turtle* attacked and attempted to sink the HMS *Eagle* in New York harbor.

The Confederacy used submarines on a limited basis in the American Civil War. By the turn of the twentieth century, all the major sea powers had submarines. Germany, with its U-boats, was the first to use them effectively. The U-boat became the scourge of the seas in both World War I and World War II.

The development of a nuclear power plant small enough to fit in the hull of a ship made the concept of a true submarine possible. In its maiden voyage in 1954, the USS *Nautilus*, the world's first nuclear powered submarine, traveled 1,381 nautical miles underwater. Its second voyage took it beneath the North Pole. Since then, submarines have circumnavigated the globe while submerged. Submarine design has expanded into specialized areas, the most notable are the deep-sea exploration submarines such as the *Alvin*.

The submarine *Resurgam* out of water on the dockside in 1879.
It was lost at sea during early tests.

TORPEDO

Self-propelled, underwater explosive device used in Battle of the Atlantic

The word *torpedo* was originally used for underwater explosive devices that could be attached to ships' hulls. During the Civil War, it also applied to underwater mines. Though torpedoes are associated with a submarine weapon, they are also launched from airplanes, helicopters, and a variety of surface ships. The basic design for a torpedo includes a warhead, the triggering mechanism, a ballast compartment, fuel flask, navigation and depth instruments, and a propeller and propulsion system.

Their effectiveness in sinking ships caused all the major sea powers to design torpedoes. Arguably the most famous users of torpedoes were the German U-boats of World War I. Because U-boat torpedo attacks were so effective in sinking ships bound for England, one of the terms of the Versailles Treaty was a ban on German submarine construction. German U-boat torpedo attacks during World War II once again almost brought England to its knees.

The most famous torpedo in World War II was the Japanese Type 93, or Long Lance, the most advanced torpedo in the world at the start of the war. Among its innovations was a compressed oxygen propulsion system that did not leave a tell-tale trail of bubbles. American torpedo design lagged the Axis powers and did not improve until after a Long Lance torpedo had been captured and studied.

As technology advanced, designers began to create specialized torpedoes that incorporated individual sonar guidance systems to help guide them to targets. Previously, torpedoes exploded either on contact or with magnetic triggers set to explode once the torpedo neared a ship's hull.

The United States presently has four types of torpedoes in its inventory. The Mark 46 and Mark 50 are lightweight torpedoes (517.6 pounds and 750 pounds, respectively) designed for antisubmarine warfare. The largest and heaviest American torpedo (19 feet, 3,434 pounds) is the Mark 48, an ADCAP (Advanced Capability) torpedo designed to sink deep-sea nuclear power submarines and high-performance surface ships. The smallest (102 inches, 509 pounds) is the Mark 54 antisubmarine torpedo, designed for use in shallower littoral waters.

A steamer comes under attack from a torpedo during World War I

Radar/Sonar

Electronic detection devices used in the Battle of the Atlantic

RADAR (Radio Detection and Ranging) and SONAR (Sound Navigation Ranging) are acronyms for a diverse group of electronic devices used to detect the presence or location of distant objects. Radar is employed on land and in the air. Sonar is used underwater.

Radar systems fall into two broad categories: monostatic and bistatic. Monostatic is the most common. It has its transmitting and receiving antennas based at the same location. In bistatic systems, the transmitters and receivers are in two separate locations, often a long distance from each other.

Radar is based on the transmission of high-frequency pulses of electromagnetic energy by means of directional antenna. All the major belligerents of World War II were developing radar systems in the 1930s. When war broke out, Prime Minister Winston Churchill immediately recognized radar's importance and ordered a crash program to develop a sophisticated radar network. The network was completed in time for the Battle of Britain and played a decisive role in the British victory. Thanks to radar tracking of Luftwaffe formations, the Royal Air Force did not have to waste valuable time getting its squadrons into intercept position. An airborne version was developed and became an important navigational aide for nighttime operations.

Sonar uses pulses of acoustic waves to detect objects under water. An early form of sonar was ASDIC, Allied Submarine Detection Investigation Committee, developed by the British in 1917. "Sonar" was the American acronym for the system and the British adopted use of it in 1943. A ship equipped with sonar would send out a series of sound waves. Detection of an underwater object and the calculation of the object's location was determined through examining the time it took for the sound wave to bounce off the object and return to its source, as well as other factors including water salinity, pressure, and temperature.

Sonar spelled the difference in the Allied victory over the U-boats in the Battle of the Atlantic, for it denied the German submarines the ability to hide undetected deep in the water.

Personnel manning radar scope during World War II

Strategic Air Campaign over Germany

The Anglo-American "aerial second front"

Until its troops could return to Europe, the only way Great Britain could strike at Germany was through the air. Initially the Royal Air Force (RAF) staged bombing raids on targets in occupied northern France, the low countries, and western Germany.

American participation in the air war over Europe began in 1942 with bombing raids in northern France staged from bases in England. A campaign of "around the clock" bombing of Germany, with Americans attacking in the day and the British at night, commenced in earnest in 1943. The centerpieces of the American strategic bombing campaign were the B-17 Flying Fortress and the B-24 Liberator heavy bombers. American strategists believed their bomber squadrons were powerful enough on their own to successfully conduct long-range missions in daylight. Heavy losses from Luftwaffe attacks in the Schweinfurt raids in August and October 1943 caused a temporary end to the deep penetration raids. It was not until 1944 and the advent of the long-range P-51 Mustang fighter equipped with auxiliary external fuel tanks that the bombers would have the necessary escort to nullify Luftwaffe defenses.

The strategic air campaign occasionally suffered from shifting priorities in which different war industries and cities were targeted. Sometimes tactical needs, for example, in support of the Overlord landings prior to D-Day, overrode strategic considerations. The most controversial use of airpower was against population centers. The most egregious example of this was the destruction of Dresden, a city that had no war industries.

After the war, claims of destruction of strategic industries, particularly aircraft production, were found exaggerated. However, there were successes. The German natural and synthetic oil industry was virtually destroyed. In the waning weeks of the war, Luftwaffe squadrons were grounded and army tanks and vehicles were stalled by a lack of gasoline.

Most importantly, without Allied strategic control of the skies over Europe, the land invasion of the continent would not have been possible.

US bombers fly over the Ruhr after a raid on a synthetic rubber factory

Airplane

Pivotal weapon in the Air Campaign over Germany

When Orville and Wilbur Wright made their successful airplane flight on December 17, 1903, at Kitty Hawk, North Carolina, the air age was born. Though the United States was the first to develop the airplane successfully, it was among the last of the great powers to explore its military applications. During World War I, it had to rely on Britain and France for its warplanes.

The biplanes of World War I were flimsy contraptions. In the beginning of the war, airplanes were unarmed and pilots literally held flying duels in which they shot at each other using pistols, rifles, and even shotguns. When Anthony Fokker designed a mechanical synchronization gear that allowed a machine gun to fire through a spinning propeller without the bullets damaging the blades, the fighter plane and air combat was born. Though air warfare captured the public's imagination, it had little real influence in the conduct and outcome of the conflict.

During the interwar years, the gangly two- and three-wing aircraft of World War I gave way to sleek, aerodynamic, single-wing, all-metal, enclosed canopy designs. These and other innovations led to airplanes that could fly faster, farther, and higher.

World War II was the first conflict in which airpower played an integral and vital part of war-making strategy. Its use in combined-force blitzkrieg attacks on land rewrote tactical doctrine. At sea, its effectiveness in sinking ships led to aircraft carriers supplanting battleships as a navy's pre-eminent warship. Its ability to destroy targets deep within an enemy's territory caused a revolution in grand strategy, with no target too remote for attack.

Aircraft speed and performance were improved by the development of the jet engine and the incorporation of computer technology. Stealth technology, perfected in the 1980s, was a major innovation. Stealth aircraft have little or no radar signature. This makes them capable of attacking and leaving a target without detection. The first stealth fighter was the F-117, used in Operation Desert Storm. Some pilots were initially skeptical of stealth capability. They were convinced only after seeing the corpses of bats lying around their parked aircraft, indicating the obvious failure of even bat radar to detect the airplane.

German flying ace Heinrich Gontermann stands near his Fokker DR-1 tri-plane in 1917. The DR-1 was designed by Anthony Fokker, known as the "Flying Dutchman."

BATTLE OF SINGAPORE

Japanese conquest of strategic British colony

Singapore, a 21-square-mile British colony located at the tip of the Malay Peninsula, was acclaimed as an "impenetrable fortress" and the "Gibraltar of the Pacific." The reality was far different. The much-vaunted harbor defense artillery was in fixed concrete emplacements facing seaward. Fortifications on land were few and incomplete, the belief being that the jungles north of the city were impenetrable to troops and armor. The British leader responsible for Singapore's defense, Lieutenant General Arthur Percival, was a career staff officer who had never before commanded troops in combat. Finally, there was Great Britain's failure to adequately defend its far-flung empire after two years of war. Having to fight for survival in Europe and the North Atlantic and keep possession of Egypt and the Suez Canal, Britain had little to send to Singapore and Hong Kong.

General Tomoyuki Yamashita and his army landed on the Malay Peninsula on the same day Pearl Harbor was attacked. The Royal Navy attempted to interdict the landings with Task Force Z, composed of the battleship *Prince of Wales* and the battle cruiser *Repulse*. But both ships were sunk on December 10 by Japanese aircraft.

Yamashita's troops and tanks steadily moved south toward Singapore, through the jungle that the British believed impenetrable. Percival dithered as the British strategic position steadily worsened. Astonishingly, he refused to authorize either the reinforcing of existing defenses or the construction of new ones.

Aggressive Japanese tactics, complete mastery of the sea and air, and British lethargy and incompetence at the command level in Singapore created a scenario that could have only one outcome. On February 12, 1942, Percival ordered his troops to retreat to the island of Singapore and form a defensive ring around the city. Three days later, on the morning of February 15, he held a conference with his commanders. Percival stated that their choices were to either mount an offensive or capitulate. That afternoon, Percival led a party under the flag of truce, met with General Yamashita, and surrendered.

The loss of Singapore was a stunning blow to the prestige of the British Empire, from which it never recovered.

A British surrender party is escorted to General Yamashita's headquarters

DOOLITTLE RAID

The surprise raid on Japan launched from a U.S. Navy aircraft carrier

An Army B-25 takes off the deck of the USS *Hornet*, on its way to take part in the first U.S. air raid on Japan.

The morale of the American public had been rocked by the many Japanese victories following the sneak attack at Pearl Harbor. The Philippines, Singapore, Hong Kong, the Dutch East Indies (Indonesia), and other countries and islands fell like ten pins to the Japanese juggernaut. Within weeks, this new Japanese empire, that they called the Greater East Asia Co-Prosperity Sphere, stretched from the border of India east to the middle of the Pacific Ocean and contained almost one-third of the globe.

At that time, there was nothing the United States could do to stop the Japanese advance. American industry and the military needed time to rearm and train the men for war. But President Franklin Roosevelt realized that the military had make some sort of dramatic action—even a symbolic one—to boost the morale of the American people.

The Doolittle Raid became that symbolic action. Senior navy planners proposed in January 1942 that Army Air Corps medium bombers be launched off the flight deck of an aircraft carrier. Since the bombers couldn't return and land on the carrier after their raid, they would land on special air bases in China.

Army Air Corps Lt. Colonel James H. "Jimmy" Doolittle commanded the top-secret mission. In early April, sixteen specially modified B-25 Mitchell medium bombers were loaded onto the flight deck of the USS *Hornet*. With Vice Admiral William Halsey on the carrier USS *Enterprise* leading the escort, the fleet headed toward Japan. It was discovered by Japanese picket ships about 700 miles from Japan, which was on the outer limits of the modified B-25's range. But the decision was made to launch. The attack took the Japanese people by surprise. Though the damage was slight, the raid caused immense embarrassment to the Japanese high command and led to the decision to attack Midway.

Doolittle returned to the United States a hero and was awarded the Medal of Honor. Every crewmember of the raid received America's second highest medal for valor, the Distinguished Service Cross.

A navy divebomber flies by the aircraft carrier *Hornet*, the launch point of the bombing raid

WILLIAM FREDERICK HALSEY JR.

American admiral and fleet commander in the Doolittle Raid (1882–1959)

"Bull" Halsey, the son of a naval captain, graduated from the U.S. Naval Academy in 1904. His exemplary action as a destroyer patrol commander in World War I resulted in his being awarded the Navy Cross. Between wars, he served as a naval attaché in Germany, Norway, Denmark, and Sweden. In 1935, he qualified as a pilot at the age of fifty-two. From that point on he was deeply involved in naval aviation.

When the Japanese attacked Pearl Harbor on December 7, 1941, Vice Admiral Halsey's flagship, the aircraft carrier USS *Enterprise*, was scheduled to be in port. However, he was luckily about 150 miles west of Hawaii. In the early months of World War II, Halsey conducted a number of hit-and-run carrier raids against Japanese-held islands. His most significant mission during this period was commander of the Doolittle Raid fleet.

A serious ailment caused him to be hospitalized during the Battle of Midway. Upon release from the hospital, he was appointed commander of the South Pacific Area and promoted to admiral. In this command, he was responsible for naval operations supporting the Marine offensive on Guadalcanal, a difficult assignment that perfectly fit his tenacious, fighting temperament.

In June 1944, Halsey was transferred to command the U.S. Third Fleet, which would become the largest and most powerful fleet in U.S. history. Halsey alternated operational command of this fleet with Admiral Raymond Spruance. When one was at sea, the other was planning the next offensive. Fleet designations reflected the alternating commands. Under Halsey, it was the Third Fleet. Under Spruance, it was the Fifth Fleet.

During the Battle of Leyte Gulf, Halsey was fooled by the Japanese decoy carrier fleet and lured away from the Philippines, leaving the landing beaches at Leyte only partially defended. By the time he returned, the surface battle had fortunately ended in an American victory.

Halsey's flagship, the USS *Missouri*, was host to the Japanese surrender ceremony on September 2, 1945. He was promoted to the five-star rank of admiral of the fleet in December 1945. In 1947, he retired from active duty. He died in 1959.

Battle of Coral Sea

The first naval battle where the opposing fleets didn't see each other

USS *Lexington* as seen from USS *Yorktown*

The Japanese planned two offensives in the spring of 1942 to expand their island defensive perimeter in the Pacific. Operation MO in the Southwest Pacific called for the capture of Port Moresby, New Guinea, and Tulagai in the eastern Solomons to further isolate Australia. The second was against Midway Island, northwest of Hawaii, designed to lure the American fleet to battle and destroy it.

Operation MO was composed of two invasion convoys. The larger was targeted for Port Moresby. The second invasion force was assigned the capture of Tulagai. Protecting both were two carrier groups, one built around the light carrier *Shoho* and a second composed of the heavy carriers *Shokaku* and *Zuikaku* and their escorts.

Admiral Chester Nimitz, commander in chief of the Pacific Fleet, had been forewarned of the Japanese plan as a result of decoded intelligence. He dispatched to the Coral Sea an intercepting fleet composed of two task forces built around carriers *Lexington* and *Yorktown* and their escorts and a third composed of three cruisers and one destroyer.

The Japanese landed unopposed on Tulagai on May 3. The invasion fleet was attacked the following day by aircraft from the *Yorktown*, inflicting some damage.

For the next three days, both carrier fleets played a deadly game of blind man's bluff. The Port Moresby invasion fleet chose to await the outcome before attempting the invasion. A series of navigational and identity errors on both sides caused air strikes from the heavy carriers to hit secondary targets. The Japanese sunk the destroyer *Sims* and damaged the oiler *Neosho*, which later sank. American planes sank the light carrier *Shoho*.

Aircraft from *Shokaku* and *Zuikaku* found the *Lexington* and *Yorktown* on May 8, damaging both. The *Lexington* was later scuttled. Meanwhile, aircraft from the American carriers damaged the *Shokaku.* Though the *Zuikaku* was not found, the engagement had severely depleted its air strength. The Japanese fleets chose to retire and the Port Moresby invasion was canceled.

Though the Americans had suffered greater losses, by saving Port Moresby it had scored an important strategic victory.

USS *Lexington* burns during Battle of the Coral Sea

BATTLE OF MIDWAY

Battle that turned the tide on the Pacific front

Navy fighters during the attack on the Japanese fleet

Following the Doolittle Raid incident, Admiral Isoroku Yamamoto, commander in chief of the Japanese Combined Fleet, received approval for his plan for the invasion of Midway, a strategic atoll 1,135 miles northwest of Pearl Harbor. The primary objective of the attack was to lure into battle what remained of the U.S. Pacific Fleet and destroy it, thus presumably paving the way for a negotiated peace with the United States.

The main Japanese blow would be struck by Vice Admiral Chuichi Nagumo, commander of the First Carrier Striking Force, which was composed of the heavy aircraft carriers *Akagi*, *Kaga*, *Hiryu*, and *Soryu*, all carrying modern warplanes. Nagumo's dual responsibility was to reduce defenses on Midway and, more importantly, find and destroy the American fleet.

To stop them, Admiral Chester Nimitz, commander in chief of the U.S. Pacific Fleet, had a fleet composed of heavy aircraft carriers *Enterprise* and *Hornet* and the damaged *Yorktown*, whose squadrons flew obsolete warplanes. Yet Nimitz had one crucial thing in his favor: U.S. Naval intelligence had cracked the Japanese codes. He had complete details of the Midway operation.

Nagumo's First Carrier Striking Force attacked Midway at dawn on June 4. Inconclusive reports from returning pilots, coupled with no news of American carriers by his scout planes, caused him to order a second attack on Midway. Meanwhile, an American scout plane had located Nagumo's carriers and radioed their position. Though the range was extreme, the American carriers launched their squadrons.

The slow Devastator torpedo squadrons attacked first and were wiped out. Yet, their attack disrupted Japanese aircraft rearmament and drew down the defensive fighter screen. When the high-flying Dauntless dive bombers arrived, they were able to attack virtually unopposed. Within minutes, three Japanese carriers were in flames and sinking. The *Hiryu* survived long enough to launch an attack that severely damaged the *Yorktown*. A strike by U.S. Navy dive-bombers later that day damaged the *Hiryu* so severely it was scuttled.

Yamamoto canceled the invasion and retreated. Despite the later loss by submarine attack of the *Yorktown*, Midway was a decisive victory that passed initiative in the Pacific from Japan to the United States.

A composite illustration of the Battle of Midway

Raymond Ames Spruance

U.S. admiral and commander during the Battle of Midway (1886–1969)

The two most famous American combat admirals in World War II were William Halsey Jr. and Raymond Spruance. The two were a study in contrasts. Halsey, who became an aviator in middle age, was an "air admiral." Spruance, whose career was spent in the traditional big gun navy, was a "surface admiral." Halsey had a reputation for aggressive action; Spruance was a quiet intellectual. Halsey grabbed headlines; Spruance simply won battles. Military historians have since credited Spruance with being the most outstanding battle admiral of the war.

Spruance graduated from the Naval Academy in 1907. He gained increasing respect from his superiors and peers for his calm leadership ability as he steadily rose through the ranks in the years leading up to World War II. Spruance served under Halsey in the early months of the war and so impressed him that, when Halsey had to be hospitalized prior to the Battle of Midway, he recommended Spruance, who had absolutely no experience in carrier operations, as his replacement.

Spruance's role in the victory over the Japanese fleet at Midway established his combat reputation and from that point on, he and Halsey alternated command of the growing fleet—under Halsey, the Third Fleet; under Spruance, the Fifth Fleet.

Spruance, who became an admiral in February 1944, led the Fifth Fleet in offensive operations against the Central Pacific islands of the Gilberts, Marshalls, and the Marianas. It was during the First Battle of the Philippine Sea in the Marianas campaign in June 1944, that Spruance's aviators fought in the "Marianas Turkey Shoot"—an engagement that destroyed the last of Japanese naval aviation.

Spruance was working on plans for the invasion of the Japanese home islands when news of Japan's surrender was announced. Though Spruance did not get promoted to the rank of admiral of the fleet, which many believed he should have received, he was showered with many honors. After the war, he became president of the War College, a post he loved. He retired in July 1948, served as ambassador to the Philippines in the 1950s, and died in 1969.

US Navy Admiral Raymond Spruance (R) with his son Cmdr. Edward Spruance aboard the captured Japanese submarine *I-401*

SECOND BATTLE OF EL ALAMEIN

The British victory in Egypt over the Afrika Korps

Italian prisoners captured during the fight

Since 1940, the conflict in the desert of North Africa had been a see-saw campaign with first one side, then the other, ascendant. Then, in the fall of 1942, General Erwin Rommel, commander of the German Afrika Korps, reached El Alamein, just 60 miles west of Alexandria. It seemed that the Axis armies would finally win.

But Rommel's army was at the end of its tether. His men were exhausted, tanks and armored vehicles were in desperate need of repair and maintenance, and fuel supplies were all but depleted. He was forced to go on the defensive. Rommel ordered the construction of "Devil's gardens," elaborate minefields composed of a half-million antitank mines interwoven with antipersonnel mines. Rommel also redeployed his combined German and Italian units into six groups designed to counterattack any breach in the minefields. Once he was resupplied, Rommel planned to resume his offensive in Egypt.

Facing Rommel was the new commander of the British Eighth Army, General Bernard Law Montgomery. Montgomery was not only determined to deny Rommel victory in Egypt, he wanted to decisively smash the Axis forces. To do so, Montgomery abandoned all offensive operations until he had built up an overwhelming and superbly trained force. His battle plan called for an attack in two stages: Operation Lightfoot, a breaching of the German/Italian positions, fighting for about a week, and then Operation Supercharge, the decisive breakout.

Operation Lightfoot began on the night of October 23–24 with an artillery barrage. Initial progress was slow due to delays in penetrating the minefields. Rommel's counterattacks were contained by constant air strikes and accurate artillery fire.

Operation Supercharge kicked off on November 2. Within hours, Rommel saw that his army faced annihilation. Retreat began on November 2. The Axis retreat would not stop until the troops reached the Tunisian border. The British had finally achieved their decisive victory in the Western Desert.

British soldiers aim at a German surrendering atop his tank as a sandstorm clouds the battlefield at El Alamein

MINES

Passive-defense explosive devices used at El Alamein

Mines are designed to prohibit or restrict enemy movement. Originally, mine warfare consisted of tunneling beneath enemy positions and destroying them with explosives. A spectacular example of this occurred during the Civil War in 1864, when Union troops used 4 tons of gunpowder to blow up a Confederate position at Petersburg. Mines are designed for use either on land or underwater. They are small, relatively inexpensive, and require little or no maintenance.

Land mines fall into two categories, anti-personnel and anti-tank (the latter can also be used against lighter, less heavily armored vehicles). They can be detonated in a number of ways, including pressure, pull, tension release, pressure release, or electrical. More sophisticated triggering systems use magnetic induction, radio frequency induction, audio frequency, and infrared. The size can range from 4 ounces to 20 pounds or more. Land mines can be complex or simple. Guerrillas, terrorists, and other irregular forces have learned to make effective land mines out of anything. The improvised explosive devices (IEDs) used in Iran, Afghanistan, and elsewhere are just the latest version of these improvised—but no less deadly—mines.

Naval mines are underwater explosive devices designed to sink ships or submarines, or to prevent them from entering strategically important waters. The first naval mines were created in the 1500s. Their first use in naval operations was in the American Revolution. Because of their low cost, the Confederacy made liberal use of sea mines (originally called torpedoes) in its harbors. By World War I, naval mines were in widespread use by all the major sea powers. Naval mines are detonated by contact or by triggering of magnetic or electronic sensors that detect the approach of a vessel. Stationary naval mines either lie on the sea floor or are suspended from tethers of pre-set lengths. The types of moving mines include drifting and homing, deep-water mobile, and those that rise.

Historically, mines were distributed by surface ships. But as their design became more sophisticated, submarines and aircraft have included mines in their arsenal for specialized missions.

An inert land mine is being buried as part of a mine detection training exercise

BERNARD LAW MONTGOMERY

British Field Marshal and victor of the Second Battle of El Alamein (1887–1976)

British Prime Minister Winston Churchill called his country's most famous general of World War II "indomitable in retreat; invincible in advance; insufferable in victory." And, indeed, the brilliant and eccentric general could be appallingly arrogant, condescending, and downright rude to his fellow generals and superiors. At the same time, he displayed a dedication and devotion to his subordinates that earned him their enthusiastic loyalty.

Montgomery was the son of the bishop of Tasmania. Following his graduation from Sandhurst (England's West Point) in 1908, he served as a junior officer in the Royal Warwickshire Regiment. He saw action in World War I; he was severely wounded and decorated for bravery. His World War I experience left an indelible impression, and he vowed that should he reach high command, he would never commit the same costly mistakes that bled the British army white.

Montgomery was a division commander in the beginning of World War II and successfully led his unit in the evacuation at Dunkirk. He assumed command of the British Eighth Army in Egypt in August 1942. Montgomery's victory over the German Afrika Korps at El Alamein in November 1942 made him world famous and earned him a promotion to general and a knighthood.

Following the Allied victory over the Axis in North Africa, Montgomery led his Eighth Army in the invasion of Sicily and later Italy. In December 1943, he returned to England to serve as the overall ground commander in Operation Overlord.

Montgomery was promoted to field marshal on September 1, 1944, and appointed commanding general of British 21st Army Group. Montgomery's campaign in western Europe was marred by the inability to close the Falaise Gap and complete the encirclement of German troops fighting in Normandy, the failure of Operation Market Garden (September 1944), an attempt to breach the Rhine by a drive through the Netherlands, and inflammatory statements about the strategic command structure. This last point almost led to his dismissal.

After the war, Montgomery was showered with honors and held a number of high commands. After his retirement, he wrote what historians regard as a self-serving memoir. He died in 1976.

Field Marshal Bernard L. Montgomery watches General Kienzl
sign the surrender of German forces in northern Germany

OPERATION TORCH

The Anglo-Allied invasion of French Northwest Africa

President Franklin Roosevelt and Prime Minister Winston Churchill were acutely aware of their need to launch an offensive in the West as a counterpoint to the war raging on the Eastern Front between Germany and the Soviet Union.

When an assault on northern France was judged premature, Operation Torch, composed of three Allied landings in Morocco and Algeria, was adopted. Lieutenant General Dwight Eisenhower was appointed as the overall commander. The politics of the pro-German Vichy French government made British leadership of Operation Torch landings more risky than normal. Therefore, American generals would lead and American troops would provide the bulk of the initial landing forces.

A top-secret diplomatic mission to Morocco was conducted to try and secure a surrender of the Vichy French forces prior to the invasion. This mission ultimately proved unsuccessful. The landings occurred on November 8, with Major General George Patton leading the troops that landed in Morocco, and Major General Lloyd Fredendall and Major General Charles Ryder commanding the two landing forces in Algeria. Though the landings were successful, they revealed a number of shortcomings due to inadequate training and lack of experience. French resistance in Morocco and Algeria was unexpectedly strong and did not end until November 11.

When he received news of the invasion, Hitler ordered the occupation of nominally independent Vichy France. When the Germans invaded Vichy, the French forces fighting in North Africa had the excuse they needed to drop their arms. The capitulation of French forces thrust the American and British political and military leaders into the snake pit of wartime French politics that would be a source of chronic problems throughout the war.

Despite this, the goal of bringing American troops into the fight against Germany and opening a Second Front in the west had been accomplished. Within six months, the entire coast of North Africa would be in Allied hands.

American soldiers aboard small landing craft during opening hours of Operation Torch

Dwight David Eisenhower

U.S. general, supreme commander of Operation Torch, and president (1890–1969)

Born in Texas and raised in Abeline, Kansas, Eisenhower was the son of a failed shopkeeper and a pacifist mother. Eisenhower graduated from West Point in 1915. Because more than fifty members of that class would eventually become generals, it came to known as "the class the stars fell on."

From the beginning, superiors noted Eisenhower's exemplary organizational and training skills. These qualities caused him to remain in the United States to train U.S. troops who fought in World War I. Like his contemporaries who remained in the service following the end of the World War I, Eisenhower endured the drudgery of a peacetime army that offered little in the way of advancement and opportunity.

Nevertheless, Eisenhower put his time to good use, serving in the peacetime staffs of Generals John Pershing, Douglas MacArthur, and Fox Connor (who became an important mentor). In the months prior to America's entry into World War II, Eisenhower found himself on the fast track as a result of excellent staff work in the rapidly expanding prewar army. Promotion came quickly. When he was appointed the allied commander of Operation Torch, he was a lieutenant general.

Eisenhower's success in North Africa was followed by Operation Husky, the invasion of Sicily, and the promotion to full general (four stars). Not long after Sicily's capture, he left for England to be the supreme allied commander of Operation Overlord, the invasion of northern France.

Eisenhower's troops landed in Normandy on June 6, 1944—D-day. Eleven months later, on May 7, 1945, he accepted the unconditional surrender of Nazi Germany. Eisenhower, now a five-star general of the army, was the leader of the greatest army in history, composed of more than four million men.

After the war, Eisenhower served as Army Chief of Staff and later as the first commander of NATO—the North Atlantic Treaty Organization. He became the Republican candidate for president in 1952 and was president of the United States from 1953 to 1961. He retired to a farm in Gettysburg and died there in 1969.

George S. Patton Jr.

U.S. general and field commander during Operation Torch (1885–1945)

Patton was a flamboyant, profane, and controversial general of World War II.

Patton was born into a wealthy Californian family that had a long tradition of military service. Though the disability was unknown then, later studies indicate that Patton had dyslexia. After flunking out his first year, Patton later graduated from West Point in 1909. Patton's first brush with fame was in the Punitive Expedition of 1917 led by General John Pershing. When he became a national hero for killing one of bandit Pancho Villa's lieutenants in a Wild West–style shootout.

Patton commanded a tank brigade with distinction during World War I, where he was also wounded. Patton remained in the army after World War I and endured the career frustrations suffered by all who stayed in uniform. In the months leading to America's entry into World War II, Patton's career took off. Patton was a major general in Operation Torch in November 1942.

Patton was promoted to lieutenant general and given command of the American Seventh Army in Operation Husky, the invasion of Sicily. Patton's success in Sicily was overshadowed by the "slapping incidents" when he lost his temper and struck enlisted men in hospitals suffering from combat fatigue.

Patton was given command of a fictitious army as part of Operation Fortitude, the deception campaign to protect Operation Overlord. Patton assumed command of the U.S. Third Army on August 1, 1944. As their commander, he achieved his greatest success. The Third Army led the spectacular drive that liberated northern France in the summer of 1944. During the Battle of the Bulge in December 1944, he raised the siege of Bastogne.

Patton was promoted to general in April 1945. After Germany's defeat, Patton was appointed military governor of Bavaria, a position for which he was temperamentally unsuited. After a series of gaffes, he was relieved of his responsibilities. In early December 1945, he suffered a broken neck in an automobile accident. He died on December 21, 1945, and was buried in the American military cemetery in Luxembourg.

Lt. General George Patton (right)

GUADALCANAL

The first American offensive campaign in World War II

Amphibious tractors on Guadalcanal island

American strategists realized that the victories at Coral Sea and Midway had to be quickly followed up with an offensive campaign in the southwest Pacific in order to prevent Japanese consolidation of the region. Guadalcanal, on the eastern edge of the Solomon Islands, was selected in order to deny the Japanese the use of a landing field then under construction.

The 1st Marine Division under Major General Archer A. Vandegrift landed on Guadalcanal and four nearby small islands on August 7 to little or no opposition. The marines created a perimeter around the airfield, which they expanded and christened Henderson Field after a marine pilot killed at Midway. For the next six months, the two sides slugged it out like two heavyweight boxers in a vicious campaign for control of Guadalcanal. Seven major naval actions and at least two major land battles were fought. Japanese warships, known as the Tokyo Express, arrived almost every night to shell marine positions and land troop reinforcements. For large stretches of the campaign, the marines were on their own.

After surviving one of the most grueling campaigns in Marine Corps history, the marines were relieved in December by army troops under Major General Alexander Patch. In January 1943, Patch led 50,000 troops in a campaign to clear the island. The Japanese successfully evacuated 13,000 troops in a brilliantly executed operation. By February 7, the island was in American hands.

The cost had been heavy on both sides. The Japanese lost more than 680 aircraft, 24 capital ships, and approximately 30,000 men. The Americans lost about 7,500 sailors, marines, and airmen and 25 capital ships sunk.

But the Guadalcanal campaign proved American resolution in battle at a time when its forces were weakest. It also sundered the myth of Japanese invincibility. Within weeks, American ship losses at Guadalcanal would be replaced and new, larger U.S. Navy fleets would prowl the ocean. Unable to match American industrial output, the Japanese would find themselves fighting on the defensive.

American marines coming ashore from landing craft at Guadalcanal

BATTLE OF STALINGRAD

The turning point in the war between Germany and the Soviet Union

Memorial in
Volgograd, Russia

Germany's oil shortage caused Hitler to focus his efforts on the Eastern Front to seize the oil fields in the Caucasus Mountains. To protect the northern flank of this drive, the German Sixth Army under General Friedrich von Paulus was ordered to capture Stalingrad (present-day Volgograd), a major industrial and transportation center on the Volga River. In addition, Hitler knew it would be a major coup to capture to the city bearing Stalin's name.

German troops entered the city on September 12. By the end of the month, it appeared that the Sixth Army would soon complete its capture. But Stalin gave orders to hold the city regardless of cost. What commenced was a nightmare of siege warfare in which soldiers fought not only from house to house but also from room to room and floor to floor. Fighting in which no quarter was asked or given even extended underground to the city's sewers.

Both sides suffered horrendous casualties. In November, von Paulus, fearful of the approaching Russian winter, requested to withdraw from Stalingrad to rest and refit. But by this time Hitler had become obsessed with capturing the city and ordered him to stay and fight.

The Russian Red Army launched a counterattack on November 19 against the weak point of the Sixth Army salient, its flanks. These were held by troops from German allies Romania and Italy and were inadequately patrolled and fortified. The Soviet divisions easily smashed through the defenses. Within days, the Sixth Army was surrounded. Attempts to supply it proved inadequate. A counterattack to open a corridor to the trapped troops was launched on December 12. This relieving force got within 35 miles of the city before it was stopped.

Despite the bitter cold and unrelenting Russian attacks, the Sixth Army continued to fight. On January 30, Hitler promoted von Paulus to field marshal in an attempt to inspire him to continue holding out. By then the situation was hopeless. The next day, von Paulus surrendered. Fighting in Stalingrad finally ended on February 2.

Stalingrad was a disaster for Germany: The entire Sixth Army, more than 300,000 men, were lost.

Red Army troops storming an apartment block amidst the ruins of war-torn Stalingrad during World War II

TOTAL WARFARE

Use of all assets of a country to wage war

When a nation-state decides on a total warfare strategy, everything within the country becomes united and subject to one concept: the prosecution of war. The impact on a nation's economy can have devastating consequences. Anything having to do with civilian life, from home construction to consumer goods, is prioritized to war making. A government has to resort to creative forms of propaganda to keep the civilian population at the high level of patriotism necessary to endure such sacrifice.

Historians credit Union General William T. Sherman as the first true practitioner of total war strategy with his march to the sea that laid waste to Georgia in 1864. The industrialization of war matured in the twentieth century and with it the expanding definition of legitimate military targets. During World War II, total war strategy was conducted on the Eastern Front. There Germany and the Soviet Union waged a "scorched earth" campaign in which civilians and cities suffered incredible atrocities.

By the 1960s technological sophistication of aircraft, missiles, and other weapon systems had advanced to the point where no location within a combatant nation's borders was safe from attack.

When U.S. and Soviet Union atomic arsenal stockpiles reached the level of what was called Mutually-Assured Destruction (MAD). The two nations confronted the epitome of total global war in which the entire planet would succumb in a nuclear holocaust.

Women workers inspect Plexiglas nose assemblies in a
bomber plant in Long Beach, California

BATTLE OF KASSERINE PASS

American defeat in North Africa

Eisenhower, commander in chief of Allied Armies in North Africa, and General Honore Girarud, with French forces

The Allied offensives in Morocco and Algeria in the west and Egypt in the east had driven the Axis armies into defensive positions in Tunisia. German Field Marshal Erwin Rommel proposed a counteroffensive against American forces located around Kasserine Pass. The objectives were to prevent the Americans from linking up with British troops in the east, thus splitting the Axis positions in two; to capture the major American supply depot at Tébessa; and to cause the Americans to retreat back into Algeria.

When Rommel launched his attack on the morning of February 14, Valentine's Day, the inexperience of American troops—from the senior command level down to the frontline soldier—was starkly revealed. The II Corps commander, Lieutenant General Lloyd Fredendall, responsible for the front at Kasserine, had provided lax and poor leadership in the weeks following the Torch landings at Oran. Miscalculations in the interpretation of intercepted German communications prior to battle caused American and French troop dispositions to be strong in areas not threatened and weak where the enemy planned to strike. Later, Eisenhower, the overall commander, would replace his intelligence chief.

The German combined air, armor, and infantry attack came as a shock to the Americans. Though some American officers rose to the challenge and organized ad hoc units out of battered forces and tenaciously fought back, often from isolated positions, others were overwhelmed. Panic gripped Fredendall's headquarters, which fell into "order, counter-order, and disorder" which only contributed to the chaos.

The Germans were unable to exploit their initial success. They suffered from a lack of unified command and the fact that their two top generals in Tunisia, Rommel and Jürgen von Arnim, hated each other. Reinforcements and supplies promised to Rommel by Arnim failed to arrive. When American resistance began to stiffen, Rommel was forced to call off the attack and retreat back into Tunisia.

Kasserine was a bloody, though necessary, setback for the Americans. It taught them hard lessons about combat that could only be learned in battle. These lessons would be applied in the subsequent campaigns in Tunisia and Sicily.

Muddy boots of infantry soldier walking along road in Kasserine Valley

BATTLE OF TARAWA

Epic Pacific battle that was the first major test of American amphibious tactics

Wounded marines being towed out to boats for transport for treatment.

Following successes in the South and Southwest Pacific, the American offensive shifted to the Central Pacific and the Japanese-held Gilbert Islands. The primary target for invasion was the Tarawa atoll and its main island, Betio. As Betio was only 2 miles long and 500 yards wide at its broadest, the American high command recognized that new tactics had to be developed for amphibious assault of fortified beaches.

On the Japanese side, previous land tactics against American troops included mass rushes called banzai charges. The Japanese commander of Tarawa, Rear Admiral Keichi Shibazaki, broke from that pattern. Instead, the 4,500 elite marines under his command would defend the island from behind camouflaged and reinforced bunkers and other hidden fortifications. He boasted that his intricate defenses were so strong that Tarawa could not be taken by a million men in a hundred years.

Following a preliminary bombardment by ships and aircraft, the 2nd Marine Division commanded by Major General Julian Smith assaulted the beaches at Betio. Inaccurate gauging of the tides caused many landing craft to get hung up on coral reefs, forcing marines to wade to shore. Though the bombardment had severed Japanese communication lines, it had not affected the hidden and well-constructed fortifications. As marines waded through the lagoon, the Japanese defenders opened up with withering fire that caused heavy casualties. The marines that reached shore took temporary shelter behind a sea wall. Eventually, they established a shallow perimeter but the situation remained critical.

Reinforcements the next day allowed the marines to slowly continue their advance. At one point during the battle that day, Admiral Shibazaki was killed in his bunker. His death caused the surviving Japanese defenders to abandon his defense tactics. That night, they resorted to the old doctrine of banzai charges and were wiped out. Mopping-up operations continued throughout November 23. Three days after they had landed, 18,000 marines had conquered Tarawa.

Tarawa was the bloodiest battle to date. The marines suffered almost 1,000 dead and 2,391 wounded. Images of the battle's aftermath shocked American civilians.

U.S. marines advance between blasted tropical palms on Tarawa in the early stages of fighting on the Japanese-held atoll

BATTLE OF KURSK

The last major German offensive in the east

Kursk war memorial
in Russia

The Soviet offensive in the winter of 1942–1943 had created a bulge 118 miles wide and 75 miles deep in the German lines. Because the city of Kursk was roughly in the middle, it was commonly called the "Kursk salient."

German plans to eliminate this bulge were first floated in April and then debated by Hitler, his generals, and war production minister Albert Speer for the next three months. Intra-service jealousy, production problems with the new Panzer tanks, and Hitler's own indecisiveness contributed to the delays. Meanwhile, the Red Army built up its forces and constructed at the shoulders of the salient six defensive belts, each consisting of three-to-five lines of trenches. These lines were supported by elaborate minefields and rows of barbed wire. When the German offensive started, the Red Army had 1.3 million men, 3,400 tanks and assault guns, and 1,800 aircraft in position.

Operation Zitadelle (Citadel) called for a simultaneous attack at the shoulders of the bulge. The two German armies, marshalling 700,000 men, 2,400 tanks and self-propelled artillery, and 21,00 aircraft, planned to cut through the base of the bulge, and then meet and envelope the trapped Soviet army in the pocket.

Zitadelle began on July 5. Both German armies drove deep into the Russian defensive lines. The greatest advance occurred in the southern shoulder. On July 12, German troops breached the last defensive line in the southern shoulder. Units were quickly assembled to exploit the breakthrough and about 600 German tanks roared through the breach, colliding with the fresh Red Army strategic reserve. An eight-hour battle ensued in which about 1,200 tanks fought.

That night, the exhausted Germans on both shoulders retreated to their start lines. When Hitler received news of the Allied landing at Sicily, he canceled the offensive. A total of about 3,000 tanks fought in the operation, making it the largest tank battle in history. When it concluded, the back of the German panzer army had been broken and the strategic initiative in the east had irrevocably passed to the Soviet Union.

Soviet soldiers near a burning T-34 medium tank during the Battle of Kursk

OPERATION HUSKY

The Allied conquest of Sicily that precipitated Italy's surrender

Wounded American private is given blood.

The decision to continue the Mediterranean campaign in 1943 with a landing at Sicily was a compromise reached during the Casablanca conference in January 1943. Code-named Husky, the operation was plagued from the beginning by poor planning, unclear objectives, and lack of firm leadership.

Originally, the British Eighth Army under General Montgomery was to land at Syracuse on Sicily's east shore and the American Seventh Army under General Patton was to land at Palermo on the north shore. But, when the landings occurred on July 10, the Seventh Army landed at Gela in the south in order to protect the Eighth Army's left flank. This change aroused deep resentment in Patton, who felt that the Seventh Army was being deliberately kept in a secondary role. Less than a week after the landings, General Sir Harold Alexander, Husky's overall commander, endorsed Montgomery's request to shift the Eighth Army's western boundary to include an important interior highway in the Seventh Army zone. This decision reflected Alexander's lack of faith in American troops fighting abilities, confirmed Patton's suspicions, and led to the latter's decision to show up the British.

From that point on, the Allies waged two separate wars against the Axis in Sicily. Montgomery conducted the British war, slowly advancing up the eastern coast of Sicily. Patton led the American war with a dramatic thrust through central Sicily to Palermo. Then he advanced east along the island's northern coast. The objective—or "prize"—for both armies was Messina, on the island's northeast tip. The Americans won, capturing it on August 16.

Publicly, the Allied victory in Sicily was hailed as a great triumph. But the value of that triumph was diminished by Alexander's inability to maintain control over Montgomery and Patton, two notoriously headstrong generals. This inability to work together enabled the Axis to evacuate approximately 100,000 troops with all their vehicles and equipment. This failure would later haunt the Allies in the Italian campaign.

Italian prisoners in trucks clog the North coast roads of Sicily following the invasion

SUTJESKA OFFENSIVE

Axis campaign to destroy Yugolsav partisans led by Tito

Hitler had invaded Yugoslavia as part of his campaign to shore up Italian dictator Benito Mussolini's failing offensive in Greece in 1941. But the invasion proved to be an enduring headache for Hitler. Chronic strong partisan activity targeted convoys, wrecked trains and rail lines and tunnels, and attacked troop concentrations. Hitler ordered a total of seven major campaigns to eliminate the partisan threat. The pivotal campaign was codenamed Fall Schwarz (Operation Black) and resulted in the month-long Sutjeska Offensive in southeastern Bosnia in late spring 1943.

The primary target for the operation was the communist partisan leader Tito (Josef Broz) and his Yugoslav National Liberation Army of approximately 18,000 men. Fall Schwarz was an immediate follow-up to a similar campaign, Fall Weiss (Operation White), which had failed. This time, Germany organized a force of 300 aircraft and an Axis army of 127,000 men composed of German, Italian, Ustache (Croatian fascist), Bulgarian, and Cossack troops.

The Axis attack was launched on May 15 and scored a number of immediate successes. Tito and a large portion of his army were surrounded and the Germans began a steady advance to eliminate their foe. At the end of May, the British, who had been the primary supplier of arms and supplies to Tito and his men, managed to parachute two officers into the shrinking pocket to assist in a breakout attempt. On June 9, a Luftwaffe bombing attack killed one of the officers and wounded Tito. According to legend, Tito's life was saved when his German shepherd, Luks, knocked Tito down just before the bomb exploded and shielded his master from the bomb blast with his body.

Tito and his army made two breakout attempts in May that were repulsed. A third, launched on June 5, succeeded. Following the breakout, Tito reorganized his army and immediately mounted a new offensive in Eastern Bosnia that cleared much of the area of Axis troops.

Like its predecessors, Operation Schwarz had failed. It was the last of the big Axis anti-partisan offensives in Yugoslavia.

Serbians march captured German prisoners through a village

Tito (Josef Broz)

Yugoslavian communist partisan leader and president (1892–1980)

Tito was one of many aliases used by Josef Broz, a Croatian peasant, after he became a communist revolutionary at the end of World War I. Tito was active in the revolutionary Yugoslavian Communist Party in the interwar years. When Axis forces invaded Yugoslavia in April 1941, he was a senior leader in the party. Because a treaty of alliance between the Soviet Union and Germany existed at that time, Tito did little against the German-led invasion. When Germany invaded Russia later that year, he became a leader in the Yugoslavian partisan movement.

Essentially two wars were fought simultaneously in Yugoslavia during World War II: The first, against the Axis invaders, was called the People's Liberation Struggle by the Communists; the second was a civil war fought primarily between Tito's partisans and the Free Yugoslav Army, a pro-royalist group led by General Dragoliub Mihailovic. Initially, the British and Americans primarily backed Mihailovic and gave little or no support to Tito. But revelations from Moscow showing that Mihailovic was cooperating with the Axis powers caused that to change. By November 1943, the British and Americans threw their full support behind Tito and his partisans.

Tito's guerrilla activities were so successful that they tied down many German divisions that might otherwise have been used in the campaigns in Italy and France. Hitler became so enraged over the partisan activity in Yugoslavia that during the course of the war he ordered a total of seven campaigns designed with the specific purpose of capturing or killing Tito and destroying partisan leadership.

Tito proved to be a master politician, as well as brilliant military leader. Not only did he forge a coalition of diverse Yugoslav ethnic communities (some which held centuries-old blood feuds against each other) to fight the Axis, but he also successfully played the Allies against each other. Unique among partisan leaders, Tito liberated his country with a minimum of Allied support.

By the end of World War II, Tito's Yugoslav Communist party was the only viable political force in the country. In 1953, he became the country's president, a position he held until his death in 1980.

Operation Avalanche

The opening Allied campaign in Italy designed to exploit Italy's surrender

The capture of Sicily in the summer of 1943 set the stage for landings on the Italian mainland. When Mussolini was overthrown and jailed in August, the new Italian government opened secret negotiations to surrender before the Germans could occupy the country. But the Allies lost the opportunity for a swift *coup de main* by haggling over capitulation conditions. By the time the surrender was accepted, the Germans, already suspicious of Italian duplicity, had deployed thirteen divisions in Italy.

The invasion of Italy began with Operation Baytown, a British landing at the toe of Italy opposite the Sicilian city of Messina on September 3. This was followed up on September 9, with the landing of the American Fifth Army under Lt. General Mark Clark at Salerno. Hours earlier, the Allies broadcast the news of Italy's capitulation. Clark believed that, like the British landing at the toe of Italy, his troops would arrive unopposed.

He was wrong.

The Germans had anticipated Italy's announcement and had placed its Tenth Army in southern Italy. A panzer division was in the immediate area and fought the landing troops at Salerno with great skill, preventing them from expanding the beachhead. When sufficient reinforcements arrived, the Germans launched a powerful counterattack on September 12. The Allied situation became so desperate that plans were drawn up for evacuation.

But emergency countermeasures, including the use of the entire Allied air force in the Mediterranean to assist the beleaguered troops at Salerno, broke the German attack. When repulse of the landing had failed, the Germans began a slow retreat up the Italian peninsula, taking advantage of the terrain to hamper the Allied advance.

Salerno came within a hairsbreadth of being an Allied disaster. It was just the first of many examples of Allied missteps in Italy.

American troops wading ashore from landing craft during the invasion of Salerno

BATTLES FOR MONTE CASSINO

The controversial Allied campaign

Monte Cassino—officially known to the Allies on their map as "Hill 5126"—was key in the German Gustav Line of defenses in Italy. When the Anzio landing failed to dislodge the German defenders, Allied attention returned to conquering Monte Cassino, which dominated the area. The rugged landscape of the small mountain was ideal for defenders and a nightmare for attackers. In all, four major assaults were launched, sometimes under appalling winter weather conditions. All were repulsed, usually with heavy casualties.

The most controversial attack was the second one, conducted in the middle of February. At the summit of Monte Cassino was an historic Benedictine abbey. The German commanders in Italy had assured the Vatican that they would respect the sanctity of the abbey and not use it as an observation post or post troops within its walls. But General Bernard Freyberg, who was given the assignment to assault Monte Cassino with his New Zealand corps, insisted that the Germans had occupied the abbey. He demanded that it be bombed. His immediate superior, American Fifth Army commander General Mark Clark, was skeptical. But when the theater commander, British General Sir Harold Alexander sided with Freyberg and approved the bombing, plans went ahead for the abbey's destruction.

Days before the bombing was to begin, Allied aircraft dropped leaflets on Monte Cassino, urging any civilians in the monastery to evacuate. Many civilians, including the Benedictine monks, chose to take refuge in the subterranean chapel. On February 15, American bombers dropped 576 tons of bombs on the monastery, destroying most of it. The only two places undamaged were St. Benedict's tomb and the cell he had used. A number of the monks survived.

The bombing evoked worldwide outrage. Ironically, the bombing caused the very situation Freyberg sought to eliminate: Prior to the bombing, the Germans had not used the abbey for military purposes—but once it had been destroyed, they invested it. Ultimately Monte Cassino was not captured until May 17.

Reconstruction of the monastery began shortly after the war's conclusion and it reopened in 1956.

Smoke from atop the ridge where the ancient Abbey Monte Cassino is being bombed by Allied forces during the push to take the town of Cassino

BATTLE OF ANZIO

The Allied amphibious landing attempt to break the stalemate in Italy

Captured German soldiers on their way to prison camp

The Allied campaign in Italy in 1943 had become deadlocked. Repeated attempts to crack the German Gustav Line defenses had failed with heavy losses. To break this deadlock, Prime Minister Winston Churchill proposed an amphibious landing behind the Gustav Line that would crush the German defenses. The port of Anzio, on Italy's western shore, was selected. Plans were quickly assembled as landing craft in the Mediterranean were scheduled to leave for participation in Operation Overlord, the invasion of Normandy in the spring of 1944.

Codenamed Operation Shingle, the Anglo-American force landing at Anzio was placed under the command of Major General John Lucas. Shingle had many problems, some of which would almost prove fatal for the operation. It was hastily conceived, objectives were vague and contradictory, the forces involved were insufficient for any inland assault, and senior Allied leaders completely underestimated the speed and strength of the German response. Allied troops landed virtually unopposed on January 22, 1944. With no guidance from his superiors for offensive operations once ashore, Lucas concentrated on building up his forces on the beachhead before attempting to move inland. By the time he was ready, the Germans had fortified the Alban Heights, which overlooked Anzio, and created an impenetrable cordon of defenses.

Allied troops were continually harassed by German heavy artillery; they had to fight off repeated attacks to dislodge their bridgehead. Repeated Allied attacks attempting to expand the bridgehead were driven back with heavy losses. As the ensuing days turned into weeks, then months, Churchill, to his despair, discovered that now instead of one stalemate in Italy, there were two.

It was not until May 25—after the weather had improved sufficiently for offensive operations; after Lucas had been replaced by Major General Lucian Truscott, one of his subordinates; and after the forces had been substantially reinforced—that the Allied forces at Anzio were able to break out and link up with the American Fifth Army.

German soldiers lying dead in the street of Anzio

OPERATION OVERLORD

The Allied landing in France that opened the Second Front in Western Europe

Eisenhower meeting the troops before the Normandy invasion

Operation Overlord was originally planned as a three-division amphibious assault in Normandy. This was expanded to a five-division landing supported by three armored brigades, as well as three airborne divisions that would be parachuted behind the landing beaches. A deception plan, Operation Fortitude, was created to make the Germans believe the landing would be further east, at the Pas de Calais.

General Dwight Eisenhower was Overlord's supreme commander. British general Bernard Montgomery was the overall ground commander. Commander of the U.S. First Army was Lt. General Omar Bradley, who was assigned the western beach landing sites codenamed Utah and Omaha. Commander of the British Second Army was General Miles Dempsey, who was assigned the eastern beach sites codenamed Gold, Juno, and Sword.

Bad weather in the last week of May helped the Allied plan. Believing that it would prevent a landing, many of the top German generals were absent from their posts. As a result, German countermeasures in the initial hours would suffer.

A break in the weather allowed the Allies to land on June 6. The British landings went relatively smoothly. The most serious challenge was a German combined armor-and-infantry counterattack in the gap between Juno and Sword beaches that was beaten back before it reached the sea.

High winds, low cloud cover, and inexperienced aircrews caused the American airborne troops dropping behind Utah Beach to be scattered over a large area, causing confusion among the German defenders. The landing at Utah Beach itself went smoothly, primarily because a navigational error caused the troops to land at an undefended location.

Americans landing on Omaha Beach faced one of the toughest battles of the war. So serious was the situation that Bradley considered abandoning it. Eventually, American troops managed to break through the thin crust of German defenders and by the end of the day, the Allies had a firm, if shallow, hold in France. Finally, a Second Front in Western Europe was a reality. Within a year, Nazi Germany would be defeated.

US troops march up the beachhead, while landing craft in rear continue to unload supplies, equipment, and men

OMAR NELSON BRADLEY

U.S. general and commander of Operation Cobra (1893–1981)

Unlike the bold and brash Patton, Bradley was quiet, thoughtful, and a teetotaler. The man who became famous in World War II as the "G.I. general" was born in Missouri. Like many of his classmates, including Dwight Eisenhower, his choice of West Point was primarily to obtain a free education. He graduated with Eisenhower in 1915, the celebrated "class the stars fell on."

Bradley saw no combat action in World War I. During the interwar years, Bradley served in the typical variety of posts and attended the necessary military schools that were the prerequisite to high command. When the United States entered World War II, Bradley was a brigadier general and commandant of the Infantry School at Fort Benning, Georgia.

In Tunisia, he began his combat career as a II Corps assistant commander under Lt. General George Patton in 1943. When Patton moved on to become commander of the U.S. Seventh Army, Bradley led the II Corps to victory in Tunisia. Bradley and II Corps were part of the Seventh Army in the Sicily campaign. When the "slapping incidents" placed Patton's career in eclipse, Bradley, then a lieutenant general, was selected by Eisenhower to be the American First Army commander for Operation Overlord.

Bradley planned Operation Cobra, the American breakout at Normandy. In August 1944, he became commander of the Twelfth Army Group that included the First Army and Third Army.

As Twelfth Army Group commander, Bradley led the largest military force in American history. His troops liberated some of the most storied territory in France, including Paris. Bradley contained the German counteroffensive in the Battle of the Bulge. His troops had the distinction of being the first to cross the Rhine River, at Remagen, Germany. In the final days of the war in Europe, his troops captured Germany's Ruhr River industrial region, became the first to link up with Soviet troops (Torgau, Germany), and drove across the region almost to Prague, Czechoslovakia.

Bradley became army chief of staff in 1948 and chairman of the Joint Chiefs of Staff in 1949, and in 1950 he was promoted to general of the army, the last individual to hold five-star rank. He retired from active service in 1953 and died in 1981.

OPERATION COBRA

The American breakout at Normandy

French crowds cheer Allied troops on the Champs Elysées after the liberation of Paris

The Allies' elation over the D-day landings on June 6 had soon been replaced by frustration and disappointment. Incredibly, Overlord planners had completely neglected the problems forces would confront once the lodgment had been established. Thus, it came as a shock to everyone when Allied troops encountered the Norman *bocage*—a latticework of centuries-old hedgerows that were farm and pastureland property borders.

The Germans made masterful use of these natural fortifications to bloodily contest every foot of the American advance. Even in the more open area around Caen in the British zone in the east, the Germans effectively shut down the British advance.

By July 10, more than a month after the D-day landing, Lt. General Omar Bradley, commander of the American First Army, wrote that the Allies were facing the real threat that the Normandy campaign would become a World War I–type stalemate. To avoid this, General Montgomery, the British Second Army commander, and Bradley prepared two offensive operations—Goodwood (July 17) and Cobra (July 20), offensives at Caen and St. Lô respectively. After some initial success, Goodwood ended on July 20, having failed to achieve a breakout.

Cobra was delayed by bad weather until July 25. A massive air strike on German positions preceded the ground attack. Bradley was disappointed by the initial slow progress. But, by July 27, an armored thrust pierced the thin German line west of St. Lô. Bradley immediately pushed through the breach more and more troops and armored vehicles.

Finally, on open ground ideal for speed and maneuvering, the Americans advanced further in less than one week than they had in a month. By July 31, American troops had reached Avranches on the Atlantic coast, thirty-four miles southeast of St. Lô. Cobra had succeeded—the breakout had become a breakthrough.

The following day, August 1, the Third Army under Lt. General George S. Patton Jr. was officially activated. The stage was set for the breathtaking campaign across northern France.

American tanks carry infantry after breaking through beyond Saint Lô

STRATEGIC AIR CAMPAIGN OVER JAPAN

American air force campaign

More than fifty Japanese planes litter the airfield after Allied bombing and strafing raids

Because of the vast distances involved, attacks against the Japanese home islands did not commence in earnest until the gigantic long-range B-29 Superfortress bomber became operational in 1944. Initially B-29 air strikes were staged out of bases in India and China. But supplying these remote airfields was a logistical nightmare. When the islands of Guam, Saipan, and Tinian in the Central Pacific were liberated in the summer of 1944, B-29 operations were shifted there.

High-level daylight B-29 missions over Japan staged out of these islands commenced in November and continued for the next two months. Because poor weather and heavy cloud cover inhibited follow-up reconnaissance flights, results were difficult to evaluate. As a result, the decision was made to incorporate firebombing raids on Japanese cities that ware largely constructed out of flammable materials.

During January and February 1945, the B-29s flew a mixture of precision and incendiary raids. The success of an incendiary raid on February 25—in which about 1 square mile of Tokyo was destroyed—caused General Curtis LeMay, commander of the strategic bombing campaign over Japan, to make all attacks incendiary raids. In addition, he made tactical changes to increase their effectiveness. Instead of high-level daylight strikes where were plagued by high winds, clouds, and Japanese fighters, the B-29s would attack at night and at low level. This shift had the additional benefit of reducing bomber engine strain and fuel consumption, allowing for increased bomb loads. These changes had enormous impact on the air war against Japan. All of the major industrial cities came under such heavy incendiary attack that by the end of July 1945, LeMay's bombers had almost run out of targets.

When the Japanese government ignored the Allied ultimatum for surrender issued at the Potsdam conference in July, President Harry Truman gave the order to drop the new atomic bomb.

The nuclear bombing of Hiroshima and Nagasaki, followed by the Soviet Union declaration of war on Japan, forced Japan to surrender and end World War II.

U.S. Navy dive bombers conducting a raid over Japan

Henry Harley "Hap" Arnold

U.S. general during the air campaigns over Germany and Japan (1886–1950)

Arnold graduated from West Point in 1907. He was a lieutenant of infantry while stationed at Governor's Island in New York when he witnessed flying demonstrations by aviation pioneers Wilbur Wright and Glenn Curtiss. He promptly signed up for flying lessons. In 1911, he and Thomas Milling became the army's first pilots. Together they created the army's first flying school. During World War I he supervised all pilot training. Arnold was a supporter of air power advocate Brigadier General William "Billy" Mitchell. After Mitchell's court martial for insubordination, Arnold vowed to achieve Mitchell's goal of an air force as a separate branch of the armed forces.

In 1939, he was appointed deputy chief of staff for air. In this role he oversaw the most dramatic air force expansion in American history. In 1942, now a lieutenant general, Arnold's responsibilities were expanded to include operational control of America's air forces throughout the world. This made him the commander of 2.5 million men and more than 95,000 aircraft from trainers to strategic bombers. In March 1944, he was promoted to full general. Though still a part of the U.S. Army, Chief of Staff General George Marshall gave Arnold so much leeway that the air force was independent in all but name. In addition to his role developing independent air force doctrine, Arnold was closely involved in the development of strategic bombing doctrine. The high point of his work in this was the 20th Air Force, which used the B-29 Superfortress bombers against Japan and which carried the atomic bombs that destroyed Hiroshima and Nagasaki.

In December 1944, he was promoted to the five-star rank of general of the army. In the final months of World War II, Arnold suffered a series of heart attacks that forced him to retire before war's end. He lived to see his dream of an independent air force created in 1947. In 1949, he was made the first, and only, general of the air force—thus becoming the only American general to hold five-star rank in two branches. Arnold died in Sonoma, California, in 1950.

Battle of Leyte Gulf

The greatest naval battle in history

LST's pouring army equipment ashore on Leyte Island

By the fall of 1944, the Japanese navy was in an untenable position. Its aircraft carriers were hollow shells. Almost all of its experienced pilots had been killed in action. Diminished fuel stocks and increasing American naval air power made any action by its surface fleet a dangerous proposition. But when the Japanese high command learned that General Douglas MacArthur had landed troops on the Philippine island of Leyte in October 1944, it knew it had no choice but to counterattack. With Sho-Go (Operation Victory) it decided to risk everything in one titanic knockout blow.

Three fleets were organized. One, built around four aircraft carriers all but empty of pilots and aircraft, was a deliberate sacrificial decoy designed to lure Admiral William Halsey's mighty Third Fleet and its aircraft carriers away from the landing beaches. Once the carrier fleet had done its job, two powerful surface fleets built around battleships and heavy cruisers would attack from the center and the south, blast their way through the smaller American Seventh Fleet guarding the landing site, destroy the thin-skinned transports and supply ships, and bombard the beaches.

The Japanese carrier decoys performed their role to perfection. Halsey's aircraft spotted the fleet and the aggressive commander immediately began pursuit. The two Japanese surface fleets then commenced to advance. But the Central Strike Force never got close to its objectives. It was intercepted by major elements of the Seventh Fleet and forced to retreat.

The Southern Strike Force came closest to success. The other two Japanese fleets had succeeded in drawing away almost all of the major American warships. Only a small screening force composed of escort carriers, destroyers, and destroyer escorts stood in the way of the modern Japanese battleships, heavy cruisers, and destroyers. Though outnumbered and outgunned, the American ships put up such a spirited fight that they drove off the Southern Strike Force when it was at the threshold of its objective.

When the battle ended, the American navy had saved the landing force. The Japanese Navy was effectively knocked out of the war. Though individual ships would see action, never again would it fight as a fleet.

Crew of USS *Birmingham* using hoses to battle a fire aboard the USS *Princeton*, which was set ablaze by a Japanese dive bomber

DOUGLAS MACARTHUR

U.S. general during the Battle of Leyte Gulf (1880–1964)

MacArthur was the son of Civil War hero and Medal of Honor recipient Lieutenant General Arthur MacArthur Jr. He attended West Point, graduating in 1903 at the top of his class. During America's military intervention in Mexico in 1914, he served with distinction in the Veracruz Expedition and was recommended for the Medal of Honor for a hazardous reconnaissance mission behind enemy lines. The recommendation was downgraded to a lesser decoration. MacArthur would later receive the Medal of Honor during World War II. During World War I, he was promoted to brigadier general and made a brigade commander. He was wounded twice and received a number of medals for valor.

In 1919, he became the youngest superintendent at West Point where he enacted much-needed reforms. MacArthur was appointed army chief of staff in 1930. He fought congressional budget cutbacks with limited success. He retired from the army in 1937 and served as military advisor to the Philippines. He was recalled to active duty in July 1941, with the rank of lieutenant general.

When war broke out, MacArthur fought a defensive campaign in the Philippines. On March 11, 1942, under orders from President Franklin Roosevelt, he left the Philippines with his family for Australia. As Supreme Commander of the South West Pacific Area, MacArthur conducted an island-hopping offensive campaign. This culminated in 1945 with the liberation of the Philippines. He was promoted to the five-star rank of general of the army in 1945 and oversaw the Japanese surrender signing ceremony in September 1945.

Historians agree that his greatest achievement was as civil administrator of postwar Japan. He oversaw the writing of a new Japanese constitution, a transformation of Japanese society, and a restoration of its economy.

MacArthur was the leader of United Nations forces in the Korean War. His greatest success was the brilliant amphibious landing in 1950 at Inchon Harbor. He was relieved of command by President Harry Truman in 1951 following a dispute over war strategy.

Upon retiring from the army, he unsuccessfully ran for the Republican nomination for president (won by former aide Dwight Eisenhower). He served on the board of directors of a number of corporations. He died in New York City in 1964.

General Douglas MacArthur (center), General Richard Sutherland (left), and Col. Lloyd Lehrbas wading ashore during landing at Lindgayen Gulf

BATTLE OF THE BULGE

Hitler's last-ditch offensive in the west

A few of the many prisoners taken during the battle

1944

Victory fever had infected the Allies in the West. The German army had been thrown back to its borders in disarray. The air campaign had devastated its major cities. Soviet armies in the east were approaching Germany's border. Predictions were made of Germany's surrender by Christmas.

Thus, on December 16, 1944, it came as a shock when 1,900 pieces of heavy German artillery began shelling American positions in the Belgian Ardennes Forest, a quiet sector in the U.S. First Army zone used as a rest and training area for battered and green troops. Then, three German armies with 250,000 troops and almost 1,000 tanks and assault guns smashed into the dazed American soldiers. The front soon disintegrated.

Hitler had succeeded so well in hiding his buildup and plans that senior American commanders initially refused to believe it was an offensive. Many believed the fighting was just a spoiling attack. Bad weather, which kept Allied aircraft on the ground, further helped the Germans. By December 24, the Germans had advanced 65 miles, creating a "bulge" in the Allied lines that gave the battle its name. The Belgian city of Bastogne, astride an important road junction, was surrounded and its defenders led by Brigadier General Anthony McAuliffe, fought to keep it out of German hands.

As the picture became clear, Allied countermeasures began to take shape. General Dwight Eisenhower, the supreme Allied commander, ordered. Lt. General George Patton, whose Third Army was south of the Bulge, to stop his own planned offensive and counterattack. Eisenhower also temporarily reorganized the front around the Bulge, putting fighting on the northern half under the command of British Field Marshal Bernard Montgomery, causing resentment among some American generals.

When the weather cleared, Allied air strikes blunted the German advance. On the ground, the Germans were being pushed back. Shortly after Christmas, elements of Patton's Third Army had opened a corridor to Bastogne. By January, the front had almost completely returned to its original line. Hitler had thrown away the last of his experienced reserves and so helped hasten the end of the war.

BATTLE FOR BERLIN

The Soviet Army captures the German capital

Field Marshal Keitel
signs the ratified
surrender terms for
Germany

Adolf Hitler's Thousand Year Reich was, after thirteen years, in its death throes. In the east, the Soviet Army was 35 miles from the outskirts of Berlin. In the west, British and American troops had advanced deep into Germany and elements of the American Ninth Army were about 45 miles west of Berlin. The capital city of the Third Reich was up for grabs. But, on April 11, General Dwight Eisenhower, the supreme commander of Allied troops in the west, ordered his troops to stop at the Elbe River. Those who had crossed it were told to return. Eisenhower feared he would suffer at least 100,000 casualties attempting to capture a city that he believed had no military value. He informed Soviet premier Josef Stalin that the Russians would have the sole honor of seizing Berlin.

Three Soviet Army Fronts (army groups), composed of 2.5 million troops, 6,250 armored vehicles, and 7,500 aircraft were poised near the city. The best situated was Marshal Georgi Zhukov's First Belorussian Front in the center. The only large German force facing Zhukov was the depleted and poorly armed German Ninth Army. Beginning in March, Zhukov's men rolled across the last natural barriers to Berlin, the Oder and Neisse Rivers.

Hitler, having decided to stay in Berlin, issued irrational tactical orders to his field troops, which only succeeded in making the Soviet advance easier. Hitler ordered the Ninth Army to be deployed south of Berlin, leaving the path before Zhukov wide open.

On April 25, Soviet troops had surrounded Berlin. Scattered fighting between Red Army troops and desperate or fanatical defenders continued in neighborhoods as the cordon tightened.

On April 29, Berlin's military commander, Lt. General Karl Weidling, reported to Hitler that his troops would run out of ammunition the next day. On April 30, the same day Zhukov's troops raised the Soviet flag over the German Reichstag parliament building, Hitler committed suicide in his bunker nearby. Weidling formally surrendered the city on May 2. Less than a week later, World War II in Europe was over.

A German soldier sits on the ruins of the Reichstag in Berlin on May 9, 1945

BATTLE OF IWO JIMA

The bloodiest battle in Marine Corps history

Wounded Marines helped to an aid station

Iwo Jima is a volcanic island in the Bonins, about 575 miles southeast of Japan. Its strategic location between the B-29 airfields on the Marianas and the Japanese mainland made it ideal as an emergency landing base for damaged B-29s and as a staging base for P-51 fighter escorts.

It was defended by about 23,000 Japanese troops led by Lt. General Tadamichi Kuribayashi. Kuribayashi had constructed an elaborate series of well-camouflaged tunnels, bunkers, and other fortifications to defend the island. His plan was to let the American invasion force land unopposed. Then, when the Americans began moving inland, his men would open fire.

The invasion was preceded by combined naval and aerial bombardment that lasted seventy-two days but ultimately caused little damage. The assault commenced on February 19, when 30,000 marines landed at the narrowest part of the island. When the marines began moving inland, they came under withering gunfire that seemed to come from everywhere. Even the most innocent hummock was discovered to contain a well-hidden machine gun bunker manned by fanatic defenders.

On the third day, the marines had reached the base of Mt. Suribachi, the extinct volcano on the southern tip of the pork chop–shaped island. Two days later, the volcano was taken and the most enduring image of World War II—the flag raising on Mt. Suribachi—was taken by Associated Press photographer Joe Rosenthal.

From beginning to end, the Japanese defenders fought with incredible tenacity. One fortified hill caused so many casualties it was nicknamed "The Meat Grinder." The defenders' last stand was in a rocky canyon later called "Bloody Gorge."

A campaign expected to take fourteen days lasted thirty-six. It was the bloodiest battle in Marine Corps history, where twenty-seven Medals of Honor were awarded—half of them posthumously. In acknowledgment of the men who participated in the invasion, Admiral Chester Nimitz said, "Uncommon valor was a common virtue."

The famous flag raising at Iwo Jima

HIROSHIMA AND NAGASAKI

The atomic bombing of these Japanese cities marked the end of World War II

Col. Paul W. Tibbets, Jr., pilot of the *Enola Gay*

Operation Downfall was the American plan for the invasion of Japan. It was composed of two parts, Operation Olympic, the invasion of Kyushu, and Operation Coronet, the invasion of Honshu. But senior American military leaders viewed the amphibious landings with dread. They expected the Japanese to fanatically defend their homeland. American casualty estimates went as high as one million men. The one weapon America had that might cause Japanese surrender without an invasion was the atomic bomb.

In what would be the last meeting of the top Allied leaders of World War II, President Harry Truman, Prime Minister Winston Churchill, and Premier Josef Stalin met in the Berlin suburb of Potsdam in late July 1945 to lay the groundwork for postwar Europe and the final offensive against Japan. On August 16, the day before the conference began, scientists of the top secret Manhattan Project successfully tested a small atomic bomb at Alamogordo, New Mexico. Shortly after Truman received news of the successful test detonation, he issued a surrender ultimatum to Japan, warning that the country risked suffering terrible destruction if it did not capitulate. When this ultimatum was ignored, Truman gave the order to use nuclear weapons against Japan.

On August 6, the B-29 *Enola Gay* piloted by Colonel Paul Tibbetts, Jr. took off from an air base at Tinian. On board was the atomic bomb nicknamed Little Boy. It was dropped over Hiroshima, an industrial town of about 250,000 people, at 8:15 A.M. local time. The explosion created a mushroom cloud 20,000 feet high. More than 80 percent of the city was destroyed. Casualty accounts range, but it's estimated that at least 60,000 people died in or immediately after the explosion and at least another 60,000 died from radiation poisoning and other causes.

When the Japanese government refused to respond, the B-29 *Bock's Car* piloted by Major Charles Sweeny, who had flown an observation B-29 on the Hiroshima attack, dropped a second atomic bomb, Fat Man, on Nagasaki, just three days later. At least 100,000 people died in that attack.

On August 14, Emperor Hirohito announced Japan's surrender.

The use of nuclear weapons on Hiroshima and Nagasaki provoked controversy almost from the moment they were dropped—a controversy that continues to this day.

Neighborhoods in Nagasaki reduced to rubble by the atomic bomb

Atomic Bomb

An explosive device caused by nuclear fission used on Hiroshima and Nagasaki

The theory of nuclear fission, the splitting of the atom, was first proposed around the turn of the twentieth century. The concept of a nuclear explosion is simple. A radioactive element, such as uranium-235, is bombarded with a stream of neutrons until it "splits"—setting free the neutrons in its core. These neutrons then collide with other uranium-235 atoms, causing a chain reaction. But, while the concept is simple, the means of making the chain reaction occur is extraordinarily complex and expensive.

In the fall of 1938, scientists in Germany were the first to successfully split a uranium atom. The following year, Albert Einstein wrote a letter to President Franklin Roosevelt urging him to put America's resources behind the development of the atomic bomb as a counter to nuclear bomb research in Germany. Impressed, Roosevelt authorized the creation of the top-secret program to develop the atomic bomb, the Manhattan Project.

The distinguished physicist Dr. J. Robert Oppenheimer headed the Manhattan Project. On his staff some of the most respected scientists in the world, including Enrico Fermi and Hans Albrecht Bethe. Brigadier General Leslie R. Groves was the top army officer responsible for security. The Manhattan Project was a massive operation spread throughout the nation. The budget for the operation eventually exceeded $2.5 billion. The Manhattan Project was so secret that Vice President Harry Truman did not learn of its existence until after he became president following Roosevelt's death in April 1945.

On July 16, 1945, at Alamagordo, New Mexico, scientists successfully tested the world's first atomic bomb, whose explosive power equivalent was about 15,000–20,000 tons of TNT. Scientists had created sufficient fissionable material to make only two bombs. One, nicknamed Little Boy was composed of uranium and was used on Hiroshima. The second, Fat Man was a plutonium bomb and was dropped on Nagasaki.

As the only nation with the nuclear bomb, the United States attempted to retain a monopoly on its secrets. But, when the Soviet Union successfully exploded its first nuclear weapon in 1949, it was later revealed that the Manhattan Project had been penetrated by a number of Soviet spies.

People hurry past a fire burning in the wake of an atomic explosion in Hiroshima, Japan

BATTLE OF INCHON

The American amphibious landing in the Korean War

Watching the shelling of Inchon from USS *Mt McKinley*

The Korean War began when the North Korean Army invaded South Korea on June 25, 1950. A United Nations resolution was passed condemning the aggression and approval was given for the United States to lead a UN coalition under the command of General Douglas MacArthur to liberate South Korea. American troops garrisoned in Japan were rushed to help the South Korean Army. But the allied troops were often overwhelmed and had to continuously retreat. By September, only a small area, on the southeastern corner of the Korean peninsula around the port city of Pusan, remained in South Korean and American hands. The situation, though stable, remained desperate. Only through Herculean effort was American Lt. General Walton Walker able to defend the Pusan Perimeter, as it was called.

MacArthur decided on a bold move to seize the initiative and drive back the North Korean Army—by attempting an amphibious landing at the South Korean port of Inchon on the west coast and about 200 miles behind enemy lines. The obstacles and risks were formidable. Inchon's tides are the second highest in the world. The channel is narrow and easily blocked. Instead of a beach, the assaulting troops would have to scale a twelve-foot-high sea wall. But through force of his formidable personality and reputation, MacArthur prevailed against all objections.

Units of the 1st Marine Division landed at Inchon on September 15 following a preliminary bombardment. As MacArthur predicted, the landing took the North Koreans by surprise. The following day, General Walker launched a coordinated offensive, attacking the North Korean troops around the Pusan Perimeter. Afraid of being cut off, the North Korean Army began a swift retreat. Within two weeks, the South Korean capital, Seoul, was liberated. Approximately 30,000 North Koreans successfully made it back across the border.

The victory at Inchon elevated MacArthur's reputation enormously and made him the unchallenged master in charge of how the Korean war would be continued.

U.S. Marines landing at Inchon as battle rages during Korean Civil War

SIEGE OF DIEN BIEN PHU

The siege that ended French colonial rule of Indochina

Ever since the end of World War II, France had attempted to reassert its colonial rule in Indochina. Their main enemy was the Vietnamese communist guerilla organization called the Viet Minh. The Viet Minh had numerous sanctuaries in the region, many of them in Laos. Dien Bien Phu was a small village in a remote section of northern Vietnam near the border with Laos. The French military leadership in Indochina decided to establish a military post there to cut off one of the main Viet Minh invasion routes. An elaborate base, including an airfield, was constructed and fortified with 16,000 troops. Its purpose was to draw the Viet Minh army led by General Vo Nguyen Giap into a set-piece battle where it would be annihilated.

But the French commanders underestimated the Viet Minh and Giap. They also made a key strategic mistake. Dien Bien Phu is in a valley surrounded by high hills. The French did not establish outposts to control the high ground and protect their base.

Giap responded to the French challenge with a force of five divisions containing about 60,000 men, and artillery that was hand-carried up trails thought impassible by anything other than lightly armed troops. Giap's siege began with a massive artillery barrage on March 13, followed by the first of many infantry assaults. From that point on, the French base was under near-constant attack and shellfire.

The French believed that even if Giap cut off road access, they'd still be able to supply the base from the air. But Viet Minh anti-aircraft artillery soon made any such attempt suicidal.

As the siege continued, the French government appealed for military assistance and political support from its allies, primarily the United States and Great Britain. In a series of top-secret meetings, U.S. senior military leaders briefly considered the use of tactical nuclear weapons, a proposal President Dwight Eisenhower rejected. Ultimately, there was little desire on the part of both countries to help in something regarded as a lost cause.

The French positions were finally overrun on May 7, 1954. The surrender of the outpost at Dien Bien Phu marked the end of French rule in Indochina. Later that year, representatives of the French government and the Viet Minh met in Geneva and signed a treaty recognizing Vietnamese independence.

Vietnamese soldiers assaulting French positions at Muong Thanh airport at the Dien Bien Phu battlefield

SUEZ CRISIS

Military intervention that caused collapse of British government

President Dwight D. Eisenhower and Secretary of State John Foster Dulles discussing the Suez Crisis

Cold War politics, pan-Arab nationalism, and misplaced British pride all combined in 1956 to produce the Suez Crisis. In the early 1950s, Egyptian President Gamel Nasser, a pan-Arab nationalist, signed military aid agreements with the Soviet Union. When England and America refused his request for funding of the Aswan Dam, he nationalized the Suez Canal on July 26, and denied Israel use of the canal and the Gulf of Aqaba. Before that, the canal had been a British protectorate and international agreements guaranteed passage for all ships. British Prime Minister Anthony Eden believed that if Britain appeased Nasser as it had Adolf Hitler in 1938, Nasser's demands would escalate and war would break out in the region.

Eden began secret talks with the governments of France and Israel for a military campaign designed to reduce Nasser's influence. Israel would land paratroopers near the canal and send armored troops into the Sinai. Britain and France would call on both sides to leave the canal, when Egypt refused (as they expected), Britain and France would militarily intervene to "protect" the canal and eventually restore control to its antebellum state.

On October 25, 1956, Nasser signed a tripartite military agreement with Syria and Jordan. On October 29, Israel attacked Egypt and by November 5 had occupied almost the entire Sinai Peninsula. Following Egypt's refusal to evacuate the canal and after blocking a UN resolution condemning the fighting, British and French troops occupied Port Said and took up positions near the canal. Neither the British nor the French governments anticipated the international firestorm that then erupted around them.

The Soviet Union, in the process of crushing a rebellion in its satellite Hungary, threatened to go to war. A furious United States blocked a $1 billion International Monetary Fund loan Britain needed to boost its economy and applied other pressure. The rare unity of effort between the two superpower rivals, the United States and the Soviet Union, was overwhelming. Fighting stopped on November 29, 1956, with troops leaving shortly afterward.

France survived without too much diplomatic damage. Israel regained use of the waterways and received some other concessions. Great Britain was humiliated. Eden's political career was wrecked and his government collapsed.

A soldier on board a tank looks out over an Egyptian street during the Suez Crisis

MOSHE DAYAN

Israeli general during the Suez Crisis and statesman (1915–1981)

Moshe Dayan was born in the first kibbutz in Palestine at a time of Ottoman Empire rule. He joined the militia Haganah at age fourteen and he received training as a guerilla. During the Arab revolt of 1936–1939, he served in Yizhak Sadeh's ambush and patrol units. At this time, he also trained under the British unconventional warfare advocate Orde Wingate. He was briefly imprisoned by the British at the outbreak of World War II and was freed to assist the British in fighting the Vichy French in Syria and Lebanon. He was wounded in action on June 8, 1941, losing his left eye. Because he could not be fitted with a glass eye, he took to wearing an eye patch. As he rose in command and responsibility, the eye patch caused him to become one of the most recognizable figures in modern history.

Dayan's fortunes rose significantly following the creation of Israel in 1947. He was a successful battalion commander in the 1948 War of Independence. He also gained experience that would later serve him well in government through participating in some important high-level diplomatic negotiations.

In 1953, he became the chief of staff of the Israeli Defense Forces and, in that capacity, planned and oversaw Israel's campaign during the Suez Crisis. He resigned from the army in 1958 and entered politics. In 1967, he was appointed minister of defense just prior to the outbreak of the Six-Day War. Though Dayan did not plan the campaign, his efficient management of it caused his reputation to soar.

Dayan came under criticism for the military's poor response in the Yom Kippur War. He resigned shortly after the war's end. He later served as foreign minister and played a crucial role in the Camp David peace settlement between Israel and Egypt. He retired in 1979 and died two years later in Tel Aviv.

TONKIN GULF INCIDENT

Clash that led to America's entry into the Vietnam War

President Lyndon B. Johnson signs Gulf of Tonkin resolution

As part of its low-level military assistance to the South Vietnamese government, the U.S. Navy conducted intelligence-gathering missions in the Tonkin Gulf off the North Vietnamese coast. Though officially conducted in international waters, the electronic warfare missions, codenamed DeSoto, were provocative in nature. Ships often deliberately entered North Vietnamese territorial waters to gather intelligence about radar defenses and other capabilities.

On the night of August 1–2, the destroyer *Maddox* entered within range of coastal defenses and was attacked by North Vietnamese patrol boats. On August 4, the *Maddox* and a sister destroyer *C. Turner Joy* reported attacks by torpedo boats. A later investigation revealed that a combination of factors, including weather conditions, sea conditions, and the inexperience of a number of the officers on both ships, indicated that the second attack may not have occurred at all.

Based on initial reports, President Lyndon Johnson petitioned Congress to give him the authority to retaliate. Specifically, he requested that Congress pass a resolution giving him the authority to conduct military operations in Vietnam—in effect, to wage undeclared war.

Johnson and his staff convinced Congress that the intent of the resolution was actually *not* to wage undeclared war, simply to retaliate against Communist aggression and to shore up the democratic government of South Vietnam. Johnson assured Congress that he had no intentions of increasing America's involvement in Vietnam. This incident, however, led to an increased involvement of U.S. military forces in Vietnam.

Years later, it was revealed that the Johnson administration withheld evidence and deliberately misrepresented and overstated details of the incidents.

The USS *Coral Sea* waiting "on station" in the Gulf of Tonkin during the Vietnam War

SIX-DAY WAR

Israeli victory that changed regional balance of power

As a small, narrow country surrounded by hostile nations, Israel's vulnerable geography dictates its strategy of survival. In May 1967, it faced one of its greatest crises ever. Egypt had kicked out the peacekeeping United Nations Emergency Force. Together with Syria and Jordan, it had mobilized its army. Israel was surrounded by 250,000 troops, more than 2,000 tanks and 700 front-line aircraft. Simultaneously, the Soviet Union and the Arab league had succeeded in diplomatically isolating Israel. With Egypt's leader, President Gamel Nasser, proclaiming he would destroy Israel, other Arab states sent contingents in support. Israeli Defense Minister General Moshe Dayan stated that Israel's survival depended on a pre-emptive strike. If they waited for their enemies to attack, Israel risked being overwhelmed.

At 7:45 A.M. June 5, 1967, fighters and fighter-bombers from the Israeli Air Force launched surprise attacks against the powerful Egyptian Air Force (EAF) and its airfield. The first strikes were timed to arrive while the pilots were having breakfast and operations continued for the next three hours. After the EAF had been crippled, operations expanded to include the smaller Jordanian and Syrian air forces.

On land, the Israeli Defense Force commenced offensive operations against Egypt in the Sinai Peninsula, against Jordan in the West Bank, and against Syria in the Golan Heights. The fact that Israel had established air superiority over the region in the opening hours of the war proved decisive. Within days, Israeli troops found themselves on the banks of the Suez Canal in the west and the banks of the Jordan River in the east. In the north, it held the strategic Golan Heights. And, for the first time in living memory, the divided Holy City of Jerusalem was completely in Israeli hands.

The Arab world had suffered a crushing defeat and had been enormously humiliated. Hostilities ceased on June 10 but attempts to create a lasting peace failed. The combination of Cold War politics through Soviet Union intrigues and Arab unwillingness to address the many unresolved issues in the region made it inevitable that another war would occur.

Israeli soldiers at the Wailing Wall in Jerusalem

THE TET OFFENSIVE

The strategic communist military campaign in South Vietnam

Refugees fleeing the fighting in Hue

Tet is the Vietnamese Lunar New Year holiday. Previously, both sides in the war agreed upon a truce to allow civilians to celebrate the most important holiday in the Vietnamese calendar. Though scattered fighting occasionally broke out, the truces were generally respected. As the 1968 Tet holiday approached, the North Vietnamese high command proposed an all-out offensive throughout South Vietnam. Key government sites and military bases were targeted. Radio stations would be seized and announcements would be made exhorting the South Vietnamese peasants to rise up against their corrupt government and join the communists. When that happened, it was assumed that the American forces would be forced to leave.

The offensive began on January 31. The American military high command had received advance warning, so it was not totally surprised. The guerilla Viet Cong was the primary military force in the Tet Offensive. As planned, Viet Cong units attacked military bases and government buildings throughout the country. One of the most publicized attacks was the assault on the U.S. embassy in the South Vietnam capital of Saigon. Though the embassy's outer wall was breached and some Viet Cong entered the courtyard, all Communist troops were killed before they reached the embassy building itself.

To the Communists' surprise, the popular uprising that was key to their offensive never occurred. The peasants sided with their government. In fact, militarily, the Tet Offensive was a colossal failure. Not one of their military objectives was attained.

Yet, the Communists won. News reports of the attacks that were aired on American network television stations conveyed a story of a powerful attack that indicated the enemy was about to win. The dramatic images of the fighting, particularly of the aftermath of the attack on the U.S. embassy, shocked the American public. Popular support for the war evaporated. Demands for an end to the war following the Tet offensive became irresistible.

A female Viet Cong soldier in action with an anti-tank gun during a fighting in southern Cuu Long delta

YOM KIPPUR WAR

Regional conflict that almost caused World War III

Ever since their defeat in the Six-Day War , Egypt, Jordan, and Syria had vowed to win back the territory they had lost. Periodically diplomatic efforts were attempted but prejudice, confrontational rhetoric, Cold War politics, and some outright mistakes caused all to fail.

In 1973, Egypt again announced that war was imminent with Israel and troops in Egypt and Syria began moving into forward positions. Israeli troops were mobilized on October 5 in a defensive response—but orders for a pre-emptive strike like the one beginning the Six-Day War were not issued because the diplomatic consequences were considered too great.

The next day, on Yom Kippur, the holiest day in the Jewish calendar—and during the Muslim holy month of Ramadan—Egypt and Syria attacked. The Arab oil-producing states intervened on the international front and, using oil as a weapon of war, imposed an oil embargo on the United States, Portugal, and Holland for their support of Israel. Petroleum shortages shook those nations. Even though many Arab states once again contributed men, arms, and financial support, this time Jordan chose to remain neutral. The decision freed Israel to shift its troops to meet the attacks in the north and south.

Meanwhile, the regional conflict soon became a test of superpower resolution as the United States and the Soviet Union began shipping arms to their respective allies. After recovering from the initial attack, Israel launched counteroffensives. On October 14, in the greatest tank battle since Kursk, Israeli armor destroyed more than 250 Egyptian tanks and routed the enemy. In the north, Israeli troops had defeated the Syrian army and was marching toward Damascus. Israel was winning the war. Tensions escalated between the Soviet Union and the United States for two weeks as they mobilized their military and exchanged high-level messages. At one point, the use of nuclear weapons was threatened.

Fortunately, cooler heads prevailed and the combatants accepted a cease-fire. Fighting ended on October 26. Egypt achieved its goal of the recovery of the Sinai through diplomatic means in 1979.

Mechanized column advancing through the Golan Heights

OPERATION EAGLE CLAW

Failed rescue of American hostages in Tehran

President Jimmy Carter announces new sanctions against Iran in retaliation for taking U.S. hostages

On November 4, 1979, a group of Iranian students stormed the U.S. embassy in Tehran and took hostage all of the Americans in the compound. Their purpose was twofold: to force the United States to return the exiled Shah of Iran; and to find documents to support their belief in a CIA-backed plot to overthrow the new, revolutionary government led by the cleric Ayatollah Ruholla Khomeini. While President Jimmy Carter attempted through diplomatic channels to free the hostages, he also authorized a top-secret military plan to extract them. Codenamed Operation Eagle Claw, it was a joint-force mission of enormous complexity that almost succeeded.

Training for the operation began almost immediately after the hostages were taken. Because no one organization or branch was capable at that time of executing the mission, it became a hodge-podge of combined operations. Personnel, weapons, equipment, and aircraft were obtained by hook, crook, begging, and outright threat. It mixed navy and marine helicopter crews, army and air force commandos, and CIA personnel, among others. Most important of all were the helicopters needed to extract the hostages.

The men, aircraft, and fleet were in place in early April. President Carter did not give final approval until April 16. On the night of April 24, tanker/transports from a secret base in Muscat Island and eight helicopters on the aircraft carrier USS *Nimitz* took off toward a rendezvous site in a remote section of Iran codenamed Desert One. The tanker/transports arrived first. Six of the eight helicopters arrived one hour late. Then, as preparations were being made for the next stage of the mission, one of the helicopters at Desert One shut down. Five helicopters were too few to successfully complete the mission. The order was given to abort. As the aircraft prepared to depart, one helicopter crashed into one of the tanker/transports and both aircraft exploded, killing eight. The rest managed to fly out safely.

President Carter publicly accepted full responsibility for the mission's failure, and the public repaid him by voting him out of office. The hostages were released the day after the United States signed of the Algiers Accords in Algeria on January 19, 1981. Operation Eagle Claw's failure led to the eventual creation of the joint-service Special Operations Command.

Helicopters take off from the deck of the USS *Nimitz* to attempt the rescue of American hostages

FALKLANDS WAR

Undeclared war between Argentina and Great Britain

The Falkland Islands is a small group of islands located in the South Atlantic Ocean, about 400 miles off the southern tip of Argentina. It is disputed territory ruled by Great Britain and claimed by Argentina. When the Argentine economy fell into crisis, the ruling military junta launched a campaign to retake the Malvinas (the Argentine name for the island group), thus diverting public attention. An Argentine invasion force seized the islands on April 2, 1982. British Prime Minister Margaret Thatcher's government was taken by surprise. The British government first learned the news of the invasion from a ham radio operator message.

As the junta expected, a wave of patriotic fervor swept the nation and the economic crisis was forgotten. An important part of the junta's calculations was the belief that Britain would accept the seizure as a fait accompli and not attempt any military response. They were wrong.

Patriotic feelings also ran high in Great Britain over the "outrageous attack." The Thatcher government ordered a naval task force to take the islands back. The counter-invasion assault included air, sea, and land battles. The British submarine *Conqueror* sunk the Argentine light cruiser *General Belgrano*, the only ship to be sunk in battle by a nuclear-powered submarine. The loss of the *Belgrano* caused the rest of the Argentine fleet to return to port.

The Argentine air force would prove more effective, sinking two destroyers and sinking and damaging nine other ships with air-to-surface missiles.

British SAS reconnaissance teams began secretly landing on the islands in the middle of May. This was followed up with British commando landings on May 20 and 21. Ground operations commenced and, after about two weeks of fighting, the Argentine troops on the Falklands surrendered.

Reaction in Argentina was swift. The public turned on the junta with a vengeance. Ongoing protests forced the junta out of office in 1983. In Britain, the war restored Prime Minister Thatcher's flagging popularity and her party handily won the 1983 election. Though sovereignty of the islands remains a touchy issue, relations between the two countries eventually normalized.

British Royal Navy frigate HMS *Antelope* explodes in the bay of San Carlos off East Falkland during the Falklands War

MISSILES AND ROCKETS
Self-propelled weapons used during the Falklands War

Rockets are not a recent invention. The Chinese used gunpowder-powered rockets as early as 300 B.C. Tipu Sultan of Mysore used the first iron rockets against the British in 1798. Sir William Congreve used samples of these rockets to develop one for the British military use in 1803. The Congreve Rocket became incorporated into America's heritage (though anonymously) when Francis Scott Key wrote the phrase "rocket's red glare" for the "Star Spangled Banner" poem during the War of 1812, which became the national anthem.

Missiles are categorized as air-to-air, air-to-surface, anti-radar, anti-ship, and airborne anti-tank guided missiles. They are either fire-and-forget, which allows the shooter to move or leave once the missile is launched, or wire-guided, which means the shooter has to keep his launch weapon aimed at the target until impact.

Air-to-air missiles were first used in World War I. French Lieutenant Y. P. G. Le Prieur invented them for use by the French and British air forces against German Zeppelins and observation balloons. Today, air-to-air missiles come in a variety of sizes, are capable of supersonic speeds exceeding Mach 4, and have a range of more than 30 miles.

Air-to-surface missiles saw widespread use in World War II. The most extreme example of an air-to-surface missile was the Japanese Ohka kamikaze aircraft launched from Mitsubishi "Betty" bombers.

Antiradar missiles were first used in the Vietnam War. Specially trained Air Force squadrons known as "Wild Weasels" were trained to attack and destroy Soviet-built North Vietnamese radars used to direct surface-to-air missiles in what amounted to a deadly game of "chicken."

Anti-ship missiles, usually fired from aircraft, are designed to penetrate the thick, armored hull of a ship before exploding. The French Exocet missile became famous during the Falklands War when Argentine fighters used the Exocet to sink two Royal Navy ships.

Airborne anti-tank guided missiles were first used in World War II. The American bazooka and German panzerfaust were the most famous. Today, the American military uses the Javelin, a fire-and-forget missile, which was used in combat for the first time in the Battle of Debecka Pass during the Second Gulf War.

Illustration of the battle of Fort McHenry, the scene of "the rockets' red glare"

Operation Eager Anvil

Special Operations Mission that preceded Operation Desert Storm

A squadron of planes patrolling the mountains

In August 1990, Iraq invaded and annexed its smaller neighbor Kuwait—an action promptly condemned by the United States and other nations. Within a week, a U.S.-led coalition army, commanded by General H. Norman Schwarzkopf, was deployed to Saudi Arabia. The campaign to liberate Kuwait broke into two stages, Operation Desert Shield, the protection of Saudi Arabia and buildup of troop strength, and Operation Desert Storm, the attack. Preceding the ground assault would be an air campaign. But before air operations could begin, part of the elaborate radar "fence" along the Iraq–Saudi border had to be knocked out. The mission to do that was codenamed Operation Eager Anvil.

Task Force Normandy, composed of two teams of Apache and Black Hawk helicopters from the 101st Airborne Division and the 20th Special Operations Squadron, lifted off from its forward operating base in northwest Saudi Arabia at 12:56 A.M. on January 17. Operation Eager Anvil called for the helicopters to fly at night using Night Vision Devices and Global Positioning System trackers near ground level, below the Iraqi radar, and annihilate two strategic Iraqi radar defense outposts, codenamed Objective California and Objective Nevada. The sites were 29 miles apart and each was about the size of a football field and well defended. The air campaign for Operation Desert Storm was timed to begin at 2:39 A.M. If Task Force Normandy didn't complete its mission as scheduled, the coalition's air squadrons would encounter a fully functioning and alert Iraqi defense system.

The teams reached their attack positions at 2:37 A.M. At 2:38 A.M., the pilots received over their headsets the order, "Party in ten." Sixteen Hellfire missiles rocketed out of helicopter launch tubes at Mach I. The American helicopters then bored in. Within four minutes, the mission was over. As the helicopters began their return trip, they radioed to the waiting squadrons the messages: "California. Alpha, Alpha. Nevada. Alpha. Alpha."—Both objectives were completely destroyed.

The attack and bomber squadrons raced through the gap in the radar defenses undetected and unopposed, fanned out, and commenced an assault of the rest of Iraq's radar defenses later dubbed "Poobah's Party." By sunrise, Iraq's radar network had been eliminated and the coalition had total air supremacy.

Military helicopter landing in desert

NIGHT-VISION DEVICE (NVD)

Vision-enhancing optical instrument used in Operation Eager Anvil

Historically, combat operations suffer a significant drop-off in effectiveness once the sun sets. The reason, of course, is that soldiers can't see in darkness. Over the centuries, commanders tried various methods to increase individual effectiveness during nighttime operations. As late as World War II, the Imperial Japanese Navy used special binoculars and sailors with superior night vision as lookouts on their ships. Artificial illumination methods from torches to searchlights were limited in their usefulness. It was not until the 1950s that technology had advanced sufficiently to provide man-portable optical devices to "turn" night into day.

Modern night-vision devices (NVDs), sometimes also known as night-vision goggles or NVGs, are sufficiently sophisticated tools that give fighters the ability to see, maneuver, and shoot at night or during periods of reduced visibility. Night-vision goggles are electro-optical devices that intensify ambient light in both the visible and infrared spectrum thousands of times by electronic means. Users do not look through NVGs as they would binoculars. Rather, the viewer looks at an amplified electronic image projected on a phosphor screen.

Though NVDs have enhanced a soldier's ability to conduct night operations, they are not the same as human eyesight in daylight. Images are monochromatic, either shades of electric green or gray. Field of view in NVDs is just 40 degrees (normal eyesight is almost 190 degrees), so the effect is like looking down a tunnel. Image sharpness is degraded, causing even objects nearby to look out of focus. Depth of field is hampered. Normal human vision is stereoscopic or two-eyed. NVG vision is essentially monocular, or one-eye, vision. This creates problems in judging distances of objects, particularly if they overlap or are beside each other and if one is significantly larger.

Yet, even with these limitations, Special Operations troops have become so proficient in the use of NVDs and NVGs that they prefer to conduct all their operations in the hours of darkness and have adopted the motto: "We own the night."

Using night vision goggles a U.S. Marine looks down a dark street while on a search operation for insurgents in the early hours of February 1, 2007 in Ramadi in Iraq's Anbar province

GLOBAL POSITIONING SYSTEM (GPS)

Satellite-based worldwide navigational system used in Operation Eager Anvil

Like the compass and the sextant, the global positioning system (almost always referred to as "GPS") is one of the greatest technological achievements in navigation. The heart of the system is an array of at least twenty-four navigation satellites (the exact number varies) orbiting Earth. These satellites constantly transmit precise microwave signals to the planet. An individual possessing a GPS receiver can use these signals to determine his location on the planet with extraordinary exactness.

GPS was developed by the United States Department of Defense and was originally only used by the military. When Korean Air Lines Flight 007 was shot down in 1983 as the result of faulty navigation that caused it to accidentally enter Soviet airspace, President Ronald Reagan directed the system be made available free for civilian use. In addition to navigation, it has become an important tool in other fields where accuracy is a premium, particularly mapmaking, surveying, telecommunications, and science. One example of GPS applications is that cellular phone makers now make phones that contain GPS chips.

A ground location is determined by the triangulated reception of signals from at least three satellites. The GPS receiver analyses the data from these satellites and then computes both location and time.

For the military, GPS has been particularly useful on the battlefield, where it allows commanders to know constantly the locations of units down to the individual soldier or vehicle. This has the additional application of helping reduce incidences of casualties as a result of so-called friendly fire. GPS has also proved valuable in search and rescue operations. One of the more famous uses of GPS was in the rescue of Air Force captain Scott O'Grady in 1995. O'Grady was shot down over Bosnia and trapped in hostile territory. A rescue force was able to extract O'Grady in a minimum amount of time thanks to location information provided by O'Grady's portable GPS receiver.

An air force lieutenant colonel uses a global positioning device during a land navigation exercise

BATTLE OF 73 EASTING

Pivotal tank battle in the First Gulf War

The squadrons participating in the air campaign against Saddam Hussein's troops in the First Gulf War had completed their mission. Now it was time for ground troops of the coalition army under command of U.S. General H. Norman Schwarzkopf to finish the job and liberate Kuwait. On January 17, 1991, coalition troops crossed the Saudi border and the offensive, Operation Desert Storm, commenced.

Desert warfare more resembles naval warfare than it does traditional land campaigns. The desert is largely featureless and has no roads; maneuvers are wide and sweeping and can only be camouflaged by artificial means like smoke; when battles are fought, the denying or seizing of a location is irrelevant—only the destruction of the enemy force matters.

Operation Desert Storm began in bad weather, in what would prove to be the coldest and wettest winter in decades. Because of a lack of landmarks, positions were identified by a series of codenamed phase lines; these include geographic coordinates—called eastings and northings—that are linked to Global Positioning System devices. The U.S. 2nd Armored Cavalry Regiment (ACR), operating west of Kuwait, had crossed Phase Line Smash on February 26 and turned right. Its mission was to find, engage, and hold Iraqi units, enabling more powerful armored units on its flanks to envelop and finish off the enemy.

At about 4:30 P.M., E Troop, an advance element of the 2nd ACR, skirmished with an Iraqi outpost at 70 Easting. Fearing a loss of surprise, Captain H.R. McMaster took the ten Abrams tanks and thirteen Bradley Armored Personnel Carriers he commanded and raced toward the large Iraqi position ahead at 73 Easting. Without waiting for reinforcements, he charged straight into a site held by the elite Republican Guard's Tawakalna Division.

Before the stunned Iraqis could react, E Troop was in its midst and within minutes had destroyed more than twenty tanks and armored vehicles. Other 2nd ACR Troops soon joined E Troop. Though heavily outnumbered, the American troops destroyed dozens of tanks—the equivalent of an Iraqi brigade—in what would be the largest tank battle in the First Gulf War.

An abandoned Iraqi tank sits in Kuwaiti desert as an oil well burns in the background

H. Norman Schwarzkopf Jr.

U.S. general and theater commander during Operation in Desert Shield/
Desert Storm (1934–)

The leader of the coalition forces in Operation Desert Shield/Desert Storm first encountered the region at the age of twelve. His father was stationed in Tehran where he was a security advisor to the Shah of Iran. Schwarzkopf graduated from West Point in 1956. He served two tours of duty in Vietnam, first as an advisor to a unit in the South Vietnamese army and later as a battalion commander. Following Vietnam, he served in a variety of posts and steadily rose in command and responsibility.

He was a major general and a deputy commander of the Joint Task Force that carried out the 1983 invasion of Grenada (Operation Urgent Fury). In 1988, he was promoted to general and appointed commander-in-chief of U.S. Central Command (CENTCOM), responsible for all U.S. military operations in the Middle East, East Africa, and Central Asia.

When Saddam Hussein invaded Kuwait, Schwarzkopf was responsible for the planning and operations for Operation Desert Shield/Desert Storm, the liberation of Kuwait. This later came to be called the First Gulf War.

Schwarzkopf directed the largest U.S. mechanized combat operation since 1945. Within 100 hours of the beginning of Operation Desert Storm, the Iraqi army was decimated and Kuwait liberated.

Known for his volatile temper and his bullish personality, "Stormin' Norman" Schwarzkopf retired from service in August 1991.

ARMOR

*Protective covering of troops, transport, and weapon systems used in
Desert Shield/Desert Storm*

Armor of one form or another has been used throughout recorded history. Broadly, there are two types of armor, for bodies and for vehicles.

Body armor was designed to protect the most vulnerable parts of the body. In ancient times this meant the head, chest and abdomen, and shins. In Medieval times, knights wore complete body suits of armor. With the advent of gunpowder, the use of armor fell into decline, as its protection proved inadequate to stop the penetration of a bullet or cannon shell fragment. Body armor began to return in limited use in the late nineteenth century with the use of metal helmets. By the end of the twentieth century, soldiers were using body armor made of composite materials to protect the chest and abdomen and head.

The principle of vehicle armor is the same as that for the body, to protect the most vulnerable parts of the vehicle. In ships, this means the area of the hull at the water line and compartments necessary for the protection and command of the ship. In aircraft and land vehicles, such as tanks, this includes the engine and transmission area as well as the workspace for the crew and ammunition storage space.

Body armor was originally composed of layers of hides, leather, and bone. As metallurgical skills developed, armor made of metal, first bronze and then steel, was added to the natural armor. Eventually metal armor supplanted natural materials. Today, most body armor is composed of ceramic plates and synthetic fabrics and woven into computer-designed thicknesses and patterns to achieve optimum protection.

One recent improvement in vehicle armor is Chobham armor, created in the 1960s and named after the British tank research center that developed it. Chobham armor is a classified design of ceramic tiles and metal plates in elastic layers designed to exploit the kinetic energy of an impacting projectile. Chobham armor literally uses the force of the projectile against it. Chobham armor is lighter than traditional steel plates and more effective against modern weapons. Though new types of vehicle armor based on the principle of Chobham armor have since been perfected, all are classified.

American soldiers adjust their body armor prior to a patrol in Iraq

PLASTIC EXPLOSIVES

Malleable explosive material used in Operation Desert Storm

Plastic explosives, once generically known as plastiques, are specialized explosives notable for their stability and flexibility. Plastic explosives can be molded into different shapes and wrapped around objects. They are not susceptible to accidental discharge due to sudden impact or extremes in temperature. These traits have made plastic explosives popular in a variety of industries and fields outside the military, from the movie industry to mining. It is also an explosive favored by terrorists.

Alfred Nobel, the inventor of dynamite, created the first plastic explosive, Gel-ignite, in 1875. It was an inexpensive explosive that acquired a notorious reputation because of its use by the Provisional IRA in terrorist attacks in Northern Ireland.

The history of plastic explosive use begins in World War II. The British Special Operations Executive branch was responsible for sabotage missions in German-occupied territory. It needed to be able to provide to clandestine partisan groups largely composed of untrained civilians safe and simple explosives for use in sabotage. The term *plastique* as the generic name for plastic explosives came into use during this time because packages dropped for use by the French Resistance were labeled *Explosif Plastique*.

Arguably the most infamous plastic explosive is Semtex. Invented in 1966, and originally manufactured in Communist-era Czechoslovakia, tons of brick-orange blocks of the versatile plastic explosive were exported. Widely used by Islamic militants, it is difficult to detect. Semtex was responsible for the destruction of PanAm Flight 103 over Lockerbie, Scotland.

One of the most common, and probably the most famous, plastic explosives in use today is C-4. It is among the most versatile of plastic explosives. In addition, C-4 batches can be tainted with chemical agents that allow law enforcement units or other parties to track pieces or postdetonation residue. Unlike many other plastic explosives, C-4, if stored properly, has an indefinite shelf life. Because C-4 burns slowly when ignited by flame, it became popular among troops (beginning with those in the Vietnam War) for heating water and rations.

U.S. Army ordnance specialists prepare to detonate C-4 plastic explosives in a training exercise

FIRST BATTLE OF MOGADISHU

Somali Civil War battle

Somali women pass by a U.S. Marine near Mogadishu's green line, separating hostile Somali factions

In August 1993, U.S. and UN troops had decamped in Somalia as part of Operation Gothic Serpent, an effort to end the Somali Civil War. A plan was developed to send a Special Operations force into the Somali capital of Mogadishu and capture two senior lieutenants of one of the powerful rebel warlords. The planned called for a helicopter drop of Special Operations teams onto the safe house where the lieutenants were staying. The teams would capture the lieutenants and then rendezvous with an armed convoy that would carry the hostages back to base. The convoy, under the code name Task Force Ranger, rolled out late in the afternoon of Sunday, October 3. The plan estimated that the total elapsed time would be no more than one hour.

The two lieutenants were captured. That was about the only thing that went right.

The convoy encountered roadblocks and got lost. A Ranger was seriously wounded during the insertion. Rocket-propelled grenades shot down two Black Hawk helicopters. Within minutes, the operation had collapsed into chaos. Two snipers, Sergeant First Class Randy Shughart and Master Sergeant Gary Gordon, were inserted by helicopter to one crash site to defend Durant, an injured pilot. A Somali mob killed Shughart and Gordon and captured Durant. Shughart and Gordon were posthumously awarded the Medal of Honor.

Task Force Ranger would spend the night fighting a desperate battle of survival. Helicopter gunships ran missions throughout the night against the waves of Somalis attacking the troops. A relief convoy arrived the following morning and by 6:30 A.M., the battle was over. Though Task Force Ranger had achieved its goal, it was a Pyrrhic victory. The battle sent a shockwave through President Bill Clinton's administration. A major shift in American foreign policy occurred. American troops were soon ordered out of Somalia and the Clinton administration would become increasingly reluctant to send any more troops for military intervention in the world's hot spots.

A batallion of U.S. Marines boards trucks in Mogadishu

SATELLITE

Unmanned orbital spacecraft used in military reconnaissance

When the Soviet Union launched Sputnik I, the world's first artificial satellite, on October 4, 1957, it ushered mankind's next great technological achievement, the Space Age. Since this occurred during the ideological struggle between democracies led by the United States and communist countries led by the Soviet Union, it also ushered in the era of the Space Race.

Initially, satellites were developed by and for the military for reconnaissance purposes. Over time, and with the help of international treaties and laws establishing use parameters of outer space and nations' territorial integrity regarding flyovers, satellite use has expanded into commerce. Presently there are roughly 8,000 manmade satellites orbiting Earth. Their purposes now include communications, navigation, scientific research applications such as Earth observation and astronomy, and other military, commercial, and scientific needs. There are also ASATS (Anti-Satellite satellites), "killer satellites" designed to seek and destroy other satellites. The entire surface of the planet has been photographed and Internet map sites can provide satellite images of any address and location with surprising detail and resolution.

An artificial satellite is basically a metal container that holds an energy source and instruments designed to perform the satellite's function (its payload). All are customized to withstand the rigors of the extremely hostile environment of outer space. Satellites are propelled into space by rockets or carried into orbit by NASA's Space Shuttle. All are programmed to fly in specified orbits and for a set period of time.

The Cold War, with its specter of global annihilation from the world's nuclear superpowers, was a major force behind the development of satellites. Within a year after Sputnik's launch, the United States had responded with the top secret CORONA satellite reconnaissance missions. CORONA missions were designed to photograph every inch of the Soviet Union in a search for all Soviet military installations, particularly nuclear missile sites. In 1983, President Ronald Reagan upped the Cold War ante with his Strategic Defense Initiative proposal, popularly known as the "Star Wars" program. It included satellites designed to intercept and destroy Soviet satellites and attacking ballistic missiles. Though it was never fully developed or deployed, its threat played a key role in the collapse of the Soviet Union in 1991.

An artist's rendering of NASA's Calipso atmosphere observation satellite in orbit

Map

Visual representation of an area used in military battle planning

In military terms, maps are accurate representations of a geographic region and include detailed topographic information including the measured height and depth of terrain and seabeds.

Military leaders in ancient times up to the sixteenth century relied on crude maps whose accuracy and detail varied widely. Abraham Ortelius is generally regarded as the cartographer who created the first modern atlas; his maps were widely used as travel aids by leaders of armies. But, as historian David Buisseret noted, "Maps that would be tactically useful had to await the completion of state programs that mapped whole countries at a relatively large scale." These began to appear in the late 1600s. France was the first country to organize cartographic staffs devoted to providing maps of potential campaign areas. By the time of the American Revolution, all the major nations had military cartographic branches.

Computer software systems, satellites, and Global Positioning Devices have led to great strides in map utility. Local terrain can now be projected on computer screens, at varying scales of resolution and detail and in 3-D or in enhanced satellite photo imagery, with unprecedented accuracy.

U.S. Marines on the field studying a map prior to operations

OPERATION ENDURING FREEDOM—AFGHANISTAN

First campaign in the War on Terrorism

A soldier smiles as he returns from front lines in the Tora Bora area of Afghanistan

Operation Enduring Freedom—Afghanistan was President George W. Bush's first response to the al-Qaeda terrorist attacks on American soil on September 11, 2001. Its objective was the capture of al-Qaeda's leader Osama bin Laden, the destruction of al-Qaeda, and the elimination of the Taliban regime ruling Afghanistan.

The operation began in October with a combined American and British air campaign against known al-Qaeda and Taliban bases. Initially, the American military presence on land was primarily Special Operations units who fought with members of the Afghan Northern Alliance. It became the largest Special Operations campaign in American history.

The land campaign kicked off in November 2001, about a month after the air campaign had started. Two days after it began, Mazari Sharif was the first major city to be captured. Kabul fell on November 12. The next day, Taliban and al-Qaeda forces regrouped at the Tora Bora cave complex near the Pakistani border. Combined air and ground attacks for about nine days ended in the last Taliban fighters surrendering on December 17. Meanwhile, a siege had commenced on the city of Kunduz. That ended with the Taliban surrendering on November 25. Kandahar, another important Taliban stronghold, fell on December 7. American and Afghan forces began to consolidate their gains and install a new government at Kabul.

The following year, Operation Anaconda was launched against al-Qaeda and Taliban strongholds in Paktia Province on the Pakistan border. By the end of 2002, it appeared that the power of al-Qaeda and the Taliban in Afghanistan had been broken.

But, when the United States began Operation Iraqi Freedom the following year, al-Qaeda and Taliban cells returned and a renewed insurgency began to destabilize the country.

U.S. Marines deploy on January 5, 2002 to Kandahar, Afghanistan

OPERATION ANACONDA

Largest offensive in Operation Enduring Freedom—Afghanistan

Operation Anaconda was the first large-scale battle in Afghanistan to involve a significant number of conventional warfare troops. The objective of the operation was to destroy al-Qaeda and Taliban troops and bases in the Shahi-Kot Valley and Arma Mountains in the Paktia Province in eastern Afghanistan. It was launched in response to intelligence reports indicating the rebels were planning a spring offensive in 2002 and that top Al-Qaeda and Taliban leaders Osama bin Laden, Ayman al-Zawahiri, and Mullah Omar might be with the bands located in the province. A multinational force of about 2,000 men, including U.S. Special Forces, SEALs, Rangers, and other Special Operations troops, was assembled for a pre-emptive attack. Major General Buster Hagenbeck of the 10th Mountain Division was chosen to command.

On March 1, 2002, the Special Operations units began infiltrating the mountainous area and setting up observation posts. The attack began the next day with troops arriving by vehicles traveling up the main highway and dropping onto strategic sites from helicopters. Original estimates were that the troops would encounter about 150–200 lightly armed enemy fighters. Instead, the Anaconda force confronted an enemy 500 to 1,000 strong, located in well-placed and well-constructed defenses. They were also well armed with heavy machine guns, mortars, and rocket-propelled grenades.

Supported by helicopters and bomb strikes that included missions flown by B-52s, the multinational force fought a bitter battle among the 8,000-to-12,000-foot-high ridges and peaks. Predator Unmanned Aerial Vehicle drones provided real-time intelligence on al-Qaeda and Taliban positions. The rebels fought bitterly but after a little more than two weeks, the fighting concluded. Though none of the rebel leaders were found, the al-Qaeda and Taliban forces suffered heavy casualties (accounts vary on the number) and a number of their sites were destroyed. Eight American servicemen were killed and eighty-two troops were wounded. Senior American leaders called the operation a success because it had eliminated a large rebel presence in the province.

Former Northern Alliance soldiers heading to the front line to join the U.S.-led coalition battling against al Qaeda and Taliban forces

Radio

Wireless communication used to control the flow of battle

Wireless communication began in the 1880s when Heinrich Hertz demonstrated the existence of electromagnetic radiation (the word *hertz* became the name for the system used to measure radio waves).

The U.S. Army Signal Corps introduced its first portable wireless field sets capable of transmitting Morse code messages in 1906. The following year, it began experiments with radio telephony (voice radio). Wireless communication saw little use during World War I, with generals preferring to transmit orders via telegraph, landline telephone, or carrier pigeon.

Technological advances in the years following the war led to the rapid integration of wireless communication into the military. Naval research included experimentation with the radio compass, airborne radio, and radio remote control. A milestone in radio communication was reached with the International Radio Convention of 1927, which adopted the U.S. Navy's plan for worldwide frequency allocation. Because the radios used vacuum tube technology, multifrequency transceivers were large and heavy and were generally found only in ships or in headquarters locations. The original army handheld walkie-talkie debuted in 1934, weighing a whopping 25 pounds.

The transistor revolutionized radio telecommunications. Radios became smaller, lighter, could communicate greater distances, and utilize more frequencies. Radio transmissions of hundreds of miles or more became possible with the development of troposcatter propagation radios. Using special antennas, these transceivers bounced radio waves off clouds of ionized particles in the higher ionosphere.

Computer chips have continued the technological breakthrough and capability of radio communications. Today, thanks to the cell phone, troops stationed in remote corners of the world can have voice communications with loved ones back home.

A wireless-operator reports to headquarters during a three days' maneuver in 1939

BATTLE OF DEBECKA PASS

Twenty-first century "Alamo" that changed Special Operations doctrine

Debecka Pass in northern Iraq was an anonymous highway junction on the strategic Highway 2 in northern Iraq. As part of Operation Iraqi Freedom, Task Force Viking arrived there on the morning of April 6. The objective of Task Force Viking was to open the way for the capture of the strategic city of Kirkuk and its oil facilities. Task Force Viking was waiting for additional troops to arrive before continuing the advance. It knew an Iraqi armored brigade was in the area and would undoubtedly attempt to retake the junction. Their vehicles were equipped with machine guns, automatic grenade launchers, and new Javelin anti-tank missiles. Despite their augmented firepower, doctrine stated the force was too small (twelve Special Forces operatives) and too lightly armed to risk a long-term pitched battle against a major enemy attack. The most Task Force Viking was expected to do was conduct a delaying action before retreating.

Within a couple of hours of their arrival, an Iraqi attack appeared. It included eight armored personnel carriers, four T-55 tanks, artillery, and at least 150 troops. The outnumbered Americans laid down covering fire. Then they retreated up Debecka Pass to a defensive location that commanded the valley below.

The Americans called for air support, but were told that it would take thirty minutes for strike aircraft to arrive. Outnumbered and outgunned, the Americans were in what was later described as a twenty-first century Alamo. Their only chance for survival lay with a weapon that had never before been used in combat, the Javelin. While some Special Forces troops laid down protective fire, others broke out the Javelins and started shooting at the Iraqi armored vehicles. Firing at extreme range, the Javelins knocked out all the armored personnel carriers and half the tanks. The initiative switched to the American forces. By mid-afternoon the battle was over and the surviving Iraqi troops were in retreat.

The Battle of Debecka Pass proved that even against superior odds, well-trained Special Operations troops utilizing such advanced weapons systems as the Javelin could hold their own against superior enemy forces.

An armored infantry division man a checkpoint on a road to Kirkuk to keep looters and gunmen out of the city

INDEX

A

Aboukir Bay, Battle of, 176–177
Abrahamson, James L., 348
Achilles, 18–19
Achtung! Panzer! (Guderian), 346
Aetius, 60
Afghanistan, 494–497
Agamemnon, 18
Agincourt, Battle of, 96–100
Ahmed, Mohammed, 286
airplanes, 376–379
Alamo, 216–217
Alaric I, 62–63
Alesia, Battle of, 50–52
Alexander, Sir Harold, 416, 424
Alexander I (Russia), 180–181, 190
Alexander the Great, 28–31, 370
Alfred the Great, 68–69
Al Ghafiqi, Abdul Rahman, 66
Ali Pasha, 128
Allen, Ethan, 170
Allenby, Edmund, 324, 326–327, 334–335
al-Qaeda, 494–497
al-Zawahiri, Ayman, 496
American Civil War, 27, 202–203, 222–269,
    310, 370, 372
American Revolution, 162–173
Anaconda, Operation, 496–497
Anderson, Charles, 262
Anderson, Robert, 222
André, John, 170
Anglo-Zulu War, 282–283
Antietam, Battle of, 240–242, 258

Antioch, Siege of, 76–79
Antony, Marc, 54–55
Anzio, Battle of, 426–427
Aphrodite, 18
Argentina, 470–471
Arminius, 56–57
armor, 22–23, 40, 136–137, 484–485.
    See also tanks
Arnold, Benedict, 12, 162, 168, 170–171
Arnold, Henry Harley "Hap," 436–437
arquebus, 132–133
The Art of War (Ping-fa) (Sun Tzu), 26–27
Asculum, Battle of, 32–33
Atahualpa, 118–123
Atlantic, Battle of the, 368–375
Attila, 60–61
attrition, 314–315, 356
Austerlitz, Battle of, 180–181
Austria, 180–181
Avalanche, Operation, 422–423
Aztec Empire, 106–109

B

Babur, Zahir ud-Din Muhammad, 110–113
Bacon, Roger, 94
Badr, Battle of, 64–65
Bannockburn, Battle of, 90–91
Barbarossa, 116
Barbarossa, Operation, 356–357, 360
barbed wire, 308, 310–311
Barclay de Tolly, Mikhail, 190
Baudricourt, Robert de, 104
Bayerlein, Fritz, 338

Beatty, Sir David, 316
Beauregard, Pierre G. T., 222, 224, 238
Beersheba, Battle of, 324–325
Belisarius, 40–41
Bennigsen, Levin August, Count von, 186
Benteen, Frederick, 276
Berlin, Battle for, 444–445
Big Foot, 288
bin Laden, Osama, 494–497
Bismarck, Otto von, 270–271, 274
Blenheim, 142–144
blitzkrieg, 342, 346, 348, 352–353
blockades, 250
Bluemenson, Martin, 338
Boer War, 310
Bohemund of Taranto, 76
Bolivar, Simon, 209, 210, 212–215
Borodino, Battle of, 190–191
Boucicaut, Marshal, 98
Bowie, James, 216
bows, 96–97
Bradley, Omar Nelson, 428, 430–431, 432
Brest-Litovsk, Treaty of, 302, 304
Britain, Battle of, 354–355
British East India Company, 154
Brown, John, 258
Brown Bess musket, 158–159, 202
Browning, John, 322
Broz, Josef, 418–421
Brueys, François-Paul, 176
Buchanan, Franklin, 246
Buell, Don Carlos, 238
Buisseret, David, 492
Bulge, Battle of the, 402, 442–443
Bull Run, First Battle of, 224–226, 268
Bunker Hill, Battle of, 158–159
Burgoyne, Sir John, 168–169
Burnside, Ambrose, 252
Bush, George W., 494
Bushnell, David, 370

C
C-4, 486–487
Caesar, Augustus (Octavian), 52, 54–57
Caesar, Gaius Julius, 50–53

Cajamarca, Battle of, 118–123
Cambrai, Battle of, 328–329, 340, 344
Canada, 160–163
Cannae, Battle of, 34–35, 36, 46
Carabobo, Battle of, 212–214
Carleton, Guy, 162
Carter, Jimmy, 468
Carthage, 34–49
Catherine the Great (Russia), 152
Chalons, Battle of, 60–61
Chancellorsville, Battle of, 226, 242, 252–253
Chapultepec, Battle of, 220–221
Chard, John, 282
chariots, 14–17, 18, 28
Charles of Lorraine, 150
Charles V (Holy Roman Emperor), 128
chemical warfare, 320–321
Chilean War of Independence, 208–211
China, 86–87, 144
Chobham armor, 344, 484
Christian wars, 76–85, 114–117, 128–129
Christie, J. Walter, 344
Churchill, John, 142–143
Churchill, Winston, 306, 344, 354, 368, 374, 396, 398, 426, 448
Clark, Mark, 422, 424
Clausewitz, Carl Philipp Gottlieb von, 196–197
claymores, 42
Cleopatra, 54
Clinton, Bill, 488
Clive, Robert, 154–157
Cobra, Operation, 430, 432–433
Cold War, 490
Cole, Horace de Vere, 294
Commentaries on the Gallic War (Caesar), 52
Congreve, Sir William, 472
Connor, Fox, 400
Conquistadors, 106–109, 118–123
containment, 250–251
Coral Sea, Battle of, 386–387
Cornwallis, Charles, 172–173
Cortés, Hernándo, 106–109, 122
Courtrai, Battle of, 88–89
Courtrai Chest, 88–89
Crassus, 52

Crazy Horse (Tashunca Uitco), 277–278, 280–281

Crécy, Battle of, 92–95

Creveld, Martin van, 96, 144

Crimean War, 244, 248

Crockett, Davy, 216

Crook, George, 280

crossbows, 96

Crusades, 76–85

Cuesta, Gregorio de la, 188

Custer, George Armstrong, 276–281

D

d'Albret, Charles, 98

Darius I, 20–21

Darius III, 28–29

Daulah, Siraj Ud, 154

Davis, Jefferson, 222

Dayan, Moshe, 458–459

D-Day, 402, 428–429

Debecka Pass, Battle of, 500–501

Deemings, 68

de la Torre, Miguel, 212

de melo, Francisco, 140

Dempsey, Miles, 428

d'Enghien, Duc, 140

Desert Shield/Desert Storm, Operation, 379, 474, 480–481

Dien Bien Phu, Siege of, 454–455

Don John of Austria, 128

Doolittle, James H., 382

Doolittle Raid, 382–384

Drake, Sir Francis, 134

Dreadnought, 294–295

Dumouriez, Charles, 174

E

Eager Anvil, Operation, 474–475

Eagle Claw, Operation, 468

Easting, Battle of 73, 480–481

economic sanctions, 250

ed-Din, Beha, 84

Eden, Anthony, 456

Edison, Thomas, 244

Edward II (England), 90

Edward III (England), 92–93

Egypt, 14–16, 286–287, 326, 456–458, 462–463, 466–467. *See also* World War II

Eisenhower, Dwight, 350, 398, 400–401, 410, 428, 440, 442, 444, 454

El Alamein, Second Battle of, 392–396

elephants, 32–33, 44–45, 46, 110–111

Ellis, Hugh J., 328

Emancipation Proclamation, 240

Emmanuel II (Italy), 284

Enduring Freedom, Operation, 494–497

engineers, 146–147

engines, 272–273

Ethelred, 68

Eudoxia, Licinia, 62

explosive reactive armor, 344

Eylau, Battle of, 199

F

Fabian strategy, 36, 38–39

Fabius Maximus Verrucosus, Quintus, 36–39, 46

Falklands War, 470–471

Farragut, David Glasgow, 262–265

Flanders, 88–89

Floyd, John B., 232

Fokker, Anthony, 378

Fontenoy, Battle of, 148–149

Foote, Andrew H., 232

Forrest, Nathan Bedford, 236–237

Forsyth, James, 288

Fort Donelson, 232–233, 234, 236

fortifications, 144–145, 146

Fort Pillow Affair, 236

Fort Sumter, Siege of, 222–223

France, 88–89, 140–149, 160–161, 178–199, 270–275, 298–335, 454–455. *See also* World War I; World War II Hundred Years' War, 92–105

France, Fall of, 352–353

Franco-Prussian War, 270–275

Franco-Spanish War, 140–141

Franks, 66–67

Frederick II, the Great, 150–153

Freeman, Douglas Southall, 226
French and Indian War, 160–161, 170
French Revolution, 174–175. *See also* Napoleon
    Bonaparte
Friedland, Battle of, 186–187
Fuller, John Frederick Charles, 328, 338, 340–341

G
Gallieni, Joseph, 298
Gallipoli, 306–307
Garibaldi, Giuseppe, 284–285
Gates, Horatio, 168, 170
Gatling gun, 322
Gaugamela, Battle of, 30–31
Gaul, 50–53
Geiseric, 62–63
Geneva Protocol of 1925, 320
Genghis Khan, 86–87
George, David Lloyd, 318
Germany, 56–57, 138, 192–193. *See also* Prussia;
    World War I; World War II
Gettysburg, Battle of, 258–260
Ghost Dance, 278, 288–289
Giap, Vo Nguyen, 454
Gibbons, John, 276
Girarud, Honore, 410
gladius, 40, 42
Gladstone, William, 286
Glidden, Joseph F., 310
global positioning system (GPS), 478–479,
    480, 492
Godfrey of Bouillon, 76–77, 80–81
Godwin, Harold, 74
Göering, Hermann, 322
Golden Spurs, Battle of the, 88–89
Gontermann, Heinrich, 379
Gordon, Charles, 286–287
Gordon, Gary, 488
Gothic Serpent, Operation, 488–489
Gqokli Hill, Battle of, 204–205
Grant, Ulysses S., 12, 228, 232–235, 238–239,
    242, 244, 254–255, 268, 314
Great Britain, 68–69, 72–75, 90–105,
    134–135, 154–157, 160–163, 176–199,
    212, 282–283, 286–287, 294–295,

456–458, 470–471. *See also* World War I;
    World War II
Great Jewish Revolt, 58–59
Great White Fleet, 294
Greece, ancient, 18–25, 32–33
Grey, Sir Edward, 298
Greyberg, Bernard, 424
Grierson, Benjamin Henry, 256–257
Griffith, Samuel B., 26
Guadalcanal, 404–405
Guderian, Heinz, 338
Guderian, Heinz Wilhelm, 346–347
guerilla warfare, 228, 230–231
Gulf War, First, 379, 474, 480–481
gunpowder, 92–95, 132–133, 144, 472–473
Gustavus Adolphus, 138–139
Guthrum, 68
Guy of Lusignan, 82

H
Hagenbeck, Buster, 496
Haig, Sir Douglas, 308, 318, 326, 328
halberds, 100–101
Halsey, William Frederick, Jr., 382, 384–385,
    390, 438
Hamilcar Barca, 46
Hamilton, Emma, 184
Hampton Roads, Battle of, 246–249
Hannibal Barca, 34–35, 36, 38, 44–47
Hardee, William J., 266
Hardrada, Harald, 72, 74
Harold of Wessex, 72
Hastings, Battle of, 72–73, 74
Hattin, Battle of, 82–84
Helen of Troy, 18
He-lu of Wu, 26
Henry I (France), 74
Henry V (England), 98–99
Herod, 58
Hicks, William, 286
Hindenburg, Paul von, 300–305, 312, 330
Hipper, Franz, 316
Hirohito, 292, 448
Hiroshima and Nagasaki, 408, 434,
    448–451

Hitler, Adolf, 318, 320, 336, 342, 346, 352, 354, 356, 360, 398, 406, 414, 418, 442, 444, 456
Hittites, 14–16
Holocaust, 320
Homer, 18, 26
Hooker, Joseph, 252, 258
hoplites, 20, 22–23, 24
Horatii, Oath of, 42–43
Hough, Daniel, 222
Houston, Sam, 216, 218–219
Howe, William, 168
Hundred Years' War, 92–105
Huns, 60–61
Husky, Operation, 416–417
Hussein, Saddam, 320, 480, 482

I

Iliad (Homer), 18
Incan Empire, 118–123
Inchon, Battle of, 452–453
India, 110–113, 154–157
indirect attacks, 348–349
infantry revolution, 88–89
The Influence of Sea Power upon History, 1660–1783 (Mahan), 296
The Influence of Sea Power upon the French Revolution and Empire (Mahan), 296
Iran, 468–469
Iraq, 474–475, 480–481, 500–501
Iraqi Freedom, Operation, 500–501
ironclad warships, 246–249, 262–263
Islamic wars, 64–67, 76–85, 114–117, 128–129
Israel, 458–459, 462–463, 466–467
Italy, 284–285. *See also* World War I; World War II
Ivan IV, 124–125
Iwo Jima, 446–447

J

Jackson, Andrew, 200–201
Jackson, Thomas Jonathan "Stonewall," 224–227, 252–253
Japan, 126–127, 130–131, 136–137, 290–293, 314, 336–337. *See also* World War II

Jellicoe, Sir John, 316
Jerusalem, Siege of, 80–81, 334–335
Jewish-Roman Wars, 58–59
Joan of Arc, 102–105
Johnson, Lyndon, 460
Johnston, Albert S., 232, 238
Johnston, Joseph E., 224, 242
Jomini, Antoine-Henri, 196, 198–199
Jones, Catesby R., 246
Jordan, 466–467
Jutland, Battle of, 316–317

K

Kadesh, Battle of, 14–15, 16
Kasserine Pass, Battle of, 410–411
Kazan, Siege of, 124–125
Kazan Khanate, 124–125
Kemel, Mustafa, 306
Key, Francis Scott, 472
Khalkin Gol, Battle of, 336–337
Khartoum, Siege of, 286–287
Khomeini, Ayatollah Ruholla, 468
Khrushchev, Nikita, 358
Kobayakawa Hideaki, 136
Korean War, 440, 452–453
Kuribayashi, Tadamichi, 446
Kursk, Battle of, 358, 414–415
Kutuzov, Mikhail, 38, 180, 190
Kuwait, 474–475, 480

L

Lamberet, John, 200
Land Pattern Musket, 158–159
Lannes, Jean, 186
Lawrence, T. E., 334
Lech, Battle of, 138
Lee, Henry "Light Horse Harry," 242
Lee, Robert E., 226, 240–242, 252–253, 258
legions, Roman, 40–41
Lehrbas, Lloyd, 441
Leipzig, Battle of, 192–193
LeMay, Curtis, 434
Lepanto, Battle of, 128–129
Lepidus, Marcus Aemilius, 54
Le Prieur, Y. P. G., 472

Leuthen, Battle of, 150–151
Lewis, Isaac Newton, 322
Leyte Gulf, Battle of, 384, 438–440
Liddell Hart, Sir Basil Henry, 338–339, 340, 348
Lincoln, Abraham, 234, 240, 254, 266, 284
Little Bighorn, Battle of the, 277–281
Lodhi, Ibrahim, 110
longboats, Viking, 70–71
longbows, 96
Longstreet, James, 258
Louis XIV (France), 142, 146
Louis XV (France), 148
Lucas, John, 426
Ludendorff, Erich, 301, 302, 304–305, 330
Lützen, Battle of, 138

M
MacArthur, Douglas, 366, 400, 438, 440–441, 452
Macedonia, 17, 28–31
machine guns, 310, 322–323
Mahan, Alfred Thayer, 294, 296–297
Maipú, Battle of, 208–210
Mallory, Stephen, 248
Manassas, First Battle of, 224–226, 268
maps, 492–493
Marathon, Battle of, 20–22
March to the Sea, 266–269
Marne, First Battle of the, 298–299
Marne, Second Battle of the, 330–333
Marshall, George Catlett, 350–351, 436
Marshall Plan, 350
Marsin, Ferdinand de, 142
Martel, Charles, 66–67
Masada, Siege of, 58–59
Masinissa, 48
Maurice, Hermann, Comte de Saxe, 148–149
Maxim, Hiram, 322
McAuliffe, Anthony, 442
McClellan, George, 228, 240–241, 258, 348
McDowell, Irvin, 224
Meade, George Gordon, 258
Mecca, 64–65
Megiddo, Battle of, 334–335
Menelaus, 18

Mexican-American War, 216–221
Mexico, 106–109, 216–221, 332
Midway, Battle of, 364, 388–391
Mihailovic, Dragoliub, 420
Military Operations Other Than War (MOOTW), 230
Miltiades, 20
mines, 394–395
missiles and rockets, 472–473
Mitchell, William "Billy," 436
Mobile Bay, Battle of, 262–264
Mogadishu, First Battle of, 488–489
Mongols, 86–87
Monitor vs. Virginia, 246–247, 249
Montcalm, Louis-Joseph, Marquis de, 160
Monte Cassino, Battles for, 424–425
Montezuma, 106–109
Montgomery, Bernard Law, 392, 396–397, 416, 432, 442
Montgomery, Richard, 162, 359
Montross, Lynn, 40
Morgan, Daniel, 168
Morgarten, Battle of, 100
Morse, Samuel F. B., 244
Mosby, John Singleton, 228–229
Moscow, Battle of, 358, 360–361
Mughal Empire, 110–113, 154–157
Muhammad, 64–65
muskets, 158–159
Mussolini, Benito, 418, 422
Mutually-Assured Destruction (MAD), 408
Muwatallis II, 14

N
Nagashino, Battle of, 130–132
Nagumo, Chuichi, 388
Napoleon Bonaparte, 46, 104, 138, 176, 178–195
Napoleonic Wars, 38, 178–199
Napoleon III, 270–275
Nasser, Gamel, 456
naval battles
    Aboukir Bay, 176–177
    Atlantic, Battle of the, 368–375
    Coral Sea, 386–387

Jutland, 316–317
Lepanto, 128–129
Leyte Gulf, 384, 438–440
Mahan on, 296–297
Midway, 364, 388–391
Mobile Bay, 262–264
Monitor vs. Virginia, 246–247, 249
Salamis, 24–25
Spanish Armada, 134–135
Trafalgar, 182–183
Viking longboats, 70–71
Nebogatov, Nicholas, 290
Nelson, Horatio, 176–177, 182–185
Nero, 58
New Orleans, Battle of, 200–201
Nicholas II (Russia), 290
night-vision devices (NVDs), 474, 476–477
Nimitz, Chester William, 366–367, 386, 388, 446
Nobel, Alfred, 486
Norman Conquest, 72–75
nuclear weapons, 408, 434, 448–451, 454

O

Octavian, 52, 54–57
Oda Nobunaga, 126, 130
O'Grady, Scott, 478
Okehazama, Battle of, 126–127
Oldenbourg, Zoé, 80
On War (Vom Kriege) (Clausewitz), 196
Operation Iraqi Freedom, 230
Orléans, Siege of, 102–105
Osorio, Mariano, 208
Ottoman Empire, 114–117, 128–129, 274, 306–307, 324–326, 334–335
Overlord, Operation, 402, 428–429

P

Pakenham, Sir Edward, 200
Palestine, 324–325, 334–335
Panipat, Battle of, 110–113
Passchendaele, Battle of, 318–320
Patch, Alexander, 404
Patton, George S., Jr., 338, 346, 398, 402–403, 416, 432, 442

Paullus, Aemilius, 34
Pax Romana, 52
Pearl Harbor, 362–364, 382
Pemberton, John C., 254
Percival, Arthur, 380
Peron, Juan D., 211
Pershing, John, 330, 332–333, 400, 402
Persian Empire, 20–21, 24–25, 28–31, 121
Pétain, Philippe, 312
Philip II (Macedonia), 30
Philip II (Spain), 134
Philip IV (France), 88–89
Philip VI (France), 92–93
Phony War, 352–353
Pickens, Francis, 222
Pickett, George, 258
Pitt, William, 156
Pizarro, Francisco, 118–123
Plains Indian wars, 277–281, 288–289
Plains of Abraham, Battle of the, 160–161
Plassey, Battle of, 154–156
plastic explosives, 486–487
Pleasonton, Alfred, 258
Plutarch, 32
poison gas, 320–321
Polish Campaign, 342–348
Pompey, 52
Précis de l'art de la guerre (Summary of the Art of War) (Jomini), 198
Prien, Günther, 368
Prussia, 150–153, 194–195, 270–275
Puckle, James, 322
Punic Wars, 34–49
Pyrrhus of Epirus, 32–33

Q

Quebec, Battle of, 160–161

R

radar, 368, 374–375
radio, 498–499
Raleigh, Sir Walter, 12
Rall, Johann, 164
Ramesses II, 14–15
Raymond of Toulouse, 76

Reagan, Ronald, 478, 490

Reno, Marcus, 276

Richard I (England), 84

rifles, 202–203

Robert II of Artois, 88

Robert the Bruce, 90–91

Rochambeau, Comte de, 172

Rocroi, Battle of, 140–141

Roman Empire, 32–45, 48–63

Rome, Sack of, 62–63

Rommel, Erwin, 338, 392, 410

Roosevelt, Franklin Delano, 350, 362, 382, 398, 440

Roosevelt, Theodore, 294, 296, 332

Rorke's Drift, 282–283

Rozhdestvenski, Zinovy, 290

Russia, 38, 124–125, 178–199, 290–293, 300–335, 336–337. *See also* Soviet Union

Russo-Japanese War, 290–293, 310

Russo-Kazan War, 124–125

Ryder, Charles, 398

S

Saladin, 82–85

Salamis, Battle of, 24–25

samurai, 126–127, 136–137

San Jacinto, Battle of, 218

San Lorenzo, Battle of, 210

San Martín, José de, 208–211, 214

Santa Anna, Antonio López de, 216–218, 229

Saratoga, Battle of, 166, 168–169, 170

satellites, 144, 490–491

Saudi Arabia, 474

Saunders, Charles, 160

Saxe, Comte de, 148–149

Scheer, Reinhard, 316

Schlieffen Plan, 298, 300

Schliemann, Heinrich, 18

Schuyler, Philip, 162

Schwarzkopf, H. Norman, 474, 480, 482–483

Scipio Aemilianus, publius Cornelius, 44, 48

Scotland, 90–91

Scott, Winfield, 220–221, 242

Sedan, First Battle of, 270–271, 274

Seeckt, Hans von, 196

Seguín, Juan Nepomucno, 216

Sekigahara, Battle of, 136–137

Semtex, 486

Seven Years' War, 150–151, 152, 154

Shaka, 204–207

Sherman, William Tecumseh, 12, 234, 236, 266–269, 408

Shibazaki, Keichi, 412

Shiloh, Battle of, 238–239

Shughart, Randy, 488

Sidinia, Medina, 134

siege, 250. *See also by location of siege*

Silva, Lucius Flavius, 58

Singapore, Battle of, 380–381

Sino-Japanese War, 292

Sitting Bull (Tatanka Yotanka), 277–279

Six-Day War, 458, 462–463

Six Nations, Battle of, 192–193

Smith, Julian, 412

Somali Civil War, 488–489

Somme, Battle of the, 308–309

sonar, 368, 374–375

Sonnino, Paul, 146

Soviet Union, 342–357, 456, 490. *See also* Russia

Spain, 106–109, 118–123, 134–135, 140–141, 188–189

Spanish Armada, 134–135

Special Operations, 500–501

Speer, Albert, 414

Spruance, Raymond Ames, 390–391

Stalin, Josef, 356, 358, 444, 448

Stalingrad, Battle of, 406–407

stealth aircraft, 379

stirrups, 120–121

Strategic Defense Initiative, 490

strategy

    attrition, 314–315

    Clausewitz, 196–197

    containment, 250–251

    Fabian, 36, 38–39

    Hannibal, 46

    indirect attacks, 348–349

    Jomini, 198–199

Mahan, 296–297
Sun Tzu, 26–27
total warfare, 408–409
Stuart, James Ewell Brown "Jeb," 228, 258,
    260–261
submarines, 368–375
Suez Crisis, 456–457
Suleiman I, 114–117
Sun Tzu, 26–27
Sutherland, Richard, 441
Sutjeska Offensive, 418–420
Sweden, 138–139, 180–181
Sweeny, Charles, 448
Switzerland, 198–199
swords, 42–43
Syria, 466–467

T

Takeda Katsuyori, 130
Talavera, Battle of, 188–189
Taliban, 494–497
Tallard, Duc de, 142
tanks, 328–329, 340, 344–345, 484
Tannenberg, Battle of, 300–301
Tarawa, Battle of, 412–413
Technology and War (Creveld), 96, 144
telegraph, 244–245
Temujin, 86–87
Tenochtitlan, Fall of, 106–109
terrorism, war on, 494–497
Terry, Alfred, 276
Tet Offensive, 464–465
Teutoburg Forest, Battle of, 56–57
Thatcher, Margaret, 470
Theodoric I, 60
Thirty Years' War, 138–139
Thompson, John T., 322
Tibbetts, Paul, Jr., 448
Tipu Sultan, 472
Tito, 418–421
Togo, Heihachiro, 290, 292–293
Tokugawa Ieyasu, 130, 136
Tonkin Gulf Incident, 460–461
Torch, Operation, 398–403
torpedoes, 372–373

total warfare, 408–409
Tours, Battle of, 66–67
Toyotomi Hideyoshi, 136
Trafalgar, Battle of, 182–184
Travis, William, 216
trebuchets, 77–79
Trenton, Battle of, 164–165
Troy, siege of, 18–19
Truman, Harry, 350, 434, 440, 448
Truscott, Lucian, 426
Tsushima, 290–293, 364

U

U-boats, 368–375
United States of America, 162–173, 200–201,
    216–269, 277–281, 288–289, 456,
    474–475, 480–481. *See also* World War I;
    World War II
Urban II (Pope), 76, 80

V

Valentinian, 60
Valentinian III, 62
Valmy, Battle of, 174–175
Vandals, 62–63
Vandegrift, Archer A., 404
Varro, Tarentius, 34
Varus, Publius Quinctilius, 56
Vauban, Sébastien le Prestre de, 144, 146–147
Venezuela, 212–215
Vercingetorix, 50–52
Verdun, Battle of, 312–314
Vicksburg, Siege of, 254–256, 310
Vienna, Siege of, 114–117
Vietnam War, 230–231, 454–455, 460–461,
    464–465
Vikings, 68–71
Villa, Pancho, 332
Villeneuve, Pierre de, 182–183
Visigoths, 60–63
von Bock, Fedor, 360
von Falkenhayn, Erich, 312–314
von Moltke, Helmuth, 298, 300
von Moltke (the Elder), Helmuth Karl
    Bernhard, 274–275

von Paulus, Friedrich, 406
von Roon, Albrecht, 274
von Sanders, Otto Liman, 334
von Schlieffen, Alfred, 298

W

Walker, Walton, 452
War of 1812, 200–201
War of the Austrian Succession, 156
War of the Spanish Succession, 142–143, 148
Washington, George, 162, 164–167, 170
Waterloo, Battle of, 194–195
weapons
    arquebus, 132–133
    bows, 96–97
    Brown Bess musket, 158–159
    gunpowder, 92–95
    halberds, 100–101
    hoplite, 22–23
    machine guns, 310, 322–323
    of mass destruction, 320–321
    mines, 394–395
    missiles and rockets, 472–473
    plastic explosives, 486–487
    rifles, 202–203
    Roman legion, 40
    swords, 42–43
    tanks, 328–329, 344–345
    torpedoes, 372–373
    trebuchet, 77–79
Weidling, Karl, 444
Wellesley, Arthur, 188–189, 194

Wellington, Duke of, 188–189, 194
Wilhelm, Karl, Duke of Brunswick, 174–175
Wilhelm II (Germany), 294–295, 296, 298,
    305, 312, 316
William I, the Conquerer, 72–75
Wilson, Woodrow, 332
Wingate, Orde, 458
Wolfe, James, 160, 162–163
Worden, John L., 246
World War I, 298–335, 378
World War II, 38–39, 230, 314, 320, 342–446,
    486
Wounded Knee, 288–289
Wright, Orville and Wilbur, 378

X

Xerxes I, 24–25

Y

Yamamoto, Isoroku, 364–365, 388
Yamashita, Tomoyuki, 380–381
Yom Kippur War, 466–467
Yorktown, Siege of, 172–173
Yoshimoto Imagawa, 126
Ypres, Battles of, 318–320
Yugoslavia, 418–421

Z

Zama, Battle of, 44–45, 46
Zhukov, Georgi, 336, 356, 358–360, 444
Zulu wars, 204–207, 282–283